Political Research and Political Theory

Political Research and Political Theory

Oliver Garceau, editor

Avery Leiserson
J. Roland Pennock
Frederick M. Watkins
M. Brewster Smith
Douglas Price
Austin Ranney
Leon D. Epstein
Duane Lockard
Merle Fainsod

Harvard University Press
Cambridge, Massachusetts
1968

To the memory of V. O. Key, Jr.

Contents

The Authors

Leon D. Epstein is professor of political science and dean of the College of Letters and Science, University of Wisconsin. He is author of *Politics in Wisconsin* and *British Politics in the Suez Crisis*.

Merle Fainsod is Carl H. Pforzheimer University Professor, Harvard University, director of the Harvard University Library, and president of the American Political Science Association, 1967–68. He was director of the Russian Research Center, Harvard University, 1959–1964, and is author of *How Russia Is Ruled* and *Smolensk under Soviet Rule*.

Oliver Garceau was a member of the Social Science Research Council Committee on Political Behavior, 1950–1964; executive associate and consultant, the Ford Foundation, 1955–1957; research professor of government, Harvard University, 1959–1960. He is author of *The Political Life of the American Medical Association* and *The Public Library in the Political Process*.

Avery Leiserson is Harvie Branscomb Distinguished Service Professor of Political Science, Vanderbilt University. He was editor of the *Journal of Politics*, 1961–1965; president of the Southern Political Science Association, 1966; vice-president of the American Political Science Association, 1966–1967. He was a member of the Social Science Research Council Committee on Political Behavior, 1950–1964, and of the Board of Directors of the SSRC, 1959–1962. He is author of *Administrative Regulation: A Study in Representation of Interests* and *Parties and Politics: An Institutional and Behavioral Approach*.

W. Duane Lockard is professor of politics at Princeton University. He is author of *New England State Politics* and *The Politics of State and Local Government*.

J. Roland Pennock is Richter Professor of Political Science and department chairman, Swarthmore College, and editor of *Nomos*. He is author of *Liberal Democracy; Its Merits and Prospects*, *Administration and the Rule of Law*, and, with David G. Smith, *Political Science: An Introduction*.

H. Douglas Price is associate professor of government, Harvard University. He is author of *The Negro and Southern Politics* and *Political Change in "Middletown" and "Yankee City."*

Austin Ranney is professor of political science, University of Wisconsin; managing editor of the *American Political Science Review;* and chairman of the Social Science Research Council Committee on Government and Legal Processes. He is author of *The Doctrine of Responsible Party Government* and *Pathways to Parliament*, and co-author of *Democracy and the American Party System*.

M. Brewster Smith is professor of psychology and chairman of the department of psychology, University of Chicago. From 1965 to July 1968 he was director, Institute of Human Development, University of California, Berkeley. He was editor, *Journal of Abnormal and Social Psychology*, 1956–1961, and is co-author of *The American Soldier* and *Opinions and Personality*.

Frederick M. Watkins is professor of political science, Yale University, and a former president, American Society for Political and Legal Philosophy. He is the author of *The Political Tradition of the West*.

Political Research and Political Theory

Oliver Garceau

Introduction

This volume of essays is written in memory of Professor V. O. Key, Jr. The authors want in this fashion to celebrate his accomplishments, his rare good judgment, his fruitful intellectual stance, his unassuming theoretical creativity, his resourceful imagination, his avoidance of sterile controversy, his gathering of fresh data, his intelligent mastery of analytical tools, his intuitive awareness of political life, his unremitting dedication to hard work, his unfailing sense of humor, and his unstinted capacity for friendship. Because Key's work was so eminently sensible, there is no occasion for it to be recapitulated in a volume such as this. His contribution is central to contemporary work in the field, and there is no better way to evaluate it than to note its widespread usefulness. Analysis of its impact must wait upon the perspective of another generation. The essays are not, therefore, about Key, but about political science.

It seemed appropriate to invite essays from people who might, at least in part, meet Key's familiar prescription of "young men in motion." The authors are observably not young; but it may appear that they are still in motion. They have written for this volume in areas close to their own current agenda. The general direction of the essays serves to point up some major characteristics and tendencies of political science at the close of Key's career, and more especially in the broad areas to which he contributed. A whole generation drew encouragement from Key's repeated demonstration that it is possible to deal with complex variables, using sophisticated analytical methods, in prose of graceful and often lighthearted style, understandable to all who would give it a hearing. The authors have tried to continue in this tradition of simple exposition.

Though the volume seeks to report something of the state of the art, it does so by illustration only, presenting examples of the kinds of analysis, the levels of generalization, the curiosities and concerns, which occupy the profession. It is not a summary of the so-called "behavioral revolution"; nor is it an inventory of the methods and materials brought to bear in studies of the "political process." It does not try to settle any of the great controversies for all time or for our time. It does report by example on present resolutions of some major debates.

Several themes recur in the essays, for example the uses of systematic and normative theory, the problems of scale in research design, and the application of the comparative method to political science. Political science has sought, since classical times, to understand the comparative method as it might be applied to the study of politics. In developing a useful taxonomy, there is need for some sort of working theory or statement of purpose. To develop a working theory, there is need for an accumulation of data. A long process of trial and error goes into determining what, of the mass of political activity, shall be considered the materials of comparative analysis. Political science a generation ago worked most intensively on the comparison of national polities in Western, urban, industrial areas. Now there is great attention to non-Western societies. Is it easier to construct structural-functional categories in these latter societies, where to the alien Western eye things seem less complicated? Where we know little or have a less personal concern, can we more easily see the important variables?

Conversely, in comparing *inter se* the party systems of Western governments, do we have the base for a more rigorous systems analysis of institutions and processes as class cleavages become less intransigeant, economic systems more uniformly industrialized, government management of the mixed economy more universal? As the societies become more homologous in the

West, internally more homogeneous, and perhaps homogenized, can we more clearly discern the marginal differences in political systems and their operational consequences? We seem to see more clearly the direction of secular change in this arena; and we are more sensitive to differences in organization and process. Does this result in more searching analysis of the function of party government?

What happens when the universe of comparison is even more controlled and uniform? State politics within the United States is narrowly defined by a common institutional and ideological framework. Gross differences in practices and public policy are few, and they are decreasing. This does not, however, make it easy to compare states with respect to the relation between party competition and public policy outputs. There are many variables, often running in parallel.

Fifty states provide few enough cases for analysis. Even more troublesome is the small number of cases available for comparing modern one-party systems. Here the focus is on what seem historically almost unique episodes. Certainly the one-party systems emerged out of widely differing contexts as to underlying economy and organization of society, and as to internal tensions and international pressures. The comparative method applied to these materials necessarily uses larger dimensions. It is in the nature of political science that comparison, and therefore generalization, must often be made on the basis of a tentatively ordered series of seemingly unique situations.

The essays by Leon D. Epstein, Duane Lockard, and Merle Fainsod are explorations into the nature of comparative work. They variously raise the recurring issues of comparison. Whose questions shall we ask? Do we pose our own dilemmas, or those articulated within the system under study? In what sense are there broad uniformities, allowing an objective structural-functional analysis? Does it make a difference whether we ask how to seize power, how to displace myths of legitimacy, or how to adapt to accelerating change, how to preserve an equilibrium of internal forces? How may we join the comparison of contemporary systems with studies of political and social history? For it is in historical materials that will always be found the richest body of data and the most apt critical cases. Austin Ranney points up one of the most pervasive difficulties in comparative method by exploring the matter of definition: What do people mean by political party? Both the striking and the subtle permutations of the idea of party in our own polity are relevant to the effort to compare party systems. The varieties of public perception of party in one system make us careful in seeking an appropriate level of generality for the definition of party in comparative study. Interestingly, both Professors Epstein and Lockard, working with comparative materials, point to the continued significance of focusing on the single situation, with insights enriched by comparative dimensions; and this is also true in a somewhat different sense of Professor Fainsod's essay.

A second theme that runs through much of the volume concerns the scale of relationships to be studied. Undoubtedly there is wide variety in the strategies open to a developing science. There is a period of data-gathering, of more or less undisciplined observation and unstructured attentiveness to apparently pertinent phenomena. There is a borrowing of tools for observing and processing data. The convenience of tools commonly influences and sometimes determines the selection of data and of scale. There is small- and middle-scale theory building, often tied to practical payoffs. There is grand generalization, sweeping over a vast canvas of past and present, over parochial concerns of many schools of thought. There is the sharpened focus on the critical experiment or the determinative episode. There is the return to the laboratory for microanalysis of the most narrowly defined and isolated phenomena. There is assuredly no immutable, recurring sequence in these shifts of scale, and no straightline progression. Change in method is unending. Dramatic revisions of strategy are provoked by success in another scientific discipline, by a sudden turning up of rich bodies of data, by new tools of analysis, usually refined or demonstrated by others, by a fresh organizing idea, or by a shift of political purpose. The contribution of a first-rate scholar or a successful school can precipitate a new departure, quickly and widely adopted in the discipline as a matter of fashion. In both the social and the physical sciences the objective sought often dictates the focus and method of research. Events, hopes, and dreams condition our perception of what needs study, what we must know, on what scale we work.

What kind of work is found respectable, what is commendable depends also upon the intellectual spirit of the times. All science is a social activity, not alone in its imitations, its borrowings, its building "on the shoulders of giants." It is intensely social in its giving and withholding of rewards. In scholarship there are fewer objective criteria of relevance or even of competence than is at any one time supposed. The bounds of social tolerance are always narrow. Little can be done beyond the current range of the respectable, because no one will be listening beyond those conventional boundaries. If no one will listen to a new departure, nothing much will happen in any science, precisely because science is a social activity, requiring the work of many minds to go very far along any road to get the work done. Political science literature is a mine of "pilot studies" that have not been systematically followed up.

For a generation, political science has yearned to build systematic theory. This has been an enormously respectable mission. There are dreams of an overarching theoretical edifice yielding truly cumulative results. Partly this is a search for "scientific" orthodoxy, partly a reaction to the nightmare that data will pile up exponentially with only a repeating cycle of intuitive, shadowy understanding. The search for theory is invited by the evident intellectual rewards of manipulating simplified, abstracted, isolated data with highly sophisticated tools, informed by a theory. This can be a refined, entertaining game which, on balance, points in the behavioral sciences to small-scale phenomena to support orderly grand theory. Convenience of research often leads to narrowed time and place of materials observed. But the resulting minutiae are less than fully relevant to the predominant concerns of political science, which deal with the very large scale of time and place: how to foment revolution or, perhaps with us, how to subvert it; how to accelerate industrialization; how to win elections against dominant élites; the characteristics of power in large aggregates of people.

Narrow generalization from rigorous data can itself be deceiving. Analysis of voting behavior in a half-dozen elections produces convincing generalizations about the determinants of choice. But after the next election these require revision with a new narrow generalization together with a more comprehensive classification of election types. Extending the time series continues to require recasting the propositions. Beyond this there is the inescapable difficulty that our carefully equilibrated scheme of politics is by no means like a biological organism that must wait upon the slow processes of natural selection to change structure and function. Democratic politics is, rather, a continuously unfolding experience, an adventure. Here, as always, organic and organismic analogy misleads. The modern political system is not a morphologically and physiologically settled species. Grand theory often seems to come unstuck in dealing with the unfolding experience.

To this relatively unstable pattern of relationships to be studied, political science may at times have brought an ideal of theory-building that was unrealistically rigid. In seeking a cumulative scientific method we have thought of reaching absolute verities. But cumulative must also be the obsolescence of ideas. Theory is never more than provisional. The value of a new hypothesis does not lie primarily in its better fit. In the fit lies its claim to be a new hypothesis; and the reward comes if it facilitates the framing of a new and more searching question, from which will come still another hypothesis with a better fit to more relevant data. A burgeoning science is untidy. It is energetically imaginative. The experience of the past generation suggests that we shall not manage, by direct assault, an overarching theory which will order all the data for all purposes and all situations for all time. Perhaps efforts to contrive this type of theory have not been sufficiently imaginative. Certainly such theory as we have designed on this order is not widely useful.

But we have from the past generation a promising flow of small-scale propositions. The footnotes of Key's *Southern Politics* show how an imaginative mind, immersed in a considerable mass of data, can come up with new ideas about relationships that warrant looking into. Despite the current acceleration in the rate of data accumulation, we are short of data appropriate to our conventional generalizations. We are far short of the data needed to evaluate alternative explanatory propositions on the level of Key's many promising proposals. There is no shortage of theory required to keep us profitably busy.

The continuity of creating and abandoning ideas that characterizes many disciplines is of a different order from that so far to be found in the agenda of political science. For example, in astronomy, "scientific evolution proceeds remorselessly; several theories may compete with each other for a while, but sooner or later all but one will fall by the wayside, leaving the victor, not necessarily 'right,' but at least surviving. . . Inevitably one must abandon most of the alternatives one investigates, and it is the process of rejection on which everything hangs. Some skill and a lot of luck are needed." [1]

Some of the difficulty with analytical theory lies in this reluctance to reject old ideas; some in uncertainty about how to judge the fit of ideas to data; some in the problem of transposing our concerns from historical perspective to contemporary clinic and laboratory. Brewster Smith, in his essay, notes interesting analogies between the present state of political science and meteorology. The geologist can be added to the list of those sharing the troublesome limitations of materials. Most geologic evidence is and always must be historical. Most of the historical record is buried, with only random outcrops available for examination and speculation; and the outcrops are strangely modified by exposure. Though the laboratory can contrive erosion of a hill or seashore, and though occasionally a Suretsy heaves out of the Atlantic, as happened in 1963 to the delight of the several sciences, yet it remains difficult to create a mountain range for study, and the Mid-Atlantic Ridge, apparently undergoing creation, continues to puzzle us the more we learn of it.

In these essays the authors show that there is a useful language of explanatory theory; that we are by no means at a theory-building impasse, however emotionally comforting it might be to some if that turned out to be the case—if we were, after all, to be saved from science, not saved by science. Douglas Price points up the necessities and the difficulties of linking the study of small-scale data to the concern for national politics. This must be done if we are to build an understanding of the political system out of the smaller and middle-gauge theoretical concepts which are now manageable and for which data are available. Professor Smith notes that, when theory does not allow us to build and manipulate tight and perfect models, we can proceed with a looser mapping operation; and he puts such a map to work as an example, analyzing the rationality of the individual in making political choices. Avery Leiserson traces the story of theory-building over the past several generations and illuminates some of the virtues of our failures to settle on a unified theory. He also reveals the enormously interesting contributions that empirical work is making both to the understanding and to the practice of constitutional democracy.

1. Fred Hoyle, *Galaxies, Nuclei & Quasars* (New York, 1965), pp. 81, 86.

This last is important to the present and future course of political science. Not all scholars have shown Key's good judgement in combining rigorous empirical work with a firm commitment to democratic and constitutional goals. The search for a "value-free science" has a point; but it need not be the whole or the only point. It is important that we avoid rigging evidence and falsifying conclusions. It is necessary that research be sensitive to the consequences of selecting the questions and framing them. Ironically, some of the most clamorous quantifiers and methodologically meticulous pollsters continue to design questions in terms of opinion dichotomies or scales having as referents particular, temporary, ill-understood, and complex policy controversies. Nor did the authoritarian-democratic personality syndrome fare a great deal better in such hands. Both have at times been used to covert political purpose. It is in the questions asked, and thus in the data selected and the criteria imposed, that values are inevitably interjected into empirical work. Political science may, by necessity, have to recognize this more explicitly than other subject matter studies. The business of government is the identification, statement, selection, and enforcement of values. The position of political science is not uniquely difficult among the social sciences, which are, every one, congenitally value-loaded and policy-oriented. True, there is in political science a body of work called "policy sciences"; but economists and sociologists are equally directed in the selection of subject matter and analytical procedures by their value premises and policy objectives. Political science may indeed have the advantage in not being so likely to misconstrue the role of moral purpose in its work.

That there can and should be a productive interplay between normative and operational or analytical theory is pointed up by the essays of Frederick Watkins, Roland Pennock, and Avery Leiserson. There have been repeated proposals, during the "behavioral revolution," that the history of normative political theories be mined for useful operational theory. Little work has so far been done in this vein. Per contra, Professor Watkins suggests that an empirical base can be established for normative theory, and presents a proposal of how this may be undertaken. Professor Pennock demonstrates the uses of reason, the possibility and the necessity of being scientific without being antiphilosophical, the obligations of political scientists to deal rationally with ethical questions.

As a whole, the volume seeks to memorialize V. O. Key's success in joining an unshakable faith in constitutional democracy with the careful gathering of reliable new data, in joining impressionistic field research with quantification where applicable, and in applying freely and with frank enjoyment the humor and imagination which lie at the heart of productive science. His work is a lesson in research strategy. There is no need to wait for an overarching theory before getting on with middle-level propositions formulated from new data. There is no need for apocalyptic revelation of the critical variables in order to study the political process. There is no need for a method purified of all residue of human value judgement in order to speak the language of a cumulative, disciplined, study of government. However, there is a continuing need to distinguish between empirical work, motivated and informed by values, on the one hand, and partisan advocacy on the other. One may hope that the generation of scholars following Key will have a good deal less trouble fruitfully interrelating empirical research and normative theory. But one may predict that they will experience continued, perhaps increased, tension between what may appear to be the essentially conservative perspectives promoted by the careful study of the complexities of political systems on the one hand and the sometimes alienated, sometimes activist, orientation of intellectuals seeking to constitute themselves a competing political élite on the other.

Grateful acknowledgment is made to the underwriting committee that initiated this volume. The committee was composed of Angus Campbell, Robert A. Dahl, Oliver Garceau, Pendleton Herring, Avery Leiserson, Duane Lockard, and David B. Truman. The Social Science Research Council made possible a meeting of this committee to discuss the project, and a meeting of the authors to compare notes on what they proposed to contribute.

Part One

On Theory

Avery Leiserson

Empirical Approaches to Democratic Theory

I. The American Tradition

The classical tradition in Western political theory posits the reality of *intellectual ideas about politics* (whether of the rationalist–empiricist, idealist–materialist, or monist–pluralist persuasions), as opposed to the practical *skills* (*wisdom, strategies, and techniques*) of rulers and politicians acting under the blind forces of events (Fortune). The distinction focuses attention upon one of several contrasts, within the Western tradition, between European and American styles of political thinking that are by no means always flattering to Americans. Representative American theorists seem to incorporate in their ideas of politics some notion of *the people*, either by implying some "public opinion" connotation of what Americans generally believe or would find acceptable, or explicitly specifying some criterion of what constitutes "legitimate" action. Their thought is permeated with an empirical standard of popular relevance and understanding that somehow identifies or connects their work with what is general or characteristic of the "common mind." This normative quality helps the publicist to explain how the American system works, but it also inhibits his ability to engage or trust in analytic abstractions, in which Americans often fall short of

European standards of conceptual inventiveness, generality, logical extension, and symmetry.[1] On the other side, to Americans European intellectualism seems radically tainted with the elitist premise that "the masses" are either incapable of theory or are so ignorant, indifferent, and incoherent that intellectuals must formulate their ideas for them; that the people's thinking and action can only be explained by categories, symbols, or attributes imputed to them by intellectuals, for otherwise their action is by definition irrational, nonrational, or nihilistic.

Let us suspend, for the moment, debate over the respective rightness or superiority of these attitudes, and admit that theory can scarcely be said to exist until distinctions are recognized between analytical categories and operational skills, between articulated purposes and determining events—in short, between political theory and constitutional history. To understand American political thought, however, it is necessary to discard the assumption that political rationality or reality consists of a battle between clearly defined sets of conceptual systems proposed by intellectual protagonists. From its seventeenth-century beginnings, America has not lacked such disputes, most of them imported and mixed with indigenous elements. For example, positive law notions of royal or imperial sovereignty competed with the natural law idea that religious and societal norms are prior to and controlling over political authority; organismic conceptions of the colonial trading corporation existed side by side with social contract theories of the political order.[2] But with the possible exception of the civil wars over independence and secession, disputes over the ultimate nature of political union and authority have not constituted the basis of enduring cleavages among the American people.[3] It may indeed be plausibly argued that these two fundamental crises were forced upon them, one by continuing errors in British revenue and commercial policy, the other by extremist "fringe" elements in the irrepressible conflict over

1. R. G. McCloskey, "American Political Thought and the Study of Politics," and Martin Diamond's comment thereon, *American Political Science Review*, 51 (March 1957), 115–134.

2. C. L. Becker, *The Declaration of Independence* (New York: Harcourt Brace, 1922); A. C. McLaughlin, *Foundations of American Constitutionalism* (New York University Press, 1932).

3. H. Agar, *The Price of Union* (Boston: Houghton Mifflin, 1950).

slavery, rather than by purposeful strategy and clear-cut organization of the major political groups in the politically active and attentive population.

If Americans reject the image of the people as a passive instrument responding to the manipulation of intellectual ideas and politicans' tactics, what alternative concept satisfies the need for both rational constructs and testing by empirical evidence? In different accents, both Madison-Hamilton in the *Federalist Papers* and Tocqueville in his *Democracy in America* suggest that the people are not merely the symbolic source of political power but active, politically participant agents and actors, more or less successful in choosing leaders, controlling their decisions, observing and judging how public officials exercise their authority, deciding whether or not their tenure of office should be continued. To Madison the "majority of the people" was so powerful that all sorts of institutional checks had to be contrived to prevent its varied factional forms from becoming tyrannical. Tocqueville described with critical detachment the numerous ways in which a vigorous, active people participate in the processes of leadership recruitment, circulation, and control, as well as the formulation of public law and policy. Not being hampered by a feudal, rigid class system, a free people in an open society were not obliged to accept the rational necessity of socially determined, clear-cut ideological divisions over the ultimate nature of the good society and the form of governing authority appropriate thereto.[4] Rather, Americans seemed to visualize themselves as being divided by a multiplicity of *both* conflicting and commonly shared interests; to perceive government as a practical necessity to regulate and achieve these converging-diverging purposes, rather than a logical consequence of enforcing an assumed unified consensus or an elite group perspective upon the whole society. If people could think of themselves as prior to both society and government, and yet recognize that they are not angels, it is quite plausible that their conception of the good political society would be one in which government, while necessary to establish a free, equal, and open society, would still re-

4. D. J. Boorstin, *The Genius of American Politics* (University of Chicago Press, 1953); L. Hartz, *The Liberal Tradition in America* (New York: Harcourt Brace, 1955).

quire the people to play a vigorous, participant, overseeing, and corrective role.[5]

If a democratic people looks with equanimity upon their society as being in a state of both agreement and tension, their conception of politics is likely to be one of necessary, perhaps disagreeable, contingency; authority is derivative rather than preordained, ambiguous and prospective rather than historically or logically determined. In a democracy, politics becomes sustained, watchful, public scrutiny, discussion, and controversy—not confined to electoral campaigns—over who shall occupy the strategic, policy-making offices of government. Popular judgment is based not only upon past performance, alternative views and opinions upon *issues,* but also upon candidate personality and ability.[6]

In organizing themselves for selection and control of their leaders (in classical terminology, establishing a "nontyrannical republic"), the Americans chose to predicate their formal representation of interests upon population and territory, rather than class or vocational lines. The effect was not to deny or to suppress conflicts of social and economic interest, but to keep them in the informal, changeable sphere of society rather than enshrine them in constitutional forms. American political structure therefore may be viewed as the differentiated, official processes of organizing and institutionalizing the public settlement of intergroup controversies.[7] It assumes and relies upon the people's support of prescribed procedures for arriving at political settlements, but this assumption does not necessitate acceptance of compromise as an absolute criterion of political judgment. The primary requirement is that in substance and process political decisions reflect the procedural principles of *participant representation* and *mutual adjustment* of interests. It is possible to

5. J. W. Prothro and C. M. Grigg, "Fundamental Principles of Democracy: Bases of Agreement and Disagreement," *Journal of Politics,* 22 (May 1960), 276–294; E. Cahn, *The Predicament of Democratic Man* (New York: Dell, 1961).

6. F. J. Goodnow, *Politics and Administration* (New York: Macmillan, 1900); J. A. Schumpeter, *Capitalism, Socialism and Democracy* (New York: Harper, 1942).

7. D. B. Truman, *The Governmental Process* (New York: Knopf, 1951); H. Eulau, "Logics of Rationality in Unanimous Decision-making," in C. J. Friedrich, ed., *Rational Decision,* NOMOS VII (New York: Atherton Press, 1964), p. 29.

state these principles in structural terms by which Americans observably relate themselves to government, and which thereby become operative criteria or expectations governing official behavior:

1. *The distinction between social and political structure in a democracy.* A free people, voluntarily associated in a *society* divided by fluid, changing economic groupings and social classes, with partly conflicting but also shared, common purposes, requires *a political system, a formal structure of legally coercive public offices and decision-making processes* based upon units of electoral organizations different from those of the social and economic structure.

2. *The indeterminate line between public and private responsibilities in a free (self-governing) political system.* Governmental power is derived not from a logical concept of supreme power (sovereignty) but from the common purposes and values shared by the members of political society (citizens) concerning the public objects of government; these objects do not extend to all personal-social relationships but to an indeterminate number of collective needs that citizens find are not satisfactorily performed in their private capacities or through voluntary associations.

3. *The procedural separation of constitutional and governmental authority.* Personal rights and liberties should be protected by subordinating and limiting the powers of government officials and agencies to those prescribed and reasonably implied in a written constitutional instrument, formulated by representative conventions acting for (and subject to ratification by) the people as the rightful source of political authority.

4. *Competitive constituencies in leadership recruitment and political representation.* Popular controls over government can be maintained by establishing different modes of electing, for fixed terms of office, political representatives to differentiated policy-making bodies, each claiming an independent line of authority and accountability to their electorates.

5. *Shared jurisdiction among autonomous authorities in law and policy formulation.* Constitutional controls can be maintained by establishing a compulsory division of authority by at least three autonomous sets of policy-making officials, requiring the concurrence of at least two in the formulation of public policy and three for final validation and enforcement (separation of powers).

6. *The federal principle (concurrent jurisdiction and cooperative administration) in inter-level relations.* The conflicting requirements of adequate central authority and competent localized responsibility in self-governing political systems can be met by dualistic, autonomous levels combining both political and administrative powers. The conditions appear to be: (a) the basic constitutional instrument delegates certain powers primarily to each, other functions jointly to both, and denies certain powers to both; (b) the lower, narrower levels, geographically speaking, are represented in the legislative

processes at the inclusive, national level; (c) the highest judicial tribunal in the system has authority to decide inter-level disputes and to establish interpretations of the unifying constitutional document binding upon all courts throughout the system.

Needless to say, these principles are not exclusively American; nor is this the place to indicate in detail how Americans have developed the operational principles of their political system. In one respect, however—the relation between political consensus and social change—American social science has suggested a fresh insight. This concerns the solidarity–conflict dilemma in society that constantly threatens the stability of all political systems, and which involves the transformation of classical thought about the role of politics in social change. The essence of this transformation consists in the relinquishment of grandiose units of analysis like "civilizations" and "cultures," together with the assumption that what is required is a linear theory of "stages" of societal evolution, and the adoption instead of a reductionist version of the Hegelian notion that political dynamics can be incorporated into empirically convenient ways of analyzing sociopolitical systems and structures.[8] Although the consequence of this choice is to relinquish the level of abstract universality desired by some advocates of general theory, the ultimate prospects of arriving at a scientifically productive schema seem to be enhanced by postulating the concept of political society as a *tension-management system, which* (1) constantly focuses attention of politicians, social scientists, and intellectual-symbol specialists upon critical points of stresses and strains in society; (2) encourages inventiveness in devising ways of identifying and measuring the significant variables associated with these tensions, (3) provides a number of mechanisms for insuring that alternative proposals will be presented to policy-makers for mobilizing public and private resources, and (4) maximizes the tendencies making for strategic, *planned adjustment* (as opposed to detailed, totalistic, central controls) of public policy and organization toward desired value-outcomes. The aim of such a polity is not necessarily to eliminate conflicts and tensions, but to

8. W. E. Moore, *Social Change* (New York: Prentice-Hall, 1963). Compare P. A. Sorokin, *Social and Cultural Dynamics* (New York: American Book, 1940) with C. E. Merriam, *The Role of Politics in Social Change* (New York University Press, 1936); E. C. Lindblom, *The Intelligence of Democracy* (Glencoe, Ill., The Free Press, 1965).

reorient human energies toward constructive rather than defensive and destructive purposes.

It is perhaps easier to visualize intellectual and managerial elites adopting such a nonideological, discriminating view of political dynamics than it is to imagine the people articulating and assuming the role(s) appropriate to their participation and support in such a system. It is at this point that the emphasis upon political parties and interest groups in American political and social science may have something to offer that supplements the traditional philosophical and public law orientations in European universities. For it was precisely to escape the confining, rationalist assumptions of political philosophy, constitutional law, and orthodox political economy, in order to study the formal-informal, sub-constitutional relations of political parties and social classes in leadership recruitment, and the relations of parties, interest groups, and bureaucracies in public opinion formation and legislative policy-making, that American political science was recognized as a separate academic discipline in the 1880's and 1890's. While for several decades its research product was primarily historical, descriptively empirical, and institutionally reformist rather than analytic and systematic with respect to method, by the 1930's a rapprochement was effected with the emerging disciplines of social organization and social psychology to make possible a renewed, interdisciplinary attack upon the comparative study of political systems, structures, and processes. In the 1950's, under the stimulus of a "behavioral" revolt within the discipline and the obvious need for functionally equivalent, analytical categories sufficiently flexible to take account of developments in the non-Western, modernizing countries, small groups of American political scientists, working both separately and in collaboration, began to devise interdisciplinary conceptual schemes for genuinely comparative study of the participant-roles of people in democratic and nondemocratic societies.[9] The importance of this development lies in the implied

9. G. A. Almond and J. S. Coleman, *The Politics of the Developing Areas* (Princeton University Press, 1960); G. A. Almond and Sidney Verba, *The Civic Culture* (Princeton University Press, 1963); D. Lerner, *The Passing of Traditional Society* (Glencoe, Ill.: The Free Press, 1958); R. Bendix, "Social Stratification and the Political Community," *European Journal of Sociology,* (1960), 3–32; Clark Kerr *et al., Industrialism and Industrial Man* (Cambridge, Mass.: Harvard University Press, 1960); S. M. Lipset, "The Changing Class Structure and Contemporary European Politics," *Daedalus,* 93 (Winter 1964).

necessity for explicitly examining the several theories (models) of democracy in the American setting with a view to assessing the limits of their relevance for comparative analysis.

II.   The Problem of a "Model" of American Democracy

Whether or not the six principles asserted in the previous section provide an acceptable statement of American constitutional axiology, it is clear that they do not presuppose an all-inclusive, unified, integrated general will on the part of the people. On the contrary, as A. L. Lowell observed long ago, they presuppose that the people, no less than a single individual, are quite capable of holding at the same time conflicting beliefs and purposes, each of which taken by itself has justifiable reasons for being regarded as valid. One supposes it is precisely this insistence upon recognizing the potential validity of logically conflicting interests and purposes, rather than trying to impose upon society an artificial, monolithic unity called government (or the State), that justified William James in the philosophical tradition, and James Madison in the constitutional, in applying the term *pluralistic* to American political culture. However, it is not sufficient simply to apply a label, or to show that on a scale of monistic-pluralistic political systems, American government lies demonstrably close to the pluralistic end of the continuum. For the normative theorist, it is essential to establish satisfactory purposive grounds on which sufficient unity exists for the system to be worth maintaining; for the empirical theorist, it is necessary to explicate a working model of political mechanics or dynamics, whereby the conflicting factual requirements of constitutional beliefs and social structure are reconciled in a logically adequate explanation of how American democracy survives as an effective (going) political enterprise. But even if we make the debatable assumption that constitutional axiology and social structure in America exclude consideration of a model which postulates absolute exclusive control of government by any political group, even a numerical majority,[10] the political scientist would still face the problem of constructing a theoretically satisfactory model of American democracy that provides a basis for comparison with others.[11]

10. R. A. Dahl, *A Preface to Democratic Theory* (University of Chicago Press, 1956).

11. M. Duverger, *Political Parties* (London: Methuen, 1954), pp. xiii–xiv.

Tocqueville, as R. Aron has recently reminded us,[12] set up a threefold categorization of causal factors: "geographic and historic," "the laws," and the "customs, manners, and beliefs" of the people. Tocqueville's general conclusion with respect to the first category was that the peculiar geographical and historical situation, including size, natural resources making possible a broad level of affluence, and the circumstances under which the several immigrant groups composing the population forged themselves into a political community, constituted necessary conditions, not a sufficient causal explanation of democracy in America. This judgment probably characterizes opinion of the present day, notwithstanding some important deviant interpretations.[13] Tocqueville's analysis of "the laws," in which he included the constitutional structure, quasi-constitutional norms, and informal, institutional practices of political life and association, was primarily normative and functional; that is, he identified certain key factors of structure and process, and showed how they contributed to and militated against freedom and equality. The causational force of Tocqueville's theory remained implicit, however, partly because of his purpose, partly because he did not recognize the distinction between "socioeconomic forces" and "customs, manners, and beliefs," and partly because his empirical observations assumed rather than proved that manners and beliefs are more determinative of the shape of democracy than "the laws." In no way is this evaluation intended to detract from the magnitude of his performance, because it applies in even greater degree to those observers who followed him: the Englishman, Bryce, the Americans Wilson, Lowell, H. J. Ford, Goodnow, Beard, Merriam, Holcombe, Herring, Key, and Schattschneider, who represent the dominant tradition in American political science. Not only did this tradition fail to clarify the relative influence of "laws" and "beliefs"; it denied

12. *Main Currents of Sociological Thought* (New York: Basic Books, 1965), pp. 184–193.

13. D. M. Potter, *People of Plenty* (University of Chicago Press, 1954); O. Handlin, *Race and Nationality in American Life* (New York: Doubleday, 1957); C. A. Beard, *An Economic Interpretation of the Constitution of the United States* (New York: Macmillan, 1913); F. J. Turner, *Frontier and Section* (New York: Prentice-Hall, 1961); S. M. Lipset, "Conditions of the Democratic Order," Chaps. 2–3, *Political Man* (New York: Doubleday, 1960); K. Deutsch, "Social Mobilization and Political Development," *American Political Science Review* 55 (1961), 493–514.

that the facts of American politics were reducible to a form that would satisfy the requirements of a formal, deductive model, and most of them were contemptuous of efforts, normative or otherwise, to describe politics in terms of a formally rigorous, internally consistent set of definitions, assumptions, conditions, and deductively derived propositions. There was no dearth of preferential standards as to how American democracy ought to work, but almost universal skepticism that an adequate analysis of American constitutional norms, when related to group and party politics, had any determinate, logical relation to such criteria as "representativeness, responsibility, and majority rule." This state of affairs may be described as the "no-theory" theory of American democracy, by which is meant not the absence but the multiplicity of normative explanations. The theoretical position as of 1950 has been acutely described by Austin Ranney in words that may be only slightly paraphrased as follows:

"American democracy as it observably exists (x) ought to be made more like some rational model of democracy (y) that doesn't exist because the American people are so deeply committed to an empirical model (z) which cannot or can only partially be articulated on logically defensible grounds." [14]

Notwithstanding the general accuracy of this indictment, certain convergences in social science research in the United States since 1940 have begun to alter the status and outlook of democratic theory. Partly because they were organized in at least five different academic disciplines—psychology, anthropology, sociology, economics, and political science—the social sciences did not produce a unified, logically coherent, or empirically satisfactory focus upon the linkages between their respective subject matters: 1) *personality* (motivation, perception, learning, attitudes); 2) *culture* (technology, psychophysical attributes of population, norms and styles of interpersonal conduct); 3) *society* (social structure, mobility, and group or class ideologies); 4) *economy* (rational valuation and allocation of resources); and 5) *politics* (the legitimate structures of public coercion for the control of violence, and the authoritative processes of leadership recruitment, communication, and decision-making). Never-

14. *The Doctrine of Responsible Party Government* (University of Illinois Press, 1953), p. 9, referring to the Report of the American Political Science Association's Committee on Political Parties, *Toward A More Responsible Two-Party System* (New York: Rinehart, 1950).

theless, several types of cross-disciplinary inquiry during the period from 1945 to 1965 have demonstrated the inadequacies of the old-fashioned dualism between Society and State, which places politics in the role of a bridge, in Ernest Barker's words, "resting at one end on Society and at the other on the State, [or] . . . in another metaphor, a conduit or sluice by which the waters of social thought and discussion are brought to the wheels of political machinery and set to turn those wheels." [15] Without attempting an exhaustive inventory, or to ascribe priorities of credit, some of the major social science contributions to political theory may be listed under the following heads:

1. Individual (citizen, voter) socialization, participation, choice
   (a) sociopsychological [16]
   (b) rational [17]
2. Leadership attributes, incentives, career patterns [18]
3. Political (group, class and party) interests and organizations [19]

15. *Reflections on Government* (London: Oxford University Press, 1942), p. 39.

16. W. L. Warner, *et al.*, *Yankee City* (1941) and *Democracy in Jonesville* (1949); T. Parsons and E. Shils, *Toward General Theory of Action* (1961); P. Larsfeld, *et al.*, *The People's Choice* (1944); B. Berelson, *et al.*, *Voting* (1954); A. Campbell, *et al.*, *The Voter Decides* (1954) and *The American Voter* (1960); R. E. Lane, *Political Life* (1959); D. Bell, *The End of Ideology* (1960); G. A. Almond and S. Verba, *The Civic Culture* (1963); L. W. Milbrath, *Political Participation* (1965).

17. K. Arrow, *Social Choice and Individual Values* (1951); H. Simon, *Models of Man* (1957); A. Downs, *An Economic Theory of Democracy* (1957); D. Black, *The Theory of Committees and Elections* (1958); J. M. Buchanan and G. Tullock, *The Calculus of Consent* (1962); M. Shubik, ed., *Game Theory and Related Approaches to Social Behavior* (1964).

18. H. D. Lasswell, *Power and Personality* (1948); T. Adorno *et al.*, *The Authoritarian Personality* (1950); C. A. Gibb, "Leadership," in G. Lindzey, ed., *Handbook of Social Psychology* (1954); A. Gouldner, ed., *Studies in Leadership* (1950); D. Cartwright and A. Zander, eds., *Group Dynamics* (1953); W. L. Warner and J. W. Abegglen, *Business Leaders in America* (1955); L. Petrullo and B. M. Bass, eds., *Leadership and Interpersonal Behavior* (1961); R. A. Dahl, *Who Governs?* (1961).

19. P. Herring, *The Politics of Democracy* (1940); E. E. Schattschneider, *Party Government* (1941); V. O. Key, *Politics, Parties and Pressure Groups* (1942); A. DeGrazia, *Public and Republic* (1951); D. B. Truman, *The Governmental Process* (1951); G. C. Homans, *The Human Group* (1950); A. Ranney and

4. Mass communications (content, media, effects) [20]

5. Collective decision-making (public and private) [21]

6. General theory of human systems [22]

A sharp caveat should be posted to warn the reader against either over- or underestimating the degree to which the evidence and conceptual innovations of empirical social science have been "received" into normative, prescriptive political theory, democratic or otherwise. Both in his professional work and personality, V. O. Key exhibited a "briny irreverence" toward empiricist and rationalist pretensions alike, as well as to the moral agonizing of the value-oriented schools of political philosophy, that is a healthy antidote to premature integration in theory-building. At this juncture, perhaps the most useful procedure is to make more explicit the several "models" of democracy that seem to be emerging from the empirical study of politics in the

---

W. Kendall, *Democracy and the American Party System* (1956); A. Leiserson, *Parties and Politics* (1958); S. J. Eldersveld, *Political Parties* (1964); G. A. Almond and J. C. Coleman, *Politics of the Developing Countries* (1960).

20. B. L. Smith, *et al.*, *Propaganda, Communication and Public Opinion* (1946); D. Riesman, *The Lonely Crowd* (1950); B. Berelson, *Content Analysis in Communications Research* (1952); C. I. Hovland, *et al.*, *Communication and Persuasion* (1953); R. K. Merton, ed., *Continuities in Social Research* (1950); S. A. Stouffer *et al.*, *The American Soldier*, 4 vols. (1949); *Communism, Conformity and Civil Liberties* (1955); E. Katz and P. Lazarsfeld, *Personal Influence* (1955); W. Kornhauser, *The Politics of Mass Society* (1960); B. Berelson, ed., *The Behavioral Sciences Today* (1963).

21. C. I. Barnard, *The Functions of the Executive* (1938); H. Simon, *Administrative Behavior* (1947), with J. G. March, *Organizations* (1958); R. Neustadt, *Presidential Power* (1960); J. C. Wahlke, H. Eulau *et al.*, *The Legislative System* (1962); G. Schubert, ed., *Judicial Decision-making* (1963); D. Braybrooke and E. C. Lindblom, *The Strategy of Decision* (1963); R. C. Snyder, "A Decision-making Approach," in R. Young, ed., *Approaches to the Study of Politics* (1958); M. Haire, ed., *Modern Organization Theory* (1959); D. Lerner and H. D. Lasswell, *The Policy Sciences* (1949).

22. R. K. Merton, *Social Theory and Social Structure* (1949); T. Parsons, *The Social System* (1951); M. J. Levy, *The Structure of Society* (1952); R. A. Dahl and E. C. Lindblom, *Politics, Economics and Welfare* (1953); K. Boulding, *Conflict and Defense* (1962); A. Kuhn, *The Study of Society* (1963); K. W. Deutsch, *The Nerves of Government* (1963); D. Easton, *A Systems Analysis of Political Life* (1965); J. A. Robinson, "The Major Problems of Political Science," in L. K. Caldwell, ed., *Politics and Public Affairs* (1962); J. C. Miller, *Living Systems* (1966).

United States, not just in academic political science, but across the whole spectrum of research into man and his sociopolitical involvements. The following classification is not based upon mutually exclusive views of the content or nature of democracy, but upon categories of writers using the indicated contexts in contemporary inquiry and discourse.

Ideological Democracy

This category refers to people who use democracy to refer to a desirable political regime with which they wish to identify. As such, it includes the most disparate political groupings: anti-political, romantic rebels, anarchists, and hard-boiled organization men who call themselves the "non-communist Left"; social-Darwinist individuals who call themselves "conservative"; political activists who believe in the populist principle of absolute majority rule and gladly accept the designation of capital-L Liberals; and believers in an imputed constitutional morality, which includes the advocates both of natural-rights liberalism and immanent historical conservatism. A common trait of the ideological democrat is that he ostensibly believes that the constitution is consistent with his preferred brand of ethico-political doctrine, but that any particular political regime is in great danger of being subverted by "bad" politics or politicians, sinister "interests," "evil" ideas, or by ignorant, apathetic, corrupt "masses."

Institutional Democracy

Persons in this category use democracy to denote certain structural attributes or symbolized principles of a constitutional (as opposed to an autocratic) political order (freedom of speech, press, and association, majority rule, universal suffrage and free elections, political opposition, and so on). In its sophisticated usage, institutional democracy may be called the model of limited majoritarianism, because its advocates are aware of and deliberately assert the possibility of having simultaneously both majority rule and minority rights. It is congenial to legal positivism in its focus upon constitutional authorities, rules, and restraints controlling public officials. There is an assumption that the formally legitimate acts, procedures, and sanctions of public coercion either exert an independent, symbolic influence upon, or correspond to, norms of expected individual and group behavior in the "voluntary" spheres of society and economy. This theory has the defects of its qualities: its supporters rely on a historical-pragmatic rather than a logically satisfactory resolution of the democratic paradox; they tend to rationalize restrictions or departures from democratic principles on ethical and historical grounds; they exhibit a theoretical weakness toward "gadgetry" and tinkering with institutional reforms; and they virtually abdicate with respect to the problems of societal forces and effects.

The institutional democrat, unless he transcends his own training, is theoretically unequipped to deal with the economic and sociopsychological determinants of democracy. Except on functional or preferential grounds, he finds it difficult to explain why presidential government is more or less democratic (representative) than cabinet government; why a multiparty system may be more or less conducive to democracy (majority rule) than a two-party system; or why centralized party organizations may be more democratic (responsible) than decentralized parties. Institutional democracy sounds very much like the old Whig–Liberal, Recht–Staat conception of a stratified "privileged" social order which placed high values on both liberty and law.[23]

Polycentric Equilibrium

Since the institutional model is weak in its overemphasis upon the politico-legal, to the neglect of the psychocultural, aspects of democracy, some theorists have attempted to construct a theory of political society in which political structure and process perform a balancing role appropriate to observable conditions, where a changing social system is being adapted to a democratic political culture. In contrast to the eighteenth-and nineteenth-century fashions, when general theories tended to postulate some sort of immanent mechanism ("the spirit of the laws," the "unseen hand," the evolutionary analogy of "the survival of the fittest," or Marxist historical materialism), to which governmental arrangements were supposed to conform, twentieth-century social theory has favored a multicentered structural concept of interacting groups, the dynamic features of which present a complex process of inter-personal and intergroup conflict and

23. H. Tingsten, *The Problem of Democracy* (Totowa, N.J.: The Bedminster Press, 1965), pp. 11–15.

adjustment.[24] This model locates the political function in the integration or "aggregation" of social interest through partly explicit, partly tacit processes of concurrent agreement-disagreement between members and elites (leaders) of influential groups representing such interest, of which society is assumed to be composed.

Certain variants of this model tend to be axiomatic and determinist, visualizing a continuing, informal, ruling class of influential individuals who, by virtue of their peak positions in the several group hierarchies, unifying all spheres of decision-making—economic, cultural, political, military.[25] Alternatively, however, under conditions of rapid economic growth, intergroup mobility, and technological displacement, modern industrial society has come to be conceived as a configuration of shifting, changing groupings (socioeconomic, demographic, scientific-professional), whose members differentially exercise legal rights of individual freedom and equality (participation, access, and communication) in political processes of choosing leaders and arriving at decisions of intragroup and intergroup policy.[26] Establishment and continuity of democratic societies are thought to depend upon the ability of governmental and nongovernmental leaders to produce and maintain a dynamic equilibrium, a moving balance, amongst the shifting alignments of influential groups, whose members must be somehow persuaded that they have a greater stake in the survival of the democratic system than in its subversion and destruction.

Outstanding features of the polycentric equilibrium model of democracy include its empirical emphasis upon the pluralistic,

24. Louis Wirth, "The Individual and the Group," *American Journal of Sociology,* 44 (May 1939), 965; Arthur Kornhauser, "Public Opinion and Social Class," *ibid.* 55 (January 1950), 333. Critics: Henry Kariel, *In Search of Authority* (1964); Peter Bachrach, *The Theory of Democratic Elitism* (1967). C. S. Hyneman, in *Popular Government in America* (1968), argues that individual liberty-in-the-group and equality-in-the-mass are inseparable in American political thought and practice.

25. G. Mosca, *The Ruling Class* (Eng. tr. 1939); G. D. H. Cole, *Social Theory* (1920); R. Michels, *First Lectures on Political Sociology* (Eng. tr. 1949); F. Hunter, *Community Power Structure* (1953); C. W. Mills, *The Power Elite* (1956).

26. G. A. Almond, *Public Opinion and Foreign Policy* (1950); D. B. Truman, *The Governmental Process* (1951); R. A. Dahl and E. C. Lindblom, *Politics, Economics and Welfare* (1953); V. O. Key, *Public Opinion and American Democracy* (1961).

interdependent, "cross-pressured" characteristics of individual interest in a technologically and economically advancing society; explicit recognition of the need for political leadership skilled in diagnosis, negotiation, and persuasion with respect to the requirements of group satisfaction and system survival in crisis situations; the opportunities for flexibility and decentralization by encouraging nongovernmental forms of initiative and devolution in public policy-making as alternatives to expanding the agenda and machinery of government bureaucracy.

Acknowledged difficulties presented by the equilibrium model are: 1) the question of priority and coordination among the multiplicity of individual interest reflected in group affiliations (family, race, nationality, geography, vocation, socioeconomic status); 2) the tensions imposed upon the system and the indeterminancy of controlling standards of conduct in situations when loyalties to their respective groups conflict with those to the larger commonwealth; 3) the loss of focus upon membership and common interests in the inclusive political community, particularly when criteria of *group* loyalty, membership, skills, or material and moral resources, are substituted for traditional symbols of *individual* freedom and equality. The empirical ambiguities and complexities of group process theory defy reduction to a few, simple, analytical concepts and a unified deductive system of derived propositions. This very empiricism, however, suggests the possibility that democratic society assumes the existence of logically irreconcilable, differentiated processes of compulsory decision-making, each of which contains elements of legitimacy under appropriate times and conditions.

Polyarchal Democracy

The fourth model of democracy we shall distinguish is methodologically the most sophisticated, because its proponents carefully refrain from identifying their formal concepts with historical institutions or empirical reality. The theory of polyarchal democracy reduces the analytical variables to individual preferences expressed in voting decisions, under postulated rules or rigorously defined conditions under which the preferences of the majority have some rational possibility of being ascertained. Through logical elaboration of the *necessary conditions* for majority decision-making, "ideal sets of societal requisites" are deduced which provide the analytical categories (indices) by which observable approximation to democracy in the world of actual human societies can be measured and evaluated.[27] By virtue of its method of abstracting formal concepts from concrete, historical situations, and seeking to explain individual behavior in terms of hypothesized relationships between a minimal number of conceptual variables, the model of polyarchal democracy conforms more closely than group-process-and-equilibrium theory to the procedure of the natural sciences, and opens up the possibilities of linkages with "utility preference" and "mathematical game theories" of decision-making and "communications theories" of organizational behavior.[28] On the other hand,

Table 1. Typology of democratic theories, related to "Key" variable emphasized by each

Model of democracy	Analytical element
Ideological	Individual value perception and identification
Institutional	Constitutional rules
Polycentric equilibrium	Societal bases of power
Polyarchal decision-making	Conditions of rational choice

its rationalist assumptions and the technical rigor of its analytical procedures tend to alienate descriptively oriented social scientists, and to restrict its vogue to the relatively small number who enjoy formal, deductive theorizing.

To summarize: we recognize first that the problem is one of constructing dynamic, operational models for political systems in general, not merely the American variety. Secondly, each of the four models identifies in its own way an apparently necessary but different element in constructing an empirically satisfactory theory of political democracy. Thus, in Table 1 the ideological

27. R. A. Dahl, *A Preface to Democratic Theory*, chs. 3–5, and the sources cited in n. 17 above. Dahl insists, as some economists and mathematically oriented theorists do not, upon the distinction between *constitutional restraints* and *social requisites* for democracy, pointing out that the Madisonian theory of democracy confined attention to the legal Constitution and neglected the problem of social structure and group relationships (in our terms, institutional democracy).

28. K. W. Deutsch, *The Nerves of Government* (1963); D. Bell, "Twelve Modes of Prediction: A Preliminary Sorting of Approaches in the Social Sciences," *Daedalus*, 93 (Summer 1964).

model stresses the importance of specifying the preferred order of public values maintained at the level of individual perception and support of the political system. The institutional model focuses upon legal-constitutional rules controlling the actors engaged in political controversy in the politico-governmental arena. The group-process theory points to the need for specifying the social and organizational bases for political leaders' authority, influence, and power. The polyarchal model of individual preference articulates the potentialities and limits of rational choice and calculation in collective decision-making.

In the third place, American social science has not yet been notably successful in integrating these (and perhaps other) elements into a unified theory of the political system.[29] Daniel Bell has documented several such attempts: for example, a monistic, psycho-cultural model of personality, or a technocratic model of militaristic mobilization, could be added to the well-known Marxian mode of production as the "prime mover" of the political system. Few social scientists today, however, would pretend that a single dominant-factor model would be quantitatively or empirically satisfactory, let alone justified by trend analysis.

III. Empirical Affirmations

Our brief foray into theory-building in American social science has brought into focus certain shortcomings of democratic theory in developing a unified framework of concepts and indices adequate to its own standards for comparative analysis of political systems.[30] It is hoped, however, that the critical difficul-

29. The foregoing was written well before the appearance of Easton's *Systems Analysis of Political Life*, Apter's *Politics of Modernization*, or Almond and Powell's *Comparative Politics*. In the writer's opinion, these works still employ the notion of "system" in the sense of a metaphoric analogy from which they derive a logical set of terms, increase their ability to translate insights into connected propositions and hypotheses, and promote more widespread adoption of common vocabularies. By scientific standards, however, the standing of general systems theory, notwithstanding these extraordinary efforts, remains no less metaphysical than the older concepts of organism, mechanism, and process. It is our empirical understanding of political behavior and organization on a comparative basis that has advanced, and the system concept has not only been associated with this development but undoubtedly has contributed to it.

30. This judgment is not intended to slight the important quantitative work of the Yale Political Data Center and similar enterprises. Cf. B. M. Russett *et al.*, *World Handbook of Political and Social Indicators* (New Haven, Conn.: Yale University Press, 1964) ; S. M. Lipset, "Some Social Requisites of Democracy,"

ties derive not from the fact–value distinction or from a desire of social scientists to "retreat from politics," as has been charged by Christian Bay and others,[31] but from (a) the assumption that a general theory of politics must be based on either logical or empirical grounds exclusively; (b) the selection of too small a number of relevant analytical categories; (c) the uncertainties in authoritative opinion over the treatment of the selected variables as axiomatic, causally dependent, or conditionally necessary in a logically coherent, explanatory theory.

Meanwhile, it remains to point out how and in what respects systematic empirical research has produced evidence that supports the assumption of constitutional democracy on grounds other than inspiring assertions of faith and appeals to personal preferences of value and vocabulary. Perhaps the first empirical finding that needs to be emphasized is that specialists in "intelligence" about human behavior in political societies have been able to produce *public data and concepts* about the *kinds and attributes of people* and *their rulers, their expectations, perceptions, and social affiliations,* which are useful both to policy-makers and to theorists seeking to understand the legal and social conditions conductive to the survival of democracy or to revolutionary reversion to authoritarian rule. Such information, to be sure, validates no assumptions about the historic necessity or inevitability of democracy, oligarchy, or dictatorship, but freedom to engage in such inquiry and the quantity, reliability, and availability of the data are markedly more noticeable in political systems which maintain the values of political opposition, freedom of speech, press, and association, and accountability of political leaders to the electorate. The importance of publicly available, reliable information about human beings in their so-

---

American Political Science Review, 53 (March 1959), 69–105; K. W. Deutsch, "Social Mobilization and Political Development," *ibid.,* 55 (September 1961), 493–514; P. Cutright, "National Political Development: Measurement and Analysis," *American Sociological Review,* 28 (April 1963), 255ff; R. H. Retzlaff, "Aggregate Data in Comparative Political Analysis," *Journal of Politics,* 27 (November 1965), 797–817.

31. "Politics and Pseudopolitics," *American Political Science Review,* 59 (March 1965), 39–51; H. J. Storing, ed. *Essays on the Scientific Study of Politics* (New York: Holt, Rinehart & Winston, 1962); B. Crick, *In Defense of Politics* (London: Penguin Books, 1964). For a more balanced view, see W. G. Runciman, *Social Science and Political Theory* (Cambridge University Press, 1963).

cial and political relationships perhaps lies less in the certainty that it will be used wisely and well, than that it makes more probable the clarification of alternative choices and consequences to the governed, as well as to their rulers and advisers. Insofar as mutual self-knowledge increases the possibility of understanding between rulers and ruled, and that technical requirements of political cohesion and survival will be reconciled with human demands and expectations, one major premise of democracy has been upheld.

Next, the concepts and methods of social science research have enabled analysts to differentiate between individuals and groups composing "the people" and so to ascertain what kinds of people exhibit what patterns of political participation, and to identify (if not always to predict specific policy outcomes of) the rational and nonrational factors in political motivation. It is useful here to discriminate between three dimensions of interpersonal relations in any political system—that is, between (1) individuals and the system as a whole, (2) individuals and their groups, (3) groups and the system. Before Tocqueville, democratic theories of politics traditionally tended to focus upon (1) and to view (2) and (3) as threatening or evil, whereas authoritarian doctrines tend to emphasize (3) and treat (1) and (2) as inconvenient obstacles justifying rule through propaganda, myth and force.

1. With respect to individual–system relationships, empirical research has demonstrated that people exhibit in varying degrees capacities for "self-rule" and "control of leaders" that in former times were dealt with by categorical (either-or) definition, belief, and speculation.[32] Political activity, information, and sense of effectiveness among the population have been measured and shown to be positively related to education and skills. All but a minority of ignorant, apathetic, hopelessly alienated people are capable of exercising (if not articulating) a *participant* role of pursuing a self- or group-motivated "cause" as well as the *sub-*

32. The following statements rely heavily upon V. O. Key, *Public Opinion and American Democracy* (New York: Knopf, 1961); G. Almond and S. Verba, *The Civic Culture* (Princeton: Princeton University Press, 1963); L. W. Milbrath, *Political Participation* (Chicago: Rand McNally, 1965); H. McClosky, "Consensus and Ideology in American Politics," *American Political Science Review*, 58: (June 1964), 361–382. On the intolerant patriotism problem, see M. M. Grodzins, *The Loyal and the Disloyal* (Chicago: University of Chicago Press, 1956).

ject role of obeying authoritative decisions with which they may specifically disagree. Consensus and generalized support for a democratic political system are not only demonstrable but compatible with a high level of participation, cleavage, and conflict, on specific issues. Democratic government seems to function better with a moderate rather than an intense, 100 per cent level of participation; also, under conditions in which not all issues are highly politicized, and when government is careful to respect the not-very-precise line between private and public responsibilities.

It has been shown that people want both government *responsive* to widespread demands for change in personnel and directions of policy and *effective* government able to symbolize, enact, and implement its program. Such ambivalent attitudes appear not only to be reconcilable but necessary conditions of government by "participant consent." Furthermore, the well-known differences between nonparticipant, passively participant, moderately active, and intensively active groups in the population are not fixed, unbridgeable gulfs, but variable attributes which are modifiable and responsive to institutional and incremental social reforms as well as to mystical, nonrational (charismatic) qualities of leaders. Finally, democratic governments are heavily dependent upon a broad minority stratum of politically informed and active citizens who perform several vitally important communication functions: criticizing the government-in-power, evaluating news and public information, and serving as a vehicle for anticipatory policy discussion between official policy-makers and the passive and the active portions of the electorate. Thus it turns out that majorities and minorities are not mutually exclusive categories of "individual–system" relationships, but may be interpreted as playing differentiated, operationally linked, functional roles, provided that the members (leaders, followers, and officials in the constitutional structure) understand their mutual needs and obligations in the system.

2. While confirming older postulates concerning symbolic attachments and differential intensities of individual relations with the larger political order, social science research has swung to the opposite pole from Rousseau's distrust and hatred of intermediate groups between the individual and the political commonwealth. Contemporary empirical theory almost accepts as truisms that (1) there is a high positive correlation between an active, aggressive, interactive associational (interpersonal and

group) life and a democratic political system; (2) groups most favorable to extremist, authoritarian political movements are those whose members are most withdrawn, most isolated, most lacking in personal relationships with peoples in other groups, occupations, modes of life.[33]

These findings do not solve the problem for democracy of intergroup conflict on the level of individual–group relationships. For one reason, individuals differentially interpret the beliefs and promises of the political system (freedom, justice, security, welfare) in terms of their varying primary and secondary group affiliations. Another problem is that individuals tend to restrict their intergroup contacts to those which are perceived as protective, rewarding, satisfying, and to regard "outside" groups as strange, threatening, evil. Interpersonal relationships which are induced or initiated by group leaders for *political purposes* tend to accentuate individual obligations to the inner and the proscribe almost as treasonable friendly contact with outsider groups. Efforts by politicians or opinion leaders to promote loyalty to a single, all-pervasive, unifying group such as race, religion, country, nation, or party arouse strong intrapersonal conflict within the individual, as well as extreme resentment among other groups who feel threatened when one arrogantly claims for itself a complete, compulsory, exclusive loyalty.

From these considerations the inferences produced by social science for democratic politics are principally negative, although not necessarily unconstructive. In democratic societies, a great many interpersonal associations are primarily economic, cultural, professional, and only indirectly political. Loyalties are recognized as being legitimately attached to a great many group affiliations, provided that the organizational leaders thereof do not promote mutually destructive attitudes of fear, hatred, and exclusion. Intergroup toleration does not require that the members of the different groups *like* each other, but it does require respect, in the sense that they recognize and work at the problem of mitigating intergroup differences, distrust, contempt, disagreements. Finally, it appears that partial, mutual realization of differing group interests and demands in specific situations may emerge out of overt conflict and disagreement quite as much as from assumed harmony and preconceived solidarity on issues.

33. H. Arendt, *The Origins of Totalitarianism* (1951); W. Kornhauser, *The Politics of Mass Society* (1959).

3. In conclusion one may ask: what evidence has empirical social science produced which throws new light on the age-old problem of "group–system" relationships, the universal possession of influence by "invisible" minorities, entrenched elites, or monopolistic organizations in democratic political systems? First of all, following Collingwood,[34] we may specify four categories for analyzing the relationships between rulers and ruled in all political systems: *replaceability, permeability* (representativeness), *diffusion* (dispersion), and *responsiveness* (both to group needs and popular demands). Secondly, we note that while these criteria are applicable to formal, constitutional rules, they must also be interpreted in an informal context of individual attitudes and intergroup relations in particular societies and cultures. Thirdly, on the level of group–system relationships, we are dealing not only with impersonal institutional factors, but also with the perceptions and influences anticipated and felt by group leaders, public officials, and politicians—powerholders and political actors—in the process of making public decisions.

The first category relates to elections as a device for choosing and controlling leaders. It is fairly well established that formal electoral arrangements are necessary but not sufficient to establish democratic government, and "free" elections are almost always a matter of degree. Nevertheless, different kinds of electoral systems have critically important effects upon the behavior of voters, office-seekers, and -holders.[35] Depending upon social conditions and such constitutional understandings as nonpersecution for official acts and subordination of the military to the civil authorities, over large areas of the world officeholders recognize the election process as determining the legitimacy of their tenure, as providing an acceptable, orderly means of transferring power, and anticipate their results as an integral factor in deciding to advocate legislative programs. Differing principles of apportionment alter the relative positions of electoral and legislative advantage for groups, sections, and parties who thereby ac-

34. R. G. Collingwood, *The New Leviathan* (New York: Oxford University Press, 1942), chaps. 25–26.
35. E. Lakeman and J. D. Lambert, *Voting in Democracies* (London: Allen and Unwin, 1955); W. J. M. Mackenzie, *Free Elections* (New York, Rinehart, 1958); F. A. Hermens, *Democracy v. Anarchy* (South Bend, Ind.: *Review of Politics*, 1941); A. DeGrazia, "General Theory of Apportionment," *Law and Contemporary Problems* (1952), pp. 256–267.

quire a great stake in retention or reform of the system. Free elections have been shown to develop a sense of political identity, drama and responsibility on the part of voters. Inquiry into the social origins and careers of elective officials has demonstrated that over extended time periods, as the suffrage expands toward universal adult inclusion, the election process produces significant changes in the composition of cabinets, chief executives, legislative bodies, and administrative hierarchies, making them more representative, although not necessarily in direct proportion to group and ideological differences in the voting population. Separated executive and legislative elections have a marked effect upon the quality of executive–legislative relations. Of central theoretical and practical attention, in the aftermath of World Wars I and II, has been the realization that electoral arrangements are a strategic technique for influencing the character of competition in political recruitment toward a multiparty or two-party system.[36] Across the entire political spectrum, both institutionally and from the standpoint of the elective elites, the electoral system acquires "constitutional" status, both as part of the formal rules and as an informal, political factor affecting their replaceability, permeability, dispersion, and responsiveness.

From the standpoint of nonelective elites, perhaps the most significant finding of empirical research is that while general elections decided by majority (the highest number) of ballots cast can produce effective, orderly government and establish general directions of public policy, they rarely constitute evidence of clear-cut majority preference on specific policies to which official decisions are obliged to conform. In addition to the influence that minority groups may bring to bear upon parties and candidates in the election process, therefore, democratic government, under conditions of free elections and political competition, not only increases the number and variety of minorities to whom elective officials must be attentive, but expands their freedom of access and maneuver in interelection periods through differentiated decision-making processes of legislation,

---

36. V. O. Key, *Southern Politics* (New York: Knopf, 1949); E. E. Schattschneider, *The Semi-Sovereign People* (1960); D. M. Duverger, *Political Parties* (1954); D. E. Butler, *The Electoral System in Britain* (1953); P. Williams, *Politics in Postwar France* (1954); J. K. Pollock, *et al.*, *German Democracy at Work* (1955); S. M. Lipset, "Party Systems and the Representation of Social Groups," *Archives of European Sociology*, 1 (1960), 50–85.

administration, and adjudication. Through a wide variety of consultative devices, interest groups are enabled to get themselves heard at one or more stages, to the point that some observers see democratic government to be ruled by "concurrent majority" or by "minorities' consent." Although this development has been accentuated in American experience, there is considerable evidence that "interest representation" of minority groups through formal or informal channels is a universal attribute of government, the principal point of comparison between democratic and authoritarian systems being that greater publicity and nonexclusivity in the democratic case accentuates problems of aggregating and reconciling particularistic or partial viewpoints.[37] With respect to the criterion of responsiveness, at least, minority group leaders appear to have little to fear from inability to get themselves heard.

Research thus has clarified "the myth" of majority will by showing that as myth its significance lies not in some assumed determinate content but in its utility as a symbol of the public interest, the common good, to which minorities have a contribution to make but no one minority the right to dominate. Research has elaborated the elements and participants in processes of democratic decision-making, showing that they comprise elective politicians, appointive politicians, and bureaucrats, scientific and professional experts, leaders of both organized interest groups and amorphous opinion movements; it has documented cases in, which the structure of decision-making was highly centralized, greatly decentralized, and combinations of both; it has revealed the process as one of continuing mutual adjustment, in which the values of the participants undergo modification as a condition of incremental, partial satisfaction and mutual recognition of needs; it has demonstrated the stability of a political system which does not centralize all decisions but allows a great deal of devolution to bureaucratic and nongovernmental levels of responsibility subject to scrutiny and review by higher political and judicial authority. Research has demonstrated that electoral processes can encourage moderation of factional spirit between political parties and intelligent selectivity on the part of voters;[38] they can set limits of tolerability to decisions made in detail by

37. See references in fn. 19 above, and H. W. Ehrmann, ed., *Interest Groups on Four Continents* (Pittsburgh: University of Pittsburgh Press, 1958).

38. V. O. Key (with the assistance of M. Cummings), *The Responsible Electorate* (Cambridge, Mass.: Harvard University Press, 1966).

opinion minorities and professional experts. If research has not produced a formal theory of political decision-making with a determinate set of criteria appropriate to all times and conditions, it has suggested in the absence of such criteria the wisdom of democracy in keeping open as long as possible the channels of access and the alternative choices available to public decision-makers.

J. Roland Pennock

Political Philosophy and Political Science

V. O. Key's posthumous book, *The Responsible Electorate*, underlines what all who were familiar with the man or his work well knew: that his concern for the scientific study of politics was paralleled by an equal concern for a particular set of political values, those we associate with liberal democratic institutions. To be sure, most of his work was devoted to the collection and analysis of political data, and no one was more determined that conclusions should be arrived at only on the basis of the maximum obtainable relevant facts and after analyzing these facts with as great impartiality and freedom from wishful thinking as could be mustered; yet he was always perfectly clear that values as well as facts are proper subjects of rational discourse and analysis. He never became a party to the controversies—one is tempted to say to the great schism—that developed during his lifetime between empiricists and normative theorists, or, better, between empiricists and nonempiricists, within the body of political scientists. It would be pointless to speculate why; a reference to his unlimited store of horse sense is probably sufficient. But why the schism? Where do we stand now? Are the differing approaches naturally antagonistic to each other? Or are they complementary? These questions may be more worth exploring.

First, what precisely is the nature of this cleft within the ranks of political scientists? Before we ask ourselves what caused it, we should be sure we are in agreement on its topography. Any discussion of this subject that begins, as this one has, with the assumption that political scientists are visibly divided into a twofold structure, that a Great Divide separates one large body of them from the rest, is a deliberate act of simplification, perhaps of oversimplification. Yet it is probably true that during most of the past twenty years, in particular, the division that has produced the strongest reactions, pro and con, has been that between behavioralists and antibehavioralists. Each camp has its own internal divisions, and many political scientists have steadily plotted a middle course, refusing to be identified with either group to the exclusion of the other. But the fact remains that a large, productive, and able group (including the bulk of the recognized leaders of the profession) has more or less self-consciously as a group attempted to revolutionize our discipline, and that many (although by no means all) of the members of the profession who did not identify with them have resisted vigorously and sometimes bitterly what they often saw as a Philistine onslaught.[1]

As to the nature of the behavioral attack (or, for that matter, as to the degree of its success) I have nothing to add to what Dahl has said so well.[2] Its aim was to apply the scientific method, vigorously and rigorously, to every nook and cranny of the discipline. Students of politics had been calling themselves scientists for decades: let them make good their claim! The ques-

1. From speaking of empiricists and normative theorists, or empiricists and nonempiricists, I have slipped over into speaking of behavioralists and antibehavioralists. Since it appears to have been between behavioralists and normative theorists that the sharpest differences (sometimes antagonisms) have arisen, I believe this terminology points in the right direction. It should not be allowed to obscure the fact that not all empirical political scientists would be properly classifiable as behavioralists. Many empirical political scientists have been sharply critical of tendencies they have noted in behavioral approaches to political science. Key himself noted a tendency to reductionism, to leaving the politics out of political science. V. O. Key, Jr. and Frank Munger, "Social Determinism and Electoral Choice: the Case of Indiana," in Eugene L. Burdick and Arthur J. Brodbeck, eds., *American Voting Behavior* (Glencoe, Ill.: Free Press, 1959), p. 281.

2. Robert A. Dahl, "The Behavioral Approach in Political Science: Epitaph for a Monument to a Successful Protest," *American Political Science Review,* 55 (December 1961), 763–772.

tion was not, for most behavioralists, at least, whether the traditional approaches had anything to contribute. Rather it was what might be accomplished by a new approach, above all by a new insistence on finding ways of studying political phenomena that admit of the application of rigorously scientific methods.

Before further discussion of what has been happening in our own discipline, however, it may be useful to seek perspective by observing what has happened in certain other disciplines, especially in some of those not too far removed from political science and political theory. Something in the nature of a revolution has been experienced in other fields as well. Each has had its own pattern and timing, but two features in particular seem frequently to recur. One is a suspicion of, and reaction against, great "systems." In an increasingly complicated world and in a world in which we have more detailed knowledge of any particular field of study, the tension between an overarching body of theory and the complex facts for which it should account often reaches the breaking point. In particular, systems based upon a series of deductions from a set of very simple assumptions have become highly vulnerable. Those who study the facts find the theories vague or dependent upon questionable assumptions. A revulsion against theory in the large is sometimes the reaction of the would-be rigorous scientist under these circumstances.

Second, among the rather vague, general assumptions often underlying system-building in the sciences of man and society, one of the commonest and most vulnerable is that of rational man. In somewhat different ways, Adam Smith and Thomas Hobbes may both serve as examples of this type of reasoning. Theories derived from this type of assumption are nowadays open to attack either on the radical ground that man is basically irrational rather than rational, or on the more limited basis that what is rational behavior cannot be agreed upon with sufficient precision to provide a starting point for deducing a general system.

In the field of economics, a largely American phenomenon that exhibits both of these features occurred early in the century, probably reaching its culmination in the twenties. I refer to the rather ill-defined movement of so-called "institutional" economists. It is not necessary here to attempt any description of this loosely defined "school," in which the name of Thorstein Veblen bulks large, and those of Walton H. Hamilton and John R. Commons should also be mentioned. It constituted a revolt against a general theoretical system; it did not attempt to substitute another system; and it did involve an emphasis on empirical studies and on inductive rather than deductive reasoning. Further, in its attack upon the individualistic and hedonistic psychology underlying orthodox economic theory, it constitutes a paradigm case of antirationalism. The "economic man" of orthodox economics was a rational man, who knew his own interest and traded and otherwise acted accordingly, at least in the economic sphere. From the behavior imputed to this man the whole system of orthodox economic theory was developed. Neither the psychological theory of the economic man nor the body of economic theory based upon him has been the same again, since this "institutionalist" revolution, though institutionalism itself has long since ceased to be a significant movement.

In fact, in economics, as in other fields—but perhaps more so—the cycle has gone full around and is in a sense repeating itself. I refer to the development of macrocosmic economics, and in particular of Keynesian theory. Here it would appear that system-making has again taken over—which is perhaps simply another way of saying that in economics, the most developed of the social sciences, the attack upon general theory was relatively short-lived. Modern economic models rely much more heavily than they did in the past upon empirical data; but economists do not have to content themselves with "narrow-gauge" theory, nor do they consider it a virtue to do so.

Psychology has also experienced movements and changes that bear resemblance to what has happened in our own field. At one time—and not too long ago—great theoretical constructs— Freudianism, Behaviorism (remember J. B. Watson?), and Gestaltism each had its large body of followers, and each tried to dominate the field. Today, unless my hearing is failing, one no longer hears the din of these battles. Psychology may be "experimental" or it may be "clinical" (and this division, of course, reflects the consequences of the battles of yore); but in either case it is more concerned with narrow-gauge theory or even with developing theory from the ground up in bits and pieces than in projecting an all-encompassing system. What part the "rational man" plays in contemporary psychology it would not be for an outsider to say, but it is clear that he has long since been tumbled from his heights, with reverberations throughout the social sciences. At the same time it would also appear to be true that the notion of rationality stands higher today than it did a generation ago. (Note the increased attention being given to cognition.)

In philosophy perhaps more strikingly than anywhere else the day of the great systems appears to have gone, at least for the time being. It would be difficult to point to a particular decade or two that witnessed the grand confrontation between system-builders and their opponents in this field. Rather it would appear that at least from the time of Hegel the system-builders have been on the decline. But it is especially characteristic of the philosophy of the past generation that philosophers have been inclined to confine themselves to more and more rigorous analysis of smaller and smaller questions. (Curiously enough, the exponents of linguistic analysis and of radical empiricism seem to have found little kinship with rigorous science and the empiricist movement in political science.) Efforts at systematic philosophizing are not unknown today; they may even be on the increase; but, in accordance with the spirit of our period, they are proceeding with great care and caution.

More specifically, the field of moral philosophy, which is of special interest to normative political theory, has witnessed a revolution against rationalism or intuitionism (that is, an ethics based on "self-evident" first principles).[3] Of course rationalism in the Cartesian sense had long since been dealt a crippling blow by Hume. More recently, however, especially since the work of G. E. Moore, naturalistic theories of ethics have for a long time been widely out of favor. The idea that the good and the right can be arrived at by calculation, or by any kind of reasoning—as held by that most popular of naturalistic ethical theories, utilitarianism—was rejected by Moore. His elaboration of the "naturalistic fallacy" provided the starting point for most subsequent ethical theorizing. Furthermore, since Moore, and especially since the work of C. L. Stevenson, the tendency has been to stress attitudes, feelings, and desires to persuade and to recommend as the crucial elements in ethics. Here again it is worthy of note, however, that we may be already experiencing another turn of the wheel. Recent developments in the realm of ethical theory tend to lay stress once more on reasoning.

3. See George C. Kerner, *The Revolution in Ethical Theory* (New York and London: Oxford University Press, 1966).

Finally, one might mention the field of jurisprudence as having undergone similar transformations. It is particularly relevant to refer to the development of "American legal realism," especially in the thirties, as an example of the attack upon rationalistic assumptions. Here again one may point to something of a reversion, or at least a reaction to previous excesses, in recent years. It is not that law men have gone back to conceptualism; but today's stress on "principled decision-making" is a far cry from the "what-the-judge-had-for-breakfast" jurisprudence that was so popular in the thirties.

Political science, then, in experiencing a "revolution," is not only true to the nature of its subject matter, but is also sharing an experience with related disciplines. The parallel goes further. In political science, too, the two major characteristics of the other revolutions have put in their appearance: the revolt against great systems and the revolt against rationalistic assumptions. Theoretical systems such as those of Hobbes and Hegel have gone out of fashion; and political scientists have been less concerned to reason from what rational men *would* do (after the fashion of Bentham or James Mill) than to try to determine what actual men (believed to be quite short on rationality) *do* do. Yet here too it is worth noting that some tendency to revert from the extremes of these tendencies may be noted. The work of James Buchanan and Gordon Tullock may be allowed to suggest to the readers a not inconsiderable movement toward the construction of systems, or models, making use of assumptions of rational behavior.[4]

But in this matter of intradisciplinary revolutions, political science has also its peculiar problems. They flow from the fact that traditionally, dating back at least to Aristotle, political scientists have dealt with both the normative and the empirical. Political scientists down to quite recent times have regularly sought both to study political institutions scientifically and to evaluate them. Whether they did a good job of keeping these separate tasks from improperly influencing each other is not the question. The fact that they had this duality of interests has made them increasingly suspect, at least within their own fraternity.

Before inquiring whether the separation should be attempted or not, perhaps it would be well to inquire why the other dis-

4. See James M. Buchanan and Gordon Tullock, *The Calculus of Consent* (Ann Arbor: University of Michigan Press, 1962).

ciplines we have discussed did not have the same problem—if indeed they did not. Economics provides the clearest case. By and large, economists do not need to bother themselves with the bases for justifying economic systems because they can *assume* general agreement on the value of maximizing production. To be sure, that leaves open the question of how to compare two systems that *distribute* the product differently, and welfare economists do deal with this question. In doing so, they find themselves treating of normative issues. Many of them, however, seek to avoid the (ethically) tough questions by the Paretian device of limiting changes to those that leave no single individual in a less favorable position than that which he enjoyed before the change. The other disciplines discussed above (except for jurisprudence, which in this respect is not different from political science) are not, in the main, "policy sciences." For this reason, the problem of maintaining a "value-free" stance does not arise to plague them in an acute form.

Not only is political science a policy science but—and this is the crucial point—its subject matter, the polity, *controls* other subsystems, and does so by means of severe sanctions, including the punishment of death. Moreover, this control is exercised by identified individuals. This combination does not prevail in the other subjects we have been discussing. It inevitably leads to the question of who *should* govern, and how. The subject that deals with (whether or not it can properly be said to be confined to) the authoritative allocation of values finds it difficult, if not impossible, to avoid consideration of the *just* allocation of values—especially on account of that word "authoritative." Doubtless the "ises" of politics *can* be discussed without the "oughts," but the "oughts" clamor so loudly for consideration that to separate them on anything but the most tentative and provisional basis provokes objection if not rejection. Furthermore, the pure scientist in politics perennially runs the risk of smuggling in his own values in a way that escapes that criticism to which all parts of scientific endeavor should be subject. On the other side of the coin, to study the "oughts" of politics without reference to, and considerable understanding of the "ises," is an open invitation to visionary speculation, unrelated to reality.

Thus the discipline of political science has found itself torn between the situation just depicted and the mounting, quite understandable, and even laudable demands for a "value-free" science. Political theorists and empirical political scientists have alike been caught in the positivist trap, and they have often gone off in opposite directions, avoiding sound, inclusive theory. More specifically, political theorists have often retreated into history, into "functionalist" explanations of what interests (consciously or subconsciously) dictated the conclusions of particular figures in the history of political theory, into studies of ideology and of the sociology of knowledge,[5] and into detailed criticism of individual writers. Also they have rightly emphasized the imponderables of politics but have wrongly sneered at efforts to measure what can be measured and to find measurable correlates for the imponderables.

Empirical political scientists have often made a fetish of measuring. Worse still, they have confused efforts to avoid bias caused by unconscious or uncriticized values with the avoidance of all evaluation. They have too frequently adopted a crude positivism that most philosophers, if they ever held it, have long since abandoned.[6] For, whatever may have been true a few years ago, philosophers today recognize, and even insist, that to maintain that a given statement or type of statement can not be proved is not to place it in the category of the whimsical and arbitrary. It is not to banish it to the realm of ejaculations,[7] or

5. For a brilliant statement of the limitations of the study of ideologies and of the sociology of knowledge, see Judith N. Shklar, *Political Theory and Ideology* (New York: Macmillan, 1966), Introduction.

6. In support of the last part of this proposition let me rely for the moment upon the statement of a respected contemporary historian of recent ethical theory. He says: "Logical positivism as known to the Thirties and to its enemies is dead or dying" (William K. Frankena, "Ethical Theory," in Roderick M. Chisholm, and others, *Philosophy* [Englewood Cliffs, N.J.: Prentice-Hall, 1964], p. 402). The extent to which political scientists have adopted this crude positivism is perhaps best left to the judgment of the reader, particularly since it is more frequently implicit than avowed. When David Easton states it as his working assumption (and one, he declares, that is "generally adopted today in the social sciences") that "values can ultimately be reduced to emotional responses conditioned by the individual's total life-experiences" he is stating an assumption with which I would not quarrel, granted my understanding of what he means by "can ultimately be reduced." (David Easton, *The Political System* [New York: Knopf, 1953], p. 221). But frequently political scientists go on to conclude that questions of value and of moral obligation are not susceptible to rational analysis and discussion. At that point they become what I have referred to as "crude positivists."

7. The reference is to A. J. Ayer's famous statement that to say "stealing money is wrong" is equivalent to saying "stealing money!!!" Alfred Jules Ayer, *Language, Truth, and Logic* (New York: Dover, 1946), p. 107.

even to that of "meaningless" statements. On the contrary, "justification" is a valid category, applicable to "ought" propositions and, many would say, also to value-judgments. For a long time the view widely prevailed that a proposition that is in principle nonconfirmable was "meaningless," or at best that it had only "emotive meaning." But today it is generally recognized that this contention was a mere dogma. Much that makes "sense," as opposed to "nonsense," falls in the realm of the nonconfirmable. To say "I find that people who govern themselves are happy: therefore I oppose self-government" would generally be regarded as nonsense, at best, although it is not logically fallacious. Of course the reason it would be regarded as nonsense is that everyone agrees, without proof, that happiness is good and, other things being equal, ought to be furthered, not "opposed." The process of justifying or vindicating an ought proposition is often simply a matter of showing that it is related as means to end to some broader proposition to which the audience is already committed. The combination of reasoning and appeal to experience may be simple or long and complicated. In other cases it may be a matter of demonstrating that a given course of action or a suggested moral rule or an evaluation is essential to the realization of the needs, interests, or aspirations of the person to whom the appeal is being made.[8]

Argumentation—reasoning, in short—is a technique for much wider application than to matters of proof. Hume's famous statement that reason is no more than "a slave to the passions" and, even more, his almost equally famous statement that reason cannot show that I should prefer saving the world from destruction to avoid pricking my finger, have been seriously misleading. Human reasoning cannot demonstrate such propositions but it can advance "reasons," good reasons as well as bad ones. Many appeals to reason are not appeals to logic. When we try to persuade our children not to bully their smaller playmates—for example, by pointing out that they don't like it when larger children bully them—we are appealing to their reason. When we argue for strict majority rule, in a given situation, on the grounds that requirement of an extraordinary majority would place great power (for obstruction) in the hands of certain vested interests, and that these interested parties possess such a strong, cohesive

8. See Herbert Feigl, "De Principiis Non Disputandum . . . ?" in Max Black, ed., *Philosophical Analysis* (Ithaca, N.Y.: Cornell University Press, 1950), esp. p. 145.

self-interest that they are not likely to be either persuaded or maneuvered into a position where, say, a two-thirds vote can be obtained against them, we are making a rational argument. When we seek to convince a group that a given course of action will result in a threat to law and order in our community, and argue further, perhaps by reference to similar experiences in similar political environments, that this development in turn is likely to encourage continuing disorder and the mobilization of illegal forces on the other side in such a way as to defeat the group's immediate objectives as well as its long-run interest in order, we are utilizing reason. Partly we are calculating probable consequences; partly we are calling attention to certain values, in this case order, and weighing them against other values—perhaps liberty, justice, or material welfare.[9]

Let us examine more carefully the kind of reasoning that takes place when we make moral judgments and value judgments about questions of public policy: I would suggest that at the core of any system of morals that has secured and retained the support of large human communities over substantial periods of time will be found some such propositions as "human life is

9. Note the word "weighing" in the sentence above. What do we do when we "weigh" one value against another? It is neither a pure exercise of reason nor is it a matter of making an arbitrary choice, as by tossing a coin. In the first place it calls for a full examination of all relevant consequences, making use of that marriage of reason and experience known as the scientific method. One moral philosopher has put it this way: "A 'neutral' mapping of consequences includes their effects upon the person who assigned the end, hence an investigation of the degree and quality of his attachment to his proposed goal. For it is elementary that a person's whims are to be distinguished from his stable and enduring goals, and that a rational man who is to be regarded as master of himself must have some insight into himself and his aims. But once this door is opened the passageway leads on and on. Ideally, full advice to the person who asked for a cost estimate of the envisaged goals would include their scope and function in his life, their mode of development, intensity points, termination points, possible transformations, relation to common ends, possible interactions with the ends of others and their mutual alteration, and so forth." (Abraham Edel, *Ethical Judgment: the Use of Science in Ethics* [Glencoe, Ill.: Free Press, 1955], p. 54). But after this procedure has been pushed to the limit—at least to the limit of time and energy!—it still remains to make a decision. Here is the final "weighing." What is its nature? It is not calculation or demonstration. But again it is not drawing lots or following whim. It is a decision made seriously, deliberately, calmly, imaginatively, and impartially, in the light of the total situation that has been elucidated by the preceding analysis. This is the essence of moral reasoning. See Richard B. Brandt, *Ethical Theory* (Englewood Cliffs, N.J.: Prentice-Hall, 1959), pp. 73–74 and 244–52.

good"; "human life is to be protected and fostered"; "neither the interests nor the desires of any human being should be harmed," "other things being equal," or "without justification." The process of justification then must involve reasoning.

Suppose it is a question of whether better schooling should be provided for the culturally disadvantaged than for other children. The affirmative might base its reasoning on the theory that society has injured these children and therefore owes them compensation. The other side might reply, "but this was not intentional injury." "Yet," comes the counter, "I am responsible for injuries that I cause inadvertently as well as for those prompted by malice." "But, surely," it is replied, "I am not responsible for all the incidental and unforeseen effects of acts or omissions the main thrust of which had nothing to do with the issue at hand." Although one could pursue this line of argument further, it is easy to anticipate that sooner or later the ground of contention is likely to be shifted. The parties will move from discussion in terms of responsibility for past actions to responsibility for the future. Reasoning turns to calculation of probable consequences. How much would an extra million put into the schools in question benefit the disadvantaged students? Obviously this is not a question that can be answered with precision. How much would a like sum spent on improved schooling for the especially talented benefit *them?* Could both benefits be translated, however crudely and uncertainly, into terms of increased social productivity? Cost-benefit analysis may lead to agreement.

At some point, however, questions may arise that do not submit to solution by this method. We may, but not necessarily, have ultimately to choose between decreasing the misery of a few and increasing the comfort (at far above the "misery" level) of a great many. If so, reasoning in terms of calculation may be at an end. It may still be possible to "reason" with interested parties on one side in terms of appealing to basic human sympathy, and by various devices to try to get them to put themselves in the shoes of the "others." But not any or all of these devices can guarantee agreement. Possibly not even the most disinterested, neutral observer would see a clear right and wrong in the situation. But this unfortunate stalemate would be reached only after a long and varied process of reasoning. In a dynamic society, with conditions and therefore considerations and calculations continually shifting, it would probably not be reached at all. For practical purposes, processes of reasoning in pursuit of rational justification can go on without limit, in an unending series of approximations. Ultimate conflicts between "justice" and "the public interest," if they exist in theory, are unlikely to develop in practice, or, if they do, to be long-lasting.[10]

Let us move on to another, more clearly political example of normative reasoning: application of the "one man, one vote" principle. We shall assume that the basic democratic premise that all sane adults should have the vote and that none should have more than one vote is accepted.[11] The question is whether that principle entails the further proposition that legislative districting and other aspects of the process of electing representatives ought to be so arranged that each voter's influence on the outcome should be exactly the same as that of every other voter. Of course as soon as one begins to think about such a proposition, difficulties sprout at every turn. Most of them I shall not pursue or even point out. I suggest that before we get very far we shall find ourselves driven to inquire as to what was the basis for our original assumption. Suppose the result of such an inquiry leads us to believe that we assumed that, in elections, each should count for one and none for more than one because, as Jeremy Bentham once declared, otherwise all political reasoning would be "at a stand." In other words, we could concoct no feasible, reliable, and not-readily abusable way of directly weighting individual votes in accordance with ability to use them wisely (either for the individual voter's own protection and advancement or for that of society as a whole). If that was the reasoning that underlay our original decision to apply the "one man, one vote" principle directly to individual voters, we should consider the matter all over again before assuming its equal applicability to the method of selecting legislative representatives. If, for example, we believe that scientific study supports the view that a competitive system of political parties, state by state, makes government more responsive to voter interests, then we must examine the effects of the allocation of legislative seats on the party system. It is at least conceivable that we might conclude on

10. A full discussion of the use of reason in the elucidation of "the public interest" is provided by Richard E. Flathman, *The Public Interest, an Essay Concerning the Normative Discourse of Politics* (New York: John Wiley, 1966).

11. Of course this assumption is also one that could be argued about in rational terms. It just is not the one being selected for discussion here.

the basis of this study that our original principle called for something other than its literal translation to the next layer of voting arrangements. We might also conclude, on the basis again of a scientific study, that legislative districts ought to be arranged so as to coincide with real communities, so as to facilitate knowledge of candidates and communication between them and their constituents.[12] One can easily think of other considerations of this kind that might indicate that the original objective could best be satisfied by departure at the legislative level from the "one man, one vote" rule.

Perhaps, however, the rationale of the "one man, one vote" rule at the voter level is different from the one hypothesized above. Suppose it was to uphold the principle of (equal) human dignity by symbolizing it at this most basic level of practical democracy. Here again no direct translation of principle would follow—even less so than on the basis of the previous hypothesis. That job (symbolization of equality) once done, we might then seek to pursue the public interest by other electoral arrangements, as long as they did not patently deny—and thus defeat— the principle of basic human dignity. What would and what would not defeat that purpose (and how much) is obviously a difficult question. Survey techniques might contribute something to its solution. They might not solve it completely to everyone's satisfaction. But until all efforts had been made to get the answer to this question we would be in no position to make a rational decision on the question of redistricting.

Much misunderstanding concerning the nature of ethical reasoning arises from the assumption that it must be done in the abstract. If one thinks of trying to decide whether "liberty" or "security" is more important, it is easy to conclude that reason can have very little to do with it. But if one rather waits to decide that issue until it arises in a particular case, the situation is altogether different. Let us suppose it is a question of whether it is justifiable to resort to preventive detention under certain (specified) circumstances in contemporary India. At least some of these circumstances can be counted or measured—the instances of disorder, the lives lost, the property destroyed, for example. One can estimate the likelihood of continued disorder leading to

12. See Lewis A. Dexter, "Standards for Representative Selection and Apportionment," in J. Roland Pennock and John W. Chapman, eds., *Representation, Nomos X* (New York: Atherton Press, 1968).

the violent overthrow of the government. One can investigate the experience with preventive detention in other Indian states: how many people detained? For how long? Does experience show that governments have grown to rely on this device rather than to attempt reforms? Have people been so intimidated that they cease to express discontent and to suggest remedies? Or has the danger of violence actually been increased? One could add many more such relevant questions.[13] If agreement could be obtained as to these and similar facts, the job of seeking agreement on values would be well advanced.

But such empirical investigation, while in many cases it may solve what at first appeared to be irreconcilable differences as to values, need not end the process. After all the relevant probabilities have been assessed as scientifically as possible, differences of opinion as to what the public interest requires may persist. While it would be Utopian to suppose that unanimity could ever be secured, it does not follow that we have yet exhausted all resources for obtaining agreement. We are no longer discussing liberty in the abstract *versus* security in the abstract. Rather we are discussing, let us assume, the liberty of X individuals for Y weeks *versus* the probability of ten riots of certain assumed proportions, and so on. At this point the original abstract concern for liberty may be modified as applied to this situation. Conversely, if ways have been discovered during the course of the investigation to cut down the likelihood of riots without resort to preventive detention, the abstract concern for security may prove irrelevant.

The current cry for "participatory democracy," and particularly the provision in our antipoverty legislation for giving a share in administration to representative members of the impoverished groups, provide a challenge to political theorists and an opportunity for fruitful collaboration between political theorists and political scientists. At least since the writings of John Stuart Mill, theorists of democracy have argued that popular participation in the political process was valuable not only because of the information it would elicit and not only as a means of giving the participants a means of enforcing their demands, but that it was also good because of the direct effects upon the participants. Give people some power and responsibility, so the argument runs, and they will broaden their moral and intellectual horizons.

13. See David H. Bayley, *Public Liberties in the New States* (Chicago, Ill.: Rand McNally, 1964).

They will find themselves compelled—or at least impelled—to learn more about their situation, their problems, and means for their solution or amelioration and to have some concern for the public interest, or at least for a wider range of interests than those of their own family. Democratic theorists since Mill's day have varied greatly as to the weight they gave to this argument, but it is probably fair to conclude that most have given it some weight. (Moreover, it is safe to say that the differences in the weight they give to the argument arise not out of differences as to the value they would attribute to moral and intellectual development but from their differing estimates as to the extent of the developmental effects that would in fact flow from participation in politics in certain ways.) Yet, to the best of my knowledge, little attempt has been made to verify it or, by the use of survey techniques, to evaluate it. Collaboration between theorist and scientist is seldom more plainly indicated. Participatory democracy clearly involves costs. How much is it worth?

At this stage, before discussing my final example, I must introduce another ethical principle—the principle of universalizability. By this is meant simply that an ethical proposition that applies in one case must apply in all other like cases, and more particularly that a rule that applies to me must apply to you, and vice versa, assuming that the situations are not dissimilar in relevant respects.[14] It is unlikely that any person who is interested in moral discourse, who is sensitive to moral issues, will deny this proposition; hence it is hardly necessary here to pursue the arguments among moral philosophers as to whether the rule is a matter of logic, as some contend, or whether we are committed to it as a matter of linguistic usage, or simply by general agreement.[15]

With this principle in mind, let us suppose that we are con-

14. "Relevant" differences must be differences that would make the rule inapplicable in one of the cases. That is to say, the rules themselves will furnish the guidance as to what is relevant. Note that the difficult question as to whether a person should consider himself on a basis of equality with (that is, in the same class as) others does not arise here. The question at issue is not how I should treat myself, but how I should be treated by others.

15. Discussions of these issues will be found in Richard B. Brandt, *Ethical Theory* (Englewood Cliffs, N.J.: Prentice-Hall, 1959), esp. chaps. 2, 9, 10; Marcus George Singer, *Generalization in Ethics* (New York: Knopf, 1961); R. M. Hare, *Freedom and Reason* (London: Oxford University Press, 1963); and George C. Kerner, *The Revolution in Ethical Theory* (New York and London: Oxford University Press, 1966).

fronted by a more radical difference in value-judgments than those we have posited thus far. Take the case of confirmed Nazis and a liberal democrat. The question is with respect to the treatment of Jews. At first, it is likely, the Nazis will rest their case on factual assumptions. These assumptions are thoroughly explored, with the result that no empirical basis for discrimination is discovered. The claims to the contrary are exploded. Perhaps most of the Nazis at this point abandon their defense of Hitler's practices. But let us further assume that one particular Nazi is of the hard-core type; he is a fanatic.[16] He insists that Jews ought to be exterminated. We then persuade him (perhaps by falsified evidence) that he himself, although he has been ignorant of the fact, is of Jewish descent. Will he accept the logical consequence, that he should be exterminated? Or will he change his mind? Or will he continue to insist that other Jews, but not he, should be put to death? If he takes the latter line, he has abandoned the rules of moral discourse, particularly that of consistency or adherence to the rule of generalizability. We are no longer disagreeing as to what morality entails; he is refusing to accept the logical consequence of a line of argument on which he had freely embarked.

On the other hand, if he changes his mind—a not unlikely consequence, we may surmise—reasoning has had an effect. Our stratagem of deceit was not crucial. It was merely a dramatic means of insuring that he played the game fairly, asserting only the validity of rules by which he was willing to be governed, and which reflected his informed, impartial, and imaginative judgment.[17] It cannot validly be objected, then, that this is an instance of persuasion but not of reasoning. Much persuasion makes use of reasoning.

Finally, if the Nazi still insisted that Jews, including himself, should be exterminated, it may be that reason has gone as far as it can: he is a fanatic; by definition he will not listen to reason. For our purposes, the important thing is that it is only at the end of this long process, at each stage of which some may be convinced, that we reach the hard core where further reasoning is of no persuasive effect.[18] Even here, it is worth noting, we attribute

16. Cf. R. M. Hare's discussion, *Freedom and Reason* (London: Oxford University Press, 1963), chaps. 8–9.

17. See note 9, above.

18. The example and line of argument are from Hare. He would stop at this point. Since I am concerned with the use of reason to obtain agreement on mat-

our failure not to a weakness of "reason" but to the individual's lack of rationality.[19] We assume at least a certain area of agreement in the matter of value-judgments, regardless of whether those judgments be based upon emotions or culturally determined attitudes; and when a person refuses to be bound by this area of agreement we call him "irrational," or even "insane." [20]

I have been arguing that normative political theory is not separated from empirical political science by such a broad gulf as we have often been led to believe. Rather, it chiefly depends upon empirical research, upon calculation of consequences (of exactly the same kind as is involved in science generally), and upon a process of reasoning which, while not solely a matter of deductive logic, is nonetheless governed by familiar principles of reasoning, and is far removed from sheer arbitrariness. Moral reasoning, in other words, is not a shouting match. Modern trends in philosophy, and in particular in moral philosophy, are in no sense out of touch with science. Political science can be scientific without being antiphilosophical and it can be empirical without shunning ethical questions. And if it is to make the contributions it should to the pursuit of public policy—and here I become dogmatic—it must deal with ethical questions. It must refuse to back away from the process of evaluation. It must not leave that task to others who are less well-informed about the empirical matters without which value-judgments must be made *in vacuo* and for that reason blindly.[21]

_____

ters of public policy, I stop here too. This is not to say that I would accept Hare's ethical theory, which makes this point in the argument the end of the line. He is not much concerned about the possibility of fanatics, because he thinks they are rare. He believes that mostly people with moral ideals that are in conflict with those held by most rational men are suffering from a lack of sensitivity or imagination, which can be overcome by some such device as that used above. Other moral philosophers contend that rational value judgments and moral rules are the product of an indefinitely extended search for an ideal moral legislator. See Kerner, *Revolution in Ethical Theory,* chap. 5.

19. Fanaticism is defined as "unreasonable enthusiasm." *Webster's New World Dictionary of the English Language,* College Edition (Cleveland and New York: World Publishing Co., 1959).

20. Cf. Sir Isaiah Berlin, "Does Political Theory Still Exist?", in Peter Laslett and W. G. Runciman, eds., *Philosophy, Politics and Society* (Oxford: Basil Blackwell, 1962), pp. 1–33, esp. pp. 26–27.

21. I have argued elsewhere that, in the case of the study of political development, political scientists have missed important opportunities for making judgments and comparisons because they overlooked the fact that evaluations

Much of what I have been saying has been in defense of political *philosophy* as a part of political theory. Before concluding,
I should like to comment briefly on the other side of the controversy. It is frequently charged against behavioral political scientists that they concentrate on the nonrational elements of politics
to the exclusion of the rational elements. This charge has been
directed especially against voting studies.[22] As is so frequently
the case with quarrelling proponents of differing methodologies,
what is being objected to is not so much what the other fellow *is*
doing as what he is *not* doing. The division of labor among specialists, essential to progress, becomes, paradoxically, the object
of attack. The fear is expressed that concentration on one element
will lead to the neglect of others. It is a charge that can be made
with equal justification by either side. One answer is for scholars
to cease being protagonists for particular methods and get about
their business. Few adhered more faithfully to this pattern than
did V. O. Key. In the present context, however, it is important to
note what it is that the political scientists who are trying to ascertain and measure some of the (nonrational) determinants of
voting behavior are doing. As I see it, they are clearing the
ground and narrowing the area for study by those who concentrate upon issues, upon policy—that is to say, upon things that
appeal to reason. It will do us no good to blind ourselves to the
fact that our room for choice is restricted—not least by psychological and sociological factors which, at any given time at least,
are largely beyond our control. Policy-oriented students, seeking
to determine what is the most rational policy in a given situation,
will be aided if they know the constraints within which alone
they can operate effectively.

It is apparent that my discussion ends as a plea—a simple

could be based upon obtainable empirical evidence. J. Roland Pennock, "Political Development, Political Systems, and Political Goods," *World Politics*, 18
(April 1966), 415–434.

22. See, for instance, Walter Berns, "Voting Studies," in Herbert J. Storing,
ed., *Essays on the Scientific Study of Politics* (New York: Holt, Rinehart &
Winston, 1962), chap. 1. The author attacks the majority of voting studies for
seeking answers to the question of why people vote as they do in the realm of
the nonrational and the nonpolitical. See, for example, p. 22. It is worthy of
note that Berns exempts V. O. Key from the charges made in this chapter,
largely on the ground that, although Key used the "research techniques and the
language of modern social science," he did so not to formulate and test generalizations but "as an aid in political interpretation" (p. 5)

one. Political science has gained a great deal from contact with other social sciences. We have borrowed heavily from them and have been wise to do so. Sometimes, however, in our eagerness to prove that we are just as "scientific" as anyone, we have gone too far. We have overlooked the special reasons why practitioners of our discipline must not only deal with values but also (some of them, at least) must themselves evaluate. For this latter task it is imperative that they keep in contact with the latest developments among those who specialize in the science and philosophy of evaluation, the moral philosophers.

V. O. Key was not a philosopher; but neither was he an evangel for "value-free" science. We may well seek to emulate his tolerant spirit and commonsensical approach, measuring the measurable, seeking means to make as many concepts as possible subject to operational testing, and at the same time neither disregarding nor denigrating the ideas and aspects of politics that are resistant to both.

Frederick M. Watkins

Natural Law and the Problem of Value-Judgment

Political theory was a branch of political science in which V. O. Key, to judge at least by his publications, was not much interested. This was no personal idiosyncracy, but was typical of the times. Traditionally, this field had always been regarded as central to the discipline. When people believed that politics was a normative science, a science capable of elucidating the rightful purposes of political action, it had been natural to think of theory as being, in a very real sense, the most practical part of the study of politics, since it defined the ends toward which all other forms of political knowledge ought properly to serve as means. By the time of V. O. Key, however, this belief had been largely abandoned. Convinced that the very idea of a normative science was a contradiction in terms, most political theorists had long since given up attempting to provide any sort of authoritative guidance in matters of value-judgment. What passed for political theory in most American universities was a subject known, more properly, as the history of political thought. The only major exceptions were the Catholic schools, which still adhered to the normative system of Thomas Aquinas. Although political theory often continued to claim pride of place, and was given preferential treatment in many political-science curricula as the sole inescapable requirement, there was no longer any real reason to re-gard it as truly central. To anyone concerned with the realities of contemporary politics, Aristotle's evaluation of the ancient *polis* was hardly a burning issue. No man with the talents and interests of a V. O. Key could have been expected to pay more than pass-ing attention to problems of this sort.

What caused political theory to lose its former preeminence was the emergence of "value-free" science. This development was not limited to politics, but was characteristic of the prevail-ing intellectual climate. In recent times one of the outstanding peculiarities of social scientists has been their unwillingness to make overt normative judgments. In this they differ from the great majority of their predecessors, who felt no like inhibition. Under the rubric of "natural law," generations of outstanding scholars and publicists had felt called upon to devote a large part of their energies to the establishment of rational standards for the comparative evaluation of political and social behavior. Ever since the days of Hume, however, the idea of natural law has been increasingly discredited. By demonstrating the logical impropriety of proceeding from "is" statements to "ought" con-clusions, the Scottish philosopher undermined the methodo-logical foundations on which, as he saw it, the natural-law tradi-tion had previously been based. Although Kant and others tried, in the light of this criticism, to find new grounds for normative judgment, their conclusions were not generally accepted. The re-sult was a progressive abandonment of the normative realm as a proper subject of scientific discourse, and an ever-growing con-centration on the task of creating social sciences that, by con-fining themselves to purely existential statements, would become, like the natural sciences, impeccably "value-free."

In a discipline so conceived, the role of the political theorist was inevitably constricted. It is true that theories, in the sense of generalizing hypotheses, or models, are indispensable to any form of scientific inquiry, including political science. But the formulation of such hypotheses is a responsibility shared, in their respective fields of specialization, by all political scientists; the only "theorists" who can claim any special competence in such matters are those who give their time and attention to prob-lems of methodology. It is also true that value-judgments, the traditional subject matter of political theory, are factors of some importance in the political behavior of men. Without compromising the value-freeness of the discipline, therefore, there was room for specialists who, by studying normative theories past and present as historically given facts, could be expected to throw some sort of light on the decision-making process. But when it came to making value-judgments of their own, political theorists were at once assailed by scientific scruples. As human beings they were bound, of course, to have some personal preferences. In the name of scientific honesty it was legitimate, even desirable, to state these preferences, for only thus could the resulting biases be properly discounted. The one thing that could not be done was to claim that such views were justified on scientific grounds. For value-preferences, after all, were simply matters of fact, and no fact, accurately stated, could be regarded as better than any other from the standpoint of a value-free science.

At the present time, this conception of methodological propriety is still widely prevalent. There are signs, however, that the idea of value-free science, as thus interpreted, is beginning to lose its appeal.[1] When political decisions are based for the most part on traditionally familiar values, the justification of those values, for practical purposes, is a matter of small importance; the political scientist can safely assert that the values he prefers are nothing more, in the last analysis, than personal prejudices, secure in the knowledge that those prejudices will in fact be shared by the audience he is addressing. This, until quite recently, was the usual situation. Having reason to believe that their own norms, which by and large were the current norms of Western civilization, were decisively preponderant, scientists felt free to investigate the ways and means of political action without bothering to argue about ends. But the easy assumption on which this attitude once could rest is no longer wholly true. Under present conditions, the ends as well as the means of politics are open to serious question. This imposes new pressures on political scientists, who would like to defend as well as to assert the values they believe in.

For many people the triumph of National Socialism was the event that first cast serious doubt on the value of value-freeness. Hitler's victories were fortunately short-lived, but while they lasted they had the unprecedented effect of subjecting the better

1. For an early critique of the traditional position, see David Easton, *The Political System* (New York, 1953). See also C. J. Friedrich, *Man and His Government* (New York, 1963), chap. 2.

part of Europe to a regime that was radically hostile to the traditions of Western civility. Most right-thinking people, including many political scientists, were horrified by the mass exterminations and other brutalities that marked the New Order. At the end of the war, the prevailing mood of moral revulsion found expression in the Nuremberg Trials, which tried to make German leaders accountable at law for their "crimes against humanity," and in the attempt to formulate and win international acceptance for a "Declaration of Human Rights." All this was quite understandable as an emotional reaction, but what was its rational basis? And what, if anything, did political scientists have to say about the matter? Could they, as exponents of a value-free discipline, claim that their distaste for extermination camps was anything more than a purely personal preference, a preference that they simply happened to share with many others brought up in the Western tradition? Could they, as scientists, assert that their views were in any way superior to those of the Nuremberg defendants, who had likewise been following preferences of their own? If not, was the trial of those defendants anything more than an exercise of pure power, an act of vengeance imposed by victors whose only demonstrable superiority lay in the fact that they had succeeded in winning a war? Such questions called for a second look at the idea of value-free science.

The liquidation of colonialism in the post-war years has given rise to similar problems. As long as the control of most of the world lay in the hands of Western nations, questions of cultural diversity were comparatively unimportant. Most of the decisions that mattered were made by men whose values came from the common store of Western political thought. But when colonial peoples began to make good their claims to independence, this was no longer true. New leaders, representing various mixtures of Western and other traditions, had assumed the responsibility of governing a large part of the human race. By common agreement, most of the new countries were in some sense "backward," or—to employ the current euphemism— "underdeveloped." To further their "development," foreign governments, both Communist and non-Communist, began vying with one another in offers of advice or assistance. How are these rival offers to be evaluated? What are the standards, political, social or economic, by which the degree of "development" ought properly to be measured? Much as value-free scientists may want to avoid the issue, anyone who tries to cope with such questions is bound to make value-judgments. Are these judgments to be presented as nothing more than statements of personal or national prejudice? If the people who mattered were still Western-trained colonial officers, this might perhaps suffice; addressed to non-Westerners, and in competition with the more objectively "rational" advice of Marxist pseudo-scientists, mere assertions of preference by Western scholars can hardly seem persuasive. Once again, in the face of contemporary pressures, "value-free" science proves wanting.

Under these circumstances it is not surprising to find that many political theorists have begun, in recent years, to question the old assumptions. Their discontent has found expression, among other things, in a marked revival of interest in the natural-law tradition. Down roughly to the time of the French Revolution, most Westerners had accepted natural law as a rational basis for the rendering of value-judgments on political and social questions. Through the use of "right" (that is, scientifically respectable) reason, so the argument ran, it is possible to discover the basic needs of human nature and to formulate general rules of morality appropriate to those needs. The idea of natural law stands poles apart, therefore, from the idea of value-free science. For increasing numbers of theorists at the present time, the thought of returning to the older conception is obviously attractive.

Attractive, but not wholly acceptable. The idea of value-freeness has attractions of its own, and attempts to challenge it are still, on the whole, distinctly tentative. It is true that there are some Catholic scholars who, unshaken in their traditional Thomism, are willing to argue that the "perennial philosophy," complete with Aristotelian teleology and Christian theism, is the necessary basis for any true science of politics;[2] but their writings have no great following. In a world where natural scientists have no use for teleology, and where even responsible theologians are prepared to dispense with God, the idea of natural law in its original form could hardly find general acceptance. When dealing with the natural-law tradition, therefore, most contemporary theorists express their interest in extremely cautious terms. Some

2. A recent example is C. N. R. McCoy, *The Structure of Political Thought* (New York, 1963).

emphasize the social utility of a value-oriented politics, and point out its advantage over disciplines which, in their rigorous interpretation of the need for value-freeness, are constrained to neutrality in the face even of a Nazi Germany. Their work often appears in the form of a history of political thought which, without committing the author to any really overt and systematic defense of the natural-law position, emphasizes the virtues of the perennial philosophy and treats the emergence of rival theories as signs of retrogression.[3] Others, usually self-styled conservatives, are more outspoken, presenting the natural-law tradition, hypothetically, as a useful ideology, one which would, *if* accepted, go far toward relieving the modern world of its gravest difficulties.[4] In neither case is there any real attempt to demonstrate that the values in question are objectively true.

Interesting and symptomatic as these various works may be, they do not manage, or even attempt, to go to the heart of the matter. For the real issue is not whether rationally verifiable principles of moral judgment would or would not be *useful;* that they would be goes quite without saying. The question is whether the discovery of such principles is *possible;* and this is precisely the point on which our writers have little to offer.

In this general context the political theory of Arnold Brecht [5] stands out as a notable exception. Unlike the theorists previously mentioned, Brecht is a thorough-going logico-positivist. This has not prevented him from showing a very real interest in the idea of natural law, and from trying to define the conditions under which a rational science of ethics might conceivably be defended in terms of contemporary thought. The conditions, as he envisages them, are extremely rigorous. According to him, the existence of natural law can be demonstrated only by comparing the behavior of all known societies, past or present, and by showing that certain common principles of justice were in fact operative in each and every one of them. Brecht himself believes that universally recognized principles may well exist, and proposes several which, as hypotheses, might be worth investigating. Empirical verification is the necessary and sufficient condition for the translation of any such hypothesis into a precept of natural law.

3. See Leo Strauss, *Natural Right and History* (Chicago, 1953).

4. See Russell Kirk, *The Conservative Mind* (Chicago, 1953).

5. Arnold Brecht, *Political Theory* (Princeton, 1959). His treatment of the problem of natural law is to be found in chap. x.

He suggests that this would be a legitimate and promising line of inquiry for contemporary political scientists.

Although Brecht deserves great credit for his willingness to approach the problem of natural law in rigorously scientific terms, it is hard to believe that much could ever be accomplished by following the procedure he suggests. The whole point of natural law, as of any other normative system, is to provide a basis for the comparative evaluation of actual behavior. It is significant only insofar as it can be used to judge, and hopefully to correct, actions which can in fact be shown to deviate from the norm. According to Brecht's principle of verification, however, the indispensable test of any proposed principle of natural law is that it must be recognized, without exception, by each and every social group, past, present or to come. If any rule at all could hope to pass so stringent a test, it would almost certainly be so devoid of specific content as to be practically meaningless. Brecht suggests, for example, that "like cases should be treated alike" might well prove to be a universally accepted principle of natural justice. If true, the proposition would not amount to much, for the operative problem still would be "what cases are alike?" To those who believe in the common humanity of Jews and Gentiles, the slightest discrimination against a Jew as such will give rise to a sense of injustice; by the same token, a man who believes that Jews as such are enemies of the human race will deplore the injustice of any single act of clemency that permits a Jew to live. Since both, in their respective judgments, are appealing to the principle that like cases should be treated alike, it may be said in a certain sense that the humanitarian and the anti-Semite are animated by a common sense of justice. To call this a principle of natural law is all very well in its way, but laws like this are too formalistic to have any real significance. Even if, by following Brecht's proposed line of investigation, it were possible to prove the universal validity of many such propositions, the result would be too trivial to repay so great an effort.

To supporters of the "perennial philosophy," the essential sterility of this attempt to combine science and morality would come as no surprise. They believe that the idea of natural law depends on a teleological conception of the universe, and that teleology is incompatible with the logico-positivist assumptions that govern modern science. In classical antiquity, when the idea first arose, the scientific verification of ethical principles was no great problem, for at that time scientific and ethical modes of thought were essentially at one. The universe then was regarded by all right-thinking men as the complete and harmonious creation of a perfectly rational creator. Each creature was endowed from the beginning with a nature which enabled it to play its appointed role in the cosmic plan. Under this system, which applied to any conceivable form of scientific inquiry, there was no place for any basic distinction between the "is" and the "ought"; what anything "is" could only be defined in terms of the goals that it "ought" to follow. To its original proponents, therefore, natural law was a body of fixed and universally valid principles that man could discover through the proper use of the rational faculties given to him for that purpose; those principles served to define both what man "is" and what he "ought" to do.

With the rise of modern empiricism, however, this organic relationship between the "is" and the "ought" was radically disrupted. Abandoning the teleological conceptions of their predecessors, scientists from the seventeenth century onward have limited themselves to the study of observable phenomena. The universe of modern science is a world of endlessly evolving and conflicting forces, a world which, so far as the scientist himself is able to determine, conforms to no rational purpose. The classical concept of natural law, with its easy transition from "is" to "ought," has no place in such a system. In a world divorced from teleology, it is natural to conclude that the logical difficulty raised by Hume is insuperable, and that normative considerations have no proper place in any empirical science.

No such conclusion was reached, however, by the founders of modern empiricism, including Hume himself. Although Hobbes, Locke, and Hume were all agreed in rejecting the theory of innate ideas, and in asserting that the function of reason was limited to the orderly classification and comparison of sense impressions, this did not prevent them from believing that the search for universally valid norms was a proper subject for rational inquiry. All three made explicit and unembarrassed attempts to incorporate new versions of natural law within their respective systems.

How was this done? The procedure is set forth most clearly in the writings of David Hume.[6] Although he rejected the older

6. David Hume, *A Treatise of Human Nature* (London, 1739–40). The sections of the work most relevant to the problem of natural law are Book III,

view of a natural teleology implicit in the rational character of the universe, he believed that human life is guided by man-made but nonetheless universally valid rules of action. The initial motive for the creation of these rules comes from the "passions," the universal and primordial impulse of all living organisms, which is to seek pleasure and to avoid pain. Reason is the "slave of the passions" which, by transforming sense-data into an increasingly reliable knowledge of cause and effect, enables man to satisfy his desires with a more than random effectiveness. Transmitted and refined over generations, these accumulated empirical discoveries constitute what is known as civilization.

Since civilization itself depends on the maintenance of social order, the advance of civilization is necessarily marked, among other things, by the discovery of increasingly effective ways of avoiding social conflict. Hume believed that the basic problems of human existence, and thus the rationally discoverable rules of civility, are everywhere the same. Although he called these rules "laws of nature," he was careful to point out that they are in fact both natural and artificial. They are artifacts in the sense that, unlike the traditional rules of natural law, they are not innate to man as such, but are a historically conditioned product of human skill and experience. In the sense, however, that they are an inevitable end product of man's innate drive to find effective, and therefore rational, means of satisfying his "passions," they are also a natural outcome of human existence. In the last analysis, therefore, Hume's view of the nature and destiny of man is essentially teleological, though not in the classical sense. Sociability to him is not a natural gift, an innate idea, but a gradually evolving skill toward which all men must strive in order to satisfy their natural purposes. Though he shared the modern view that teleology has no place in natural science, his recognition of the purposive character of human action made it possible for him, as a social scientist, to bridge the logical gap between the "is" and the "ought" in a natural-law system that is, at one and the same time, both empirical and normative in effect.

The contrast between Hume and Brecht is instructive. Though both were logico-empiricists, with essentially similar conceptions

---

Parts 1 and 2. These sections, together with an introductory commentary, are to be found in *Hume: Theory of Politics*, ed. Frederick Watkins (Edinburgh, 1951).

of the nature and limits of human knowledge, Hume was able to set forth a genuinely meaningful series of natural-law principles, whereas Brecht failed to do so. To Brecht, any normative belief that has ever been held is an empirically verifiable fact, scientifically indistinguishable from any other like fact. This led him to propose a number of hypotheses which would be hard to verify in the first place and which would, if verified, be much too formalistic to perform the critical functions that are required of natural law. Hume's approach is very different. While recognizing that any belief is as much of a fact as any other, he is also prepared to demonstrate empirically that some beliefs are more nearly true, and therefore more valid, than others. Since the basic purpose of human nature is to satisfy the "passion" for pleasure, actual serviceability to that purpose is an objective standard by which all human acts may properly be judged. Hume's natural laws are general rules of action which, if followed, will in fact maximize the probability of maximizing pleasure. Even though a given individual or society, through ignorance or intemperance, may fail to recognize or abide by them, these rules stand as empirically verifiable statements of what man ought to do. Unlike Brecht's hypotheses, therefore, they are genuine laws of nature. As such they provide a common standard by which it is possible to evaluate, not simply to accept as given, the wide discrepancies of normative judgment that actually occur among men.

The details of Hume's natural-law system need not concern us here. Our author was, after all, a man of the eighteenth century, and his ideas at this late date are understandably outmoded. Although his view of human nature, with its crudely oversimplified hedonism, was in line with the best psychological findings of his own times, it would hardly pass muster today. The range of his empirical information was also distinctly narrow. Like most of his contemporaries, he was disposed to accept the standards of "enlightened" Europe as the culmination of human achievement, and showed none of that appreciation for the accomplishments of primitive or exotic cultures that was already being fostered by Herder and other forerunners of the romantic movement. His experience and interests were those of an enlightened eighteenth-century gentleman, confident in the belief that the ideas of his own age and class were universal dictates of right reason. In its essential parochialism, indeed, his position was not unlike that of the classical and medieval philosophers, who had developed the idea of natural law on the basis of their own familiar standards and had discounted the divergent usages of other peoples as barbarous or corrupt. In terms of modern social science, his views are almost as badly dated as those of his more ancient predecessors.

Hume's work is still instructive, however, because of the light it throws on the weakness of most present-day approaches to the problem of value-judgment. In order to be meaningfully normative, a theory of natural law must be based on some defensible conception of the purposes that govern human action. The teleological cosmos of the classical theorists and the rational hedonism of Hume were significant precisely because they provided an acceptable definition of those purposes, thus making it possible to judge social acts and institutions by a common rational standard. Each system in its own time was convincing because it proceeded from a view of human nature that coincided with the observations and conclusions of contemporary science. Any modern version of natural law, if such a thing is possible, must likewise be based on the current state of scientific knowledge about the nature and potentialities of the human race as such. If Hume is interesting to us today it is because he is still the clearest example of a man who, while accepting logico-empirical standards of scientific verification, was able in his own time to satisfy this requirement. For all their interest in normative problems, the political theorists of the present day can hardly be said to have done so.

This comparative failure may be due, of course, to the increasing rigor of contemporary science. Natural scientists now, including biologists, are rightfully disdainful of anything that smacks of teleology. Even at the level of high school science, the naive suggestion that ears are for the "purpose" of hearing is greeted with careful derision; what organs have is not "purposes" but "functions." To speak of the "purposes" that govern human action might well seem, on the face of it, to be hopelessly unscientific. But from the standpoint of the social sciences, the idea cannot well be avoided. Regardless of its ultimate physical explanation, man's consciousness of acting in pursuit of purposes is a basic fact. Thus there is nothing intrinsically improper or obscurantist about discussing human nature in these terms. The question is whether or not it is possible to identify any purpose so basic to human behavior that it can truly be said to be characteristic of the human race as such. To Hume and other social scientists of the seventeenth and eighteenth centuries—centuries which had already abandoned the older teleology—the "passion" for seeking pleasure and avoiding pain had seemed to be identifiable as a characteristic of this sort. Does the present state of the social sciences justify any comparable hypothesis about the unity of human nature? If so, there is no reason why it should not likewise be used as a basis for value-judgments.

The idea that all men share common purposes is fully in line, with the findings of contemporary scholarship. True, the first impact of the modern historical and anthropological sciences was to produce an overwhelming impression of the complexity and diversity of human experience, encouraging many people to adopt a position of absolute cultural relativism. Greater familiarity with this new wealth of information has led, however, to ever new awareness of the underlying unity of human nature. This awareness was inhibited, in earlier times, by the kind of parochialism that limited the vision of even so recent and perceptive a thinker as David Hume. Though the ancient Greeks were able to conceive of mankind as a single species pursuing a single goal, their view of man was so closely bound up with their own experiences of life in the *polis* that they were constantly tempted to deny the essential humanity of slaves, barbarians, and others who had no part in that life. Sixteenth-century Christians and nineteenth-century liberals were hardly less parochial. Without wholly denying the humanity of non-Europeans, they likewise tended to use their own partial experience as a universal standard, and to interpret all deviations from that standard as a consequence of ignorance or sin. With the advent of modern communications the complacent ethnocentrism of the Western world has been very much reduced. Scientific findings fail to support theories of racial inequality that once enjoyed wide acceptance. Primitive and exotic cultures which once seemed merely irrational and arbitrary have come to be recognized as reasonable adaptations to the requirements of a particular time and place. Men have come increasingly to be seen as creatures of like capacity, trying, under widely diverse conditions, to employ the resources of a common human nature for the satisfaction of common human needs. Modern science, by vastly expanding our knowledge of that nature and of those needs, provides the basis for a number of verifiable propositions which enable us, more adequately than ever before, to define the potentialities and limits of human action. These propositions, I believe, are entirely adequate to provide a basis for the kind of normative enquiry that former ages followed in their discussions of natural law.

I shall conclude, by way of illustration only, with three such propositions. The first may be stated thus: The primary function of any organism is to maintain its own existence and to perpetuate its kind. In terms of human consciousness this may be described as man's most basic natural purpose, more basic than that old favorite, the pursuit of happiness. In so behaving, man is responding to a drive which would seem, in fact, to be characteristic of life itself. A living organism may be defined, indeed, as a piece of more or less complexly organized matter with certain mechanisms which enable it to preserve its own specific pattern of organization against the pressures of the environment, and to maintain and duplicate itself by imposing that pattern on extraneous materials drawn from that same environment. Species are constantly changing in an evolutionary process which would seem, according to the best available evidence, to be random rather than purposive in character. This evolutionary process is so slow, however, that the basic characteristics of the human species may be taken, for all practical purposes, as something given. Each species has its own genetically determined form, and its own specific resources for self-perpetuation and reproduction. Individuals are naturally perfect or imperfect in proportion as they do or do not exemplify the full potentialities of their own species. By the use of logico-empirical methods, human beings are capable of identifying imperfections of this sort. Thus the idea of organic perfection is a scientifically meaningful concept that can be used, for human purposes, as a basis for normative judgment.

The second proposition may be stated thus: The distinctive characteristic of the human species, in its bid for organic survival, is its rational faculty. All organisms are characterized by mechanisms that enable them to make more or less flexible and adequate adjustments to the pressures of the environment. In comparison even with the higher animals, however, man is unique in the degree to which he depends on reason for the accomplishment of this result. By means which as yet are far from being fully understood, he is able to organize the raw materials of experience into usable general concepts. Through the empirical verification and logical manipulation of these concepts he acquires an understanding of his environment which, without being different in kind from that of other organisms, is unique in the degree of its adaptability to changing circumstances. Man's particular form of rationality does, to be sure, involve some disadvantages. The inordinate prolongation of human infancy, with all its attendant risks, is an unfortunate biological concomitant of the protracted educational process that human beings must undergo in order to bring their mental powers to a useful level of accomplishment. The rational process, moreover, is subject to errors and inadequacies which may lead to dangerous misconceptions and thus to dysfunctional choices from which more purely instinctive creatures are happily exempt. The survival and proliferation of the human species would seem to indicate, however, that the net organic advantage lies on the side of human reason. In any case, it is man's most distinctive feature—a feature on which, for better or for worse, his future must depend.

The third proposition may be stated thus: The optimum effectiveness of human reason depends on the creation and maintenance of social institutions that provide the widest possible opportunities for communication between men. In a very special sense of the term, man is a social animal. To point up the difference between him and other social animals it might perhaps be more accurate to say that man is a cultural animal, and that culture is indispensable to him because of his rationality. Although the potentialities of reason are endless, the realization of those potentialities is a slow and difficult business. The discovery and verification of useful concepts demands a great deal of time and calls for the pooling of large quantities of experience. This in turn calls for an effective social setting. The various languages and cultures of mankind are the present outcome of man's past attempts to conceptualize and control his various environments. Each society, building on its own inherited skills and experiences, develops a culture which it tries to transmit and improve from generation to generation. To accomplish this it must achieve a degree of stability sufficient to enable its members to retain and transmit their cultural heritage, and a degree of openness and flexibility sufficient to encourage the discovery and acceptance of useful innovations. Without a society to instruct him in its accumulated skills, including the all-important skill of language, and to safeguard his communications with other men and societies, no individual would be in a position to make any significant use of his rational powers; without placing inventive individuals in a position to explore and test new hypotheses, no society would be able to increase its cultural heritage, or to remain flexible enough to maintain itself in the face of changing circumstances. Thus reason and culture go hand in hand. In the absence of either one, the other is meaningless.

The three preceding empirical propositions lead to the following normative conclusion: Men ought, in their relations with one another, to regulate their actions in such a way as to maximize the efficiency of society as an agency of human culture. Knowledge of the best ways and means of accomplishing this can only be acquired by experience. Like other products of human culture, it will vary from society to society and will never be complete. To the extent that it is available, however, such knowledge must always be taken to imply a corresponding obligation. Actions which fail, through ignorance, to conform to the best available standards of social action are empirically erroneous; actions performed in conscious violation of such standards are not only empirically erroneous, but also morally wrong.

The virtue of the normative conclusion here set forth is that it avoids the parochial inflexibility of earlier natural-law formulas without leading to the morally paralyzing conclusions implicit in absolute cultural relativism. Since all human societies are made up of men trying, under diverse conditions, to find rational means of coping with their own particular experiences, there can be no legitimate basis for identifying rationality itself with the practices of any one society, using these practices as a common standard by which to judge all others. This does not mean, however, that there is no common standard of judgment. The maximization of man's rational potentialities is the natural goal of every culture. Insofar as the achievements of any one individual or culture can be shown, on scientifically verifiable grounds, to be more or less conducive to this end, they ought to be adopted or rejected by others. To say that all cultures are equally valid is just as much of an insult to the principle of human rationality as to say that any one culture alone is wholly right. The normative principle here proposed avoids both difficulties.

The effect of this principle is to provide an empirical basis for value-judgments. Would it be proper, then, to describe it as a natural-law principle? Our answer to this question should be the same as that of David Hume, whose theory of normative empiricism was not, in principle, very different from the one just given. In describing his own general rules he said that he had no objection to their being called laws of nature, but that he did not insist on it either.

It is all a question of terminology, which in turn depends on the degree of fixity appropriate to natural law. Although the classical theorists recognized the need for a wide range of variety and experiment in the realm of human law, they tended to think that the principles of natural law itself were to be taken as given. Since most of these principles, as set forth by earlier theorists, can be shown on empirical grounds to be necessary conditions for the maintenance of effective societies, the general consequence of any sort of normative empiricism is to reinforce the actual conclusions of the natural-law tradition. That is why Hume was willing to describe his own basic norms as "laws of nature." As a product of social experience, however, these norms must always be provisional. Existing norms may well prove, in the light of further experience, to be inadequate or wrong. Empiricism can never provide guides to action that are absolutely inflexible. If the essence of natural law is thought to reside in its timeless certainty, the term cannot rightfully be applied to the findings of any sort of normative empiricism.

No matter what terms we may use to describe it, the importance of the normative principle just laid down lies in the fact that it serves, like earlier theories of natural law, to justify the use of rational means for the establishment of value-judgments. This theoretical conclusion is in line, moreover, with the way scholars actually behave. When a social scientist, following the rules of verification appropriate to his own discipline, discovers ways of enabling men to make a more rational response to their environment, he can hardly fail, as a human being, to feel that his discoveries *ought* to be put into practice. But even though this natural impulse can never be wholly suppressed, the idea that all science must be value-free has often served to weaken it. If values are just a matter of personal preference or, at most, of traditional prejudice, they become quite simply matters of taste, immune to rational discourse. Our modern emphasis on value-free science has led, therefore, to a curious sort of paralysis. At a time when the use of reason has been crowned with unprecedented scientific achievements, scientists have felt compelled, in an access of modesty that is no less unprecedented, to disclaim any sort of rational competence to evaluate the ends toward which their own achievements are being applied. In a sense that Hume himself never gave to the phrase, reason now is truly "a slave of the passions." This is a most unnatural situation in the very basic sense that it discounts the rational nature of man. Natural law is the rubric under which men once were called upon to assume the normative responsibilities implicit in their nature as rational beings. Call it natural law or not, the responsibility is the same.

Part Two

On Method

M. Brewster Smith

Personality in Politics: A Conceptual Map, with Application to the Problem of Political Rationality [1]

Progress in the social and behavioral sciences has in general not been marked by major theoretical "breakthroughs." As those of us who profess one or another of these disciplines look upon the succession of research and theoretical interests that capture the center of the stage, we may sometimes wonder if indeed there has been any progress at all. Particularly if we are fixated on the physical sciences [2] as models of what a good science should be, we can easily become discouraged. As therapy for this depressive mood, however, one has only to scan the text-

1. The first half of this essay has been adapted, with minor changes, from my paper "A Map for the Analysis of Personality and Politics," *Journal of Social Issues*, 24 (1968). I am grateful to the editor of that journal and to the Society for the Psychological Study of Social Issues for permission to draw upon it here. The final section of the present essay is wholly new.

2. Other than meteorology, which in some respects offers such an appropriate model that I am puzzled that social scientists have not picked it up. The natural history of cloud formations, the precise physics of atmospheric microprocesses, the statistical treatment of macroprocesses, all have their homologies in the social sciences. The parallel even extends to the continued prominence of folk wisdom in both fields. Yet meteorologists seem to have been spared the self-doubts and soul-searchings to which social scientists are prone.

books of former generations and some of the earlier landmark contributions to our fields: the fact of progress, of the cumulativeness of understanding that is the hallmark of science, is immediately apparent.

The progress that we see, however, is not on the pattern according to which Einstein included and supplanted Newton, or even on that by which the modern theory of the chemical valence bond makes sense of Mendeleyev's descriptive table of elements. In addition to the development and refinement of research methods and the accretion of facts, our kind of progress has involved developing some more or less satisfactory "theories of the middle range," [3] and, especially, a steady increase in the sophistication of the questions that we ask and in our sensitivity to the variables that are likely to be relevant to them.

To codify this kind of progress, and to make our gains readily accessible as we face new problems of research and application, we need something other than grand theory in the old literary style. We are not ready for genuinely theoretical integration, and to pretend that we are is to hamper rather than to aid ourselves in attacking new problems with an open mind. Conceptual mapping operations that have only modest pretensions better fit the state of our theoretical resources, and can often be helpful in organizing these resources to bear upon particular problems. The sort of conceptual map that I have in mind starts from a particular intellectual or practical problem and attempts to link the pertinent islands of knowledge discovered in the pursuit of middle-range theories and to disentangle relationships among the kinds of variables that current knowledge points to as relevant. When the variables are drawn from the home territory of different academic disciplines (and the concepts of a context-defined field like political science inevitably have such a heterogeneous provenience), ventures in mapping become particularly important. They are the best we can do toward interdisciplinary integration, which in these instances is required of us by the nature of the task.

This essay sketches such a map for the analysis of personality and politics, an outgrowth of my attempts to apply the approach developed in *Opinions and Personality* [4] to the analysis of vari-

3. Robert K. Merton, *Social Theory and Social Structure* (rev. ed.) (Glencoe, Ill.: The Free Press, 1957).

4. M. Brewster Smith, Jerome S. Bruner, and Robert W. White, *Opinions and Personality* (New York: Wiley, 1956). See also M. Brewster Smith, "Opinions,

ous problems involving social attitudes and behavior, particularly McCarthyism, civil liberties, and anti-Semitism.[5] While it obviously bears the marks of its origins, I have had to go considerably beyond the range of variables, mainly psychological ones, that Bruner, White and I were dealing with.

A map like this is *not* a theory that can be confirmed or falsified by testing deductions against evidence; it is rather a heuristic device, a declaration of intellectual strategy, that is to be judged as profitable or sterile rather than as true or false. On my own part, I have found it useful in coming to grips with topics that were new to me, and in organizing what I think we know for my students in teaching. Placing particular variables and relationships as it does in larger context, it may have the further virtue of counteracting one's natural tendency to stress the exclusive importance of the variables or theories that one happens momentarily to be interested in. Many persisting disputes in the social sciences are like the story of the Blind Men and the Elephant. A good map helps us to keep the whole Elephant in view.

In offering this essay in homage to the memory of V. O. Key, I am keenly aware of Key's rare talent for grasping the Elephant whole without recourse to such arid conceptual baggage. It was part of Key's artistry to keep much of his conceptual sophistication implicit, as he brought empirical analysis shrewdly to bear on theoretical and normative problems. The rest of us may need more explicit aids if we are to emulate his openness to the contributions of adjacent disciplines, his distrustfulness of the simplistic explanation.

In the final section of the essay, I seek to illustrate the utility of the map by applying it in an attempt to clarify some of the meanings of political rationality—a theme with which Key was preoccupied up to his death. If the map turns out to help reduce some of the confusions prevalent at this cross-roads of normative

Personality, and Political Behavior," *American Political Science Review*, 52 (March 1958), 1–17.

5. In the area of McCarthyism and civil liberties, I prepared an unpublished memorandum for Samuel A. Stouffer in connection with planning for the studies leading to his book, *Communism, Conformity, and Civil Liberties* (Garden City: Doubleday, 1955). The application to anti-Semitism is embodied in my pamphlet, *Determinants of Anti-Semitism: A Social-Psychological Map* (New York: Anti-Defamation League of B'nai B'rith, n.d. [1965]), on which I draw heavily here. I am grateful to the Anti-Defamation League for support of the project of which it was a by-product.

and empirical concern, I would regard it as an appropriate if partial repayment of debt to Key.

The Map

Schematic as it is, the map is too complicated to take in at a glance. Figure 1 presents the gross outlines—the continents in their asserted relationships. In Figures 2 and 3 we will look in more detail at particular segments of the terrain. The full map, given in Figure 4, should then become intelligible. Certain intentional omissions and simplifications must finally be noted by way of qualification. Illustrative examples will be provided casually en route, for the most part without documentation from the literature.

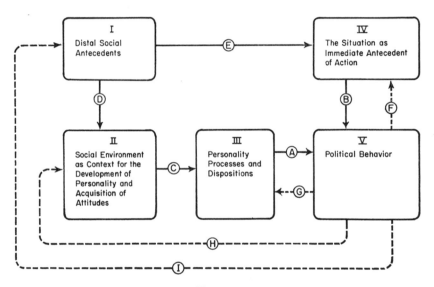

Figure 1

Figure 1 diagrams the major components of a framework for the analysis of personality and politics in terms of five major panels. In keeping with the psychological focus of the map, Panel III (personality processes and dispositions) occupies the center of the stage. Causal relationships are indicated by arrows. Because we are used to reading from left to right, I have put the payoff in actual behavior (Panel V) at the extreme right. This panel is concerned with personal political decisions as carried into action: voting, information-seeking, policy formation or implementation, influence attempts, or—the source of much of our psychological data—question-answering. The data that come from our observations of people, what they say as well as what they do, belong here; only by reconstruction and inference do we arrive at the contents of the central personality panel.

Panel IV represents the person's behavioral situation as an immediate antecedent of action; Panel II includes features of the person's more enduring social environment to which we turn to explain how he has happened to become the sort of political actor that we find him to be; and Panel I represents the more remote, or distal, facts of politics, economics, culture, social structure, and history that contribute to the distinctive features of the environment in which he was socialized and of the immediate situations in which he acts. From the standpoint of the behaving individual, the contents of Panel I are conceptually distal but may be temporally contemporaneous: an historically given political system (Panel I), for example, affects (Arrow D) the political norms—such as those concerning democracy, authority, and legitimacy—to which a person is socialized (Panel II); it also affects (Arrow E) the structure of the immediate situations of action that he is likely to encounter (Panel IV)—the alternatives offered on a ballot, the procedural rules in a legislative body, and so on. Temporally distal determinants are also assigned to Panel I: thus the history of slavery, the plantation economy, the Civil War and Reconstruction, as determinants of the politically relevant environments in which participants in Southern politics have been socialized, and of the immediate situations that comprise the stage on which they perform as political actors.[6]

If we start with behavioral outcomes in Panel V, the arrows (marked A and B) that link them with Panels III and IV represent the methodological premise emphasized by the great psychologist Kurt Lewin:[7] All social behavior is to be analyzed as a joint resultant of characteristics of the *person,* on the one hand, and of his psychological *situation,* on the other. The behavior of the same political actor may differ substantially as he faces

6. Cf. V. O. Key, Jr., with the assistance of Alexander Heard, *Southern Politics in State and Nation* (New York: Knopf, 1949).

7. Kurt Lewin, "Field Theory and Experiment in Social Psychology: Concepts and Methods," in Kurt Lewin, *Field Theory in Social Science,* ed. Dorwin Cartwright (New York: Harper, 1951), pp. 130–154.

differently structured situations; conversely, different persons who face the same situation will respond differently. Both the contribution of the person and that of his situation, in interaction, must be included in any adequate analysis. To specify the contribution of either requires taking that of the other into account.

For a long time there was a disciplinary quarrel between psychologists and sociologists about the relevance and importance of personal dispositions (primarily *attitudes*) versus that of situations in determining social behavior. To take this feature of our map seriously is to regard the argument as silly and outmoded: both classes of determinants are jointly indispensable. The study of "personality and politics" cannot afford to neglect situational factors, which must in principle be taken into account if only by holding them constant, if we are to isolate the distinctive contributions of personality. In concrete cases in which analysis along these lines is undertaken for the guidance of social action, one may ask, of course, whether the personal or the situational component is more *strategic* in terms of the variance it controls and its accessibility to major influence. It may be more feasible, for example, to influence the normative structure that pertains to interracial relations by authoritative legal action than to carry through a program of mass psychoanalysis to reverse authoritarian personality trends that predispose people toward prejudice and discriminatory behavior. The practical questions of strategic importance and accessibility do not seem to be as charged with disciplinary *amour-propre* as are the theoretical issues that still tend to divide the proponents of personality-oriented and of situational approaches.

The dotted arrows of relationship that leave the behavioral panel require special mention. Political behavior has consequences as well as causes, and for the sake of formal completeness some of these are suggested by the dotted "feedback loops" in the map. As Leon Festinger has argued on the basis of considerable evidence, self-committing behavior may have effects in turn upon a person's attitudes (Arrow G).[8] A political actor who adopts a position for expedient reasons may be convinced by his

8. See *A Theory of Cognitive Dissonance* (Chicago: Row, Peterson, 1957); also Jack W. Brehm and Arthur R. Cohen, *Explorations in Cognitive Dissonance* (New York: Wiley, 1962).

own rhetoric, or—similar in result though different in the process that is assumed—he may shift his attitudes to accord with his actions in order to reduce feelings of "dissonance." The dotted Arrows F, H, and I merely recognize that individual behavior also has effects in the social world. What the person does in a situation may immediately change it (Arrow F); as we integrate across the behavior of many individuals, the joint consequences of the behavior of the many eventually alter the social environments that shape and support the attitudes of each (Arrow H). In the longer run (Arrow I), the behaviors of individuals constitute a society and its history.

To be sure, this is a psychologist's map that focuses on the attitudes and behavior of individual persons. A political sociologist would have to give explicit attention to matters that remain implicit in the feedback arrows—to the social structures according to which individual behaviors are integrated to have political effects. His map would necessarily be differently centered and elaborated than the present one. V. O. Key has given particular attention to the problems of "linkage" between aggregated individual political orientations as a social psychologist studies them and governmental action as the political scientist's ultimate concern.[9]

With the broad framework laid out, we can now look at the details of Panels III and IV, still working from the proximal to the distal determinants of behavior (see Figure 2). The contents of Panel IV (the situation as immediate antecedent of action) remind us that an important component of any behavioral situation is the set of norms or prescriptions for behavior that are consensually held to apply in it. Students of political behavior at the various levels of governmental organization are concerned with recurring types of situations that confront the citizen, whether as constituent, voter, or petitioner; or as legislator, executive, administrative functionary, or party leader. Much of the variation in personal behavior, not only across types of situations but within the same type in different political structures and at different historical periods, will be attributable to differences and changes in the norms that prevail. Apart from the norms, there are of course many other situational features that are also important as codeterminants of action—among them,

9. V. O. Key, Jr., *Public Opinion and American Democracy* (New York: Knopf, 1963), p. 411 ff.

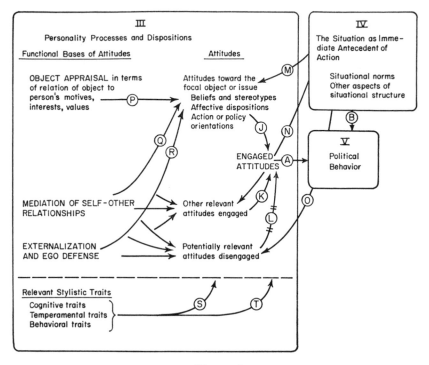

Figure 2

the competitive or cooperative relations that hold with other actors who participate in the situation, the degree of urgency with which decision or action is required, the contingencies of cost and benefit that obtain.[10] Lore about the relevant features of political situations is a principal currency of political science.

Turn now to Panel III, personality processes and dispositions. We are concerned here with inferred dispositions of the person that he brings to any situation he encounters, and with their basis in his experience and motivational processes. Social psychologists have come to use the term *attitudes* to refer to such dispositions, when they represent integrations of cognitive, emotional, and conative tendencies around a psychological object such as a political figure or issue. Our problem is a dual one: to formulate how a person's attitudes come to bear on his political behav-

10. See John W. Thibaut and Harold H. Kelley, *The Social Psychology of Groups* (New York: Wiley, 1959).

ior,[11] and how these attitudes arise and are sustained in relation to their part in the ongoing operations of the person's psychological economy.

A first point suggested in Figure 2 is that we cannot take for granted just which of a person's attitudes will become engaged as a codeterminant of his behavior in a political situation. Political scientists are probably less naive than psychologists about this. A citizen's presidential vote for one or another candidate depends, as we know,[12] not only on his focal attitude toward that candidate, but also on attitudes toward the alternative candidates, toward party, and toward issues. As for situational factors, the privacy of the voting booth is expressly designed to neutralize them insofar as possible, but the weather may keep the voter from the polls, and the form of the ballot also has its effects. For another example, a legislator's vote on a bill will depend not only on situational factors (including whether or not a roll call is involved) and on his attitudes toward the focal issue, but also on other relevant attitudes that become engaged—toward tangential issues, toward the party leadership, toward political survival, or whatever. The situation plays a dual role here: both as a codeterminant, together with his engaged attitudes, of what he does (B)—for example, the legislator may want to vote for a bill but not dare to—and as differentially activating certain of the actor's attitudes (M and N) while allowing or encouraging other potentially relevant attitudes to remain in abeyance (O). In recent years, issues concerning Negro civil rights have come to be posed in the Congress and elsewhere in such pointed terms that political actors probably find it less feasible than formerly to isolate their attitudes of democratic fair play from engagement—attitudes embodied in the American Creed to which most citizens have been socialized to some degree.[13]

Social psychological research may elect to measure and ma-

11. Key remarks (*ibid.*, p. 233) on the unsatisfactory state of basic knowledge concerning the broad problem of the bearing of attitude on behavior. To formulate the problem correctly, I think, is half the battle. The aspects of the map under discussion here are my attempt to do this.

12. See Angus Campbell, Philip E. Converse, Warren E. Miller, and Donald E. Stokes, *The American Voter* (New York: Wiley, 1960).

13. See Gunnar Myrdal, with the assistance of Richard Sterner and Arnold Rose, *An American Dilemma. The Negro Problem and Modern Democracy*, 2 vols. (New York: Harper, 1944).

nipulate one attitude at a time for good analytic reasons, but people rarely behave in such a piecemeal fashion. What gets into the mix of a person's engaged attitudes, and with what weighting, makes a big difference. Given the complexity of these relationships, there is no reason to suppose that people's political behavior should uniformly correspond to their attitudes on a single focal issue. It is surprising that some psychologists and sociologists have been surprised at the lack of one-to-one correspondence between single attitudes and behavior, and have questioned the validity of attitude measurement on these irrelevant grounds.

Moving toward the left of Panel III, we turn from the problem of how attitudes are differentially aroused to that of how they are formed and sustained. The approach taken here is the *functional* one which posits that a person acquires and maintains attitudes and other learned psychological structures to the extent that they are in some way useful to him in his inner economy of adjustment and his outer economy of adaptation. The scheme for classifying the functional basis of attitudes is one that I have discussed in greater detail elsewhere.[14] It answers the question, "Of what use to a man are his opinions?", under three rubrics: *object appraisal, mediation of self–other relationships,* and *externalization and ego defense.*

Under object appraisal, we recognize the ways in which a person's attitudes serve him by "sizing up" significant aspects of the world in terms of their relevance to his motives, interests, and values. As Walter Lippmann[15] long ago made clear, all attitudes, not just "prejudice," involve an element of "prejudgment": they are useful to the person in part because they prepare him for his encounters with reality, enabling him to avoid the confusion and inefficiency of appraising each new situation afresh in all its complexity. In the most general way, holding *any* attitude brings a bit of order into the flux of a person's psychological world; the specific content of a person's attitudes reflects to varying degrees his appraisal of how the attitudinal object bears upon his interests and enterprises. This function in-

14. See Smith, Bruner, and White, *Opinions and Personality;* also M. Brewster Smith, "Attitude Change," *International Encyclopedia of the Social Sciences* (New York: Macmillan and Free Press, 1968), I, 458–467.

15. Walter Lippmann, *Public Opinion* (New York and London: Macmillan, 1922).

volves reality testing, and is likely to be involved to some minimal degree in even the least rational of attitudes.

A person's attitudes not only embody a provisional appraisal of what for him is significant reality; they also serve to mediate the kind of relationships with others and the kind of conception of self that he is motivated to maintain. Is it important to the decision-maker to think of himself as a liberal Democrat? Then his adopting a liberal stand on any of a variety of issues may contribute to his self-regard. Does he rather set much stock in being right in the light of history? Such motivation, by orienting him toward an ideal reference group, may make him relatively independent of immediate social pressures. To the extent that, by self-selective recruitment, politicians are disproportionately likely to be "other-directed" in Riesman's sense,[16] however, they may be predisposed by personality to be especially vulnerable to such pressures.

Finally comes the class of functions to which psychoanalytic depth psychology has given the closest attention, here labeled externalization and ego defense. This is the functional basis to which Lasswell [17] gave exclusive emphasis in his classic formula for the political man: private motives displaced onto public objects, rationalized in terms of the public interest. It also underlies the conception of the "authoritarian personality" [18]—a posture in which an essentially weak ego puts up a facade of strength that requires bolstering through identification with the strong, the conventional, the in-group, and rejection of the weak, the immoral, the out-group. Given the appeal of depth interpretation in the study of personality and politics, there is little need to expand on these themes; it is more necessary to insist that externalization and ego defense are only part of the story.

The arrows P, Q, and R raise the functional question about the motivational sources of any attitude that a person holds. Arrows S and T, near the bottom of the panel, reflect on their part a different kind of relationship. A person's attitudes and the way

16. David Riesman, *The Lonely Crowd* (New Haven, Conn.: Yale University Press, 1950).

17. Harold D. Lasswell, *Psychopathology and Politics* (Chicago, Ill.: University of Chicago Press, 1930).

18. T. W. Adorno, Else Frenkel-Brunswik, Daniel J. Levinson, and R. Nevitt Sanford, *The Authoritarian Personality* (New York: Harper, 1950); John P. Kirscht and Ronald C. Dillehay, *Dimensions of Authoritarianism: A Review of Research and Theory* (Lexington: University of Kentucky Press, 1967).

they engage with particular political situations bear the mark of his stylistic traits of personality as well as of the purposes that they serve for him. Intelligence or stupidity, incisiveness or vagueness, zest or apathy, optimism or pessimism, decisiveness or hesitation—cognitive, temperamental, and behavioral traits like these have their own history and may perhaps partly be attributed to residues of the person's previous motivational conflicts, but their immediate relevance for his political attitudes and behavior is hardly motivational. His attitudes and actions in the sphere of politics, as in other realms, inevitably reflect such pervasive personal qualities, which can have momentous behavioral consequences. A purely functional account is likely to neglect them.

The foregoing analysis provides us with leverage for identifying aspects of the person's social environment that are relevant to the development, maintenance, and change of his political attitudes and his stylistic personality traits, as we turn to Panel II at the left of Figure 3. To the extent that a person's attitudes in a

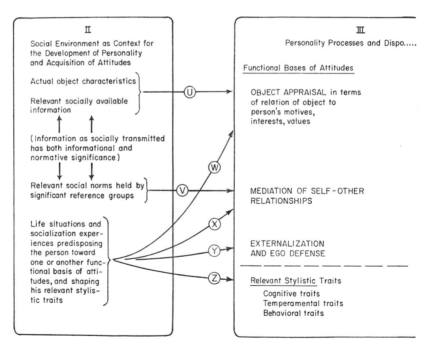

Figure 3

particular political context reflect processes of object appraisal, he should be responsive to the information that his environment provides about the attitudinal object or issue (Arrow U). The actual facts about it will be important in this connection only as they affect the information that is socially available to him, and, as we know, the quality and quantity of this information vary widely from issue to issue and across the various niches that people occupy in society.

The information on a topic that reaches a person through the channels of communication has a dual relevance, as the internal arrows in Panel II are intended to suggest: not only does it feed into his processes of object appraisal, but it carries further information—a second-order message, so to speak—about the social norms that prevail. When discussions of birth control begin to percolate through Catholic channels, or debates about the pros and cons of China policy through American ones—to take two examples in which, in the mid 1960's, controversy is superseding a previous state of affairs in which one policy position had monopolistic advantages—not only is new grist provided for object appraisal; the important news is conveyed that these previously taboo topics have become moot and discussable. As Arrow V indicates, the second motivational basis of attitudes—the mediation of self–other relations—then may lead to attitudinal consequences that point to a different resultant in behavior. It becomes safe to think in new ways.

Besides providing the environmental data that the first two attitudinal functions can work with to generate new attitudes or to sustain or change established ones,[19] the person's life situation and socialization experiences may predispose him—in general, or in a particular topical domain—toward one or another of the functional bases of attitudes (Arrows W, X and Y). What makes the rational man, in whom the first function predominates? The Utopia has not yet arrived in which we know the answer, but recent studies of socialization are beginning to become relevant to the question, and it is a good guess that part of the story is rearing by loving and confident parents who give reasons for their discipline. In the shorter run, environments that augment one's self-esteem and allay one's anxiety should also favor

19. Environmental data play a much more incidental and erratic role in relation to the function of externalization and ego defense.

object appraisal. Research in the wake of Riesman,[20] including the Witkin group's studies of field dependence-independence,[21] and Miller and Swanson's work on child rearing and personality in entrepreneurial and bureaucratic families,[22] contains suggestions about the sources of primary orientation to the second function, mediation of self-other relationships. As for externalization and ego defense, again the picture is not clear, but conditions that subject the developing person to arbitrary authority, that deflate self-esteem, that arouse vague anxiety, that provoke hostility but block its relatively direct expression toward the source of the frustration, seem likely sources.

The final arrow Z is drawn not to complete the alphabet but to make place for the findings of personality research, as they emerge, concerning the determinants in socialization of personal stylistic traits.

The entire map can now be reassembled in Figure 4. Arrows U to Z, taken together, replace Arrow C in Figure 1.

The usefulness of a map and its inherent limitation are two sides of the same coin: its status as a simplification and schematization of reality. There are many complexities that the present map does not attempt to handle. Some of the major omissions, which I note briefly here, arise from the fact that the roles of the basic psychological apparatuses and processes of motivation, perception, and learning are assumed implicitly rather than explicitly delineated.

The triadic functional classification attempts to sort out the ways in which a person's attitudes are rooted in his underlying motives and their fusions and transformations, whatever they may be. It assumes but does not spell out a conception of human motivation.

As for perception, it would elaborate the map to an incomprehensible tangle to give due recognition to what we know about perceptual selectivity—the ways in which a person's existing expectations, motives, and attitudes affect what he will attend to and how he will register and categorize it. A perceptual screen-

20. *The Lonely Crowd.*

21. Herman A. Witkin, R. B. Dyk, Hanna F. Faterson, Donald R. Goodenough, and Stephen A. Karp, *Psychological Differentiation. Studies of Development* (New York: Wiley, 1962).

22. Daniel R. Miller and Guy E. Swanson, *The Changing American Parent* (New York: Wiley, 1958); *Inner Conflict and Defense* (New York: Holt, 1960).

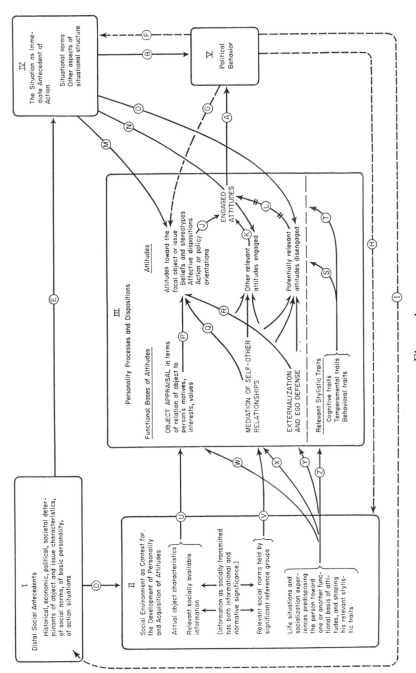

Figure 4

ing process intervenes between the environmental facts (Panel II) and what the person makes of them (Panel III); likewise between the immediate behavioral situation as it might appear to an objective observer (Panel IV) and how the person defines it for himself, which in the last analysis is the guise in which it affects his behavior.

In regard to learning, the present formulation makes the broad functionalist assumption that people in general acquire attitudes that are useful, that is, rewarding, to them. But it ignores the details of the learning process, and such consequences of learning as the persistence of learned structures beyond their original point of usefulness. A person may acquire much of the content of his political attitudes quite incidentally, moreover, in his unfocused, only mildly attentive effort to make sense of his world. The culture says, in effect, "This is how things are with (Russia) (China) (Republicans) (Southerners) (Negroes) (socialized medicine)," and in the absence of better information, he takes note. Such incidentally learned, psychologically marginal "information," may at the time have little real payoff in object appraisal or social adjustment (the person may have no occasion for dealing with the object or issue, and it may not matter enough to his significant reference groups to become part of the currency of his self–other relationships); yet, should the occasion arise, the basis for resonance to certain political positions rather than others has been laid.

The Problem of Political Rationality

In illustrative comments along the way, I have tried to indicate how the map draws distinctions that help to clarify thinking about personality and politics. But these have been hit-and-run examples. A clearer view of its usefulness—or sterility—should come from applying the map to the elucidation of some major problem of political theory and research. A good one for the purpose should be the problem of political rationality, in which V. O. Key was persistently interested and to which he made substantive contribution in his posthumous book.[23]

In setting the scene for his study of rationality in American presidential voting, Key depicted the current antirational climate of political analysis thus:

23. V. O. Key, Jr., with the assistance of Milton C. Cummings, Jr., *The Responsible Electorate. Rationality in Presidential Voting, 1936–1960* (Cambridge, Mass.: Harvard University Press, 1966).

By and large, the picture of the voter that emerges from a combination of the folklore of practical politics and the findings of the new electoral studies is not a pretty one. It is not a portrait of citizens moving to considered decision as they play their solemn role of making and unmaking governments. The older tradition from practical politics may regard the voter as an erratic and irrational fellow susceptible to manipulation by skilled humbugs . . . Nor does a heroic conception of the voter emerge from the new analyses of electoral behavior. They can be added up to a conception of voting not as a civic decision but as an almost purely deterministic act.[24]

As Key sees it, such an irrationalist view itself has political consequences:

In short, theories of how voters behave acquire importance not because of their effects on voters, who may proceed blithely unaware of them. They gain significance because of their effects, both potentially and in reality, on candidates and other political leaders. If leaders believe the route to victory is by projection of images and cultivation of styles rather than by advocacy of policies to cope with the problems of the country, they will project images and cultivate styles to the neglect of the substance of politics. They will abdicate their prime function in a democratic system, which amounts, in essence, to the assumption of the risk of trying to persuade us to lift ourselves by our bootstraps.[25]

Psychological theory has also contributed its bit to the antirationalist trend that has had the upper hand since the emergence of modern social science. The realization brought by Darwin that man is a member of the animal kingdom has often carried with it a degraded conception of human nature, instead of focusing scientific curiosity on how man is sometimes capable of qualities and achievements that surpass those he once ascribed to the angels. In psychoanalysis Freud, who himself was ironically devoted to rational values and their promulgation, greatly advanced our understanding of irrational aspects of human behavior, but also showed the way for lesser followers to engage in facile debunking of all human pretensions to rationality. The behaviorists, who for more than a generation dominated academic theorizing in American psychology, held dogmatically to a mechanistic view of man that left no place for rational action. Until recently, only psychologists in the minority Gestalt tradition [26] and humanistically inclined mavericks like Gordon All-

24. *Ibid.*, pp. 4–5.
25. *Ibid.*, p. 6.
26. For instance, Solomon E. Asch, *Social Psychology* (New York: Prentice-Hall, 1952).

port [27] held to a model of man as a rational actor that would be recognizable to the liberal proponents of democratic political institutions.[28]

But what do we mean by rationality in such contexts? Our answer will depend on the weight we give to evaluating the *products* of individual and social decision processes, as compared with our interest in evaluating the decision *processes* themselves. Rational decisions viewed as products are ones that select appropriate means to attain specified goals at acceptable costs, within a self-consistent framework of positive and negative goal values and in terms of an accurate appraisal of the situation of action. The complexities and competing models of modern decision theory [29] testify to the ambiguities that are latent in common-sense notions of rationality as an objective property of decisions themselves. Yet if we are ultimately concerned with evaluating the political consequences of decisions, we cannot avoid a perspective that looks on the rationality of decisions, as it were, from the outside.

An alternative emphasis, on criteria that pertain to the decision processes as such viewed from the "inside," makes readier contact with the process-oriented predilections of contemporary political scientists and psychologists. In the case of important classes of social decisions, conceptions of "due process" specify minimal norms for properly considered—thus rational—decision-making, setting deliberately aside the correctness of the decision reached. Are there analogous conceptions that apply in the sphere of individual decisions?

In terms of the distinctions in my map, the crux of a processual conception of individual political rationality, it seems to

27. Gordon W. Allport, *Becoming* (New Haven, Conn.: Yale University Press, 1955).

28. The conception that *determinism* is incompatible with a model of man as a responsible actor is wrong, and seriously misleading. The best discussion I know of this problem at the border between philosophy and psychological theory, and incidentally a trenchant criticism of mechanistic theory and a cogent defense of a view of man as a rational animal, is offered by Isidor Chein, "The Image of Man," *Journal of Social Issues*, 18 (October 1962), 1–35. For a social psychological interpretation of rationality as an outcome of symbolic interaction, see my paper, "Rationality and Social Process," *Journal of Individual Psychology*, 16 (May 1960), 25–35.

29. See Gordon M. Becker and Charles G. McClintock, "Value: Behavioral Decision Theory," *Annual Review of Psychology*, 18 (1967), 239–286.

me, lies in the relative preponderance of object appraisal in the person's attitudes that enter into his political decisions and actions. As products, his decisions may be defective and irrational if they are based on the appraisal of erroneous or deficient information. But to the extent that they are grounded in processes of object appraisal, they are rational in the sense that they represent a weighing of means–end relationships that is corrigible in principle given the availability of better information.

From the same processual point of view, externalization and ego defense are definitely irrational. To the extent that this function prevails as a basis for a person's attitudes, he is distracted from relevant considerations of ends and means. He is likely to cling rigidly to his political postures in disregard of available information, and if he changes at all, the change is likely to be saltatory and "unreasonable." Rather than yielding gradually to the pressure of new facts, he may leap unpredictably from a no longer tenable position to another position that is its symbolic or dynamic equivalent for him, different as its realistic political implications may be. The ardent Communist becomes the equally ardent anti-communist Catholic convert.

The remaining functional basis of attitudes, mediation of self–other relationships, is neutral in rationality from this processual perspective. The motivational agenda that it implies has nothing intrinsically to do with how the person appraises the bearing of a focal object or issue on his interests and values, but neither does it necessarily operate at cross-purposes with rational object appraisal, as is the case with externalization and ego defense. And we shall see that there are conditions under which it may lead to decisions which, as products, must be judged as rational.

The functional analysis of attitudes that is embodied in the map of Figure 4 thus makes room for rational processes—and for nonrational and irrational ones as well. It does not settle the problem of rationality by assumption, but leaves it open to empirical inquiry. It avoids treating either the rational or the irrational propensities of man—both consequences of his unique symbolic attainments—as residual. It does not rule out the plausible view that at the individual level most political acts and decisions have both rational and irrational ingredients.

Intermediate between conceptions of individual rationality as process and as product is a characteristic that would commonly be ascribed to rational decisions and judgments: they are reached in a context of relevant considerations that is broad, not narrow, and includes a time perspective in which consequences are viewed in the longer run. Thus personality traits (also placed in Panel III of the map) that characterize the contextual breadth with which a person customarily views new problems become relevant to his level of political rationality. Practically, the narrowness, concreteness, and low sophistication that *The American Voter* [30] found in the political thinking of average Americans set stringent limits on the rationality of their political decisions viewed as products, however reasonable these may appear from a person's own limited perspective. A theory of the democratic polity must therefore give special place to the role of opinion elites and attentive publics whose attitudes are freer from such limitations, and to their interplay with the less sophisticated mass.[31]

To make a place on the map for process rationality, according to which people's decisions and judgments are reasonable within the limits of their grasp of relevant considerations, may restore a view of the human condition in which democracy is conceivable. But as the foregoing discussion suggests, the practical functioning of democracy depends as well on the factors apart from process rationality that affect the extent to which individual judgments meet the criteria of rationality as products. The map finds a place for several such factors.

In regard to Panel IV (the situation as immediate antecedent of action), for example, we may ask: Does the situation pose a meaningful and intelligible political choice? Is information relevant to the choice readily available? How is the citizen to distinguish information from misinformation? All of these considerations should affect whether, in my jargon, process rationality leads to product rationality. And does the situation present the issue in a context of threat and stress, or in a way more conducive to thoughtful deliberation?

If we turn to Panel II (the social environment as context of socialization) again the question of adequacy and accuracy of political information arises. Most people's political attitudes, even when they are predominantly grounded in object appraisal,

30. Angus Campbell *et al. The American Voter*, pp. 216–265.

31. See V. O. Key, Jr., *Public Opinion and American Democracy* (New York: Knopf, 1963), p. 536 ff.

surely rest on a scanty and haphazard informational base. If such be the nature of most people's attitudes, what kinds of decisions can they be asked to make, then, with the greatest likelihood of rational outcomes? V. O. Key suggests that the basic electoral decision—in or out with the incumbent—is most likely to be within people's range.

In Panel II we also encounter the social norms held by the person's significant reference groups. If these norms are congruent with the person's own real interests (and of course this is a notoriously treacherous matter to judge), rational political outcomes may result even when his attitudes are grounded in the mediation of self–other relationships rather than in object appraisal. I can follow my crowd to good advantage *if* my crowd happens to be right from my standpoint. If, however, the person is linked through his reference groups to norms that conflict with his real interests, this functional basis of attitudes becomes a source of irrational outcomes for him. The extent to which a person's reference groups correspond to his membership groups is a related matter. A Smith who is keeping up with the Joneses may form attitudes and make decisions that would be rational enough for a Jones, but not for a Smith.

Finally, Panel II calls attention to the role of life situations and socialization experiences in preferentially orienting the person toward one or another functional basis for his political attitudes, and in forming his politically relevant traits. The paranoid style of the radical right—surely a mark of irrational externalization—has been described as a defensive posture of the dispossessed, the sidetracked, and downwardly mobile.[32] What is the effect on the characterological basis of political rationality of living in lifelong practiced denial of the threat of atomic catastrophe? Of living in economic insecurity or affluence in a marginal, or in an affluent society? Of being one of the powerless in a time of rising aspirations? And what, for that matter, are the long-term political consequences of trends toward less authoritarian child-rearing? Though it may be impossible in the nature of the case to disentangle such strands of recent history, the idea of ebbs and flows in the bases of political rationality seems entirely plausible.

Just as my map dealt with the antecedents of political behav-

32. Daniel Bell, ed., *The Radical Right*, rev. ed. (Garden City: Doubleday, 1963).

ior at the individual level, leaving the problems of articulation in a political system to the political sociologist, so my discussion of political rationality thus far stops short of the questions that would most concern a student of the functioning of democratic governmental institutions. But the map may be suggestive even in regard to matters that fall outside its explicit range.

Beyond the level of the single individual, one may approach relevance to governmental institutions by dealing with persons in the aggregate, or by dealing with them as they articulate in social structures. As I have already remarked, the latter type of analysis requires a different sort of map, and V. O. Key's treatise on public opinion is cogently addressed to considerations of articulation that would be involved in drawing it.[33] But for some problems the mere aggregation of individual data is appropriate, and because that is indeed how votes are counted, it is especially appropriate to the study of voting behavior. This is the strategy followed by Key in his posthumously published study of presidential voting that I quoted at the outset of this section.

In intent and conclusion, *The Responsible Electorate* asserts and adduces evidence for a considerable degree of rationality in American presidential voting. Key summarizes the book prospectively as follows:

> The perverse and unorthodox argument of this little book is that voters are not fools . . . In the large the electorate behaves about as rationally and responsibly as we should expect, given the clarity of the alternatives presented to it and the character of the information available to it. In American presidential campaigns of recent decades the portrait that develops from the data is not one of an electorate strait-jacketed by social determinants or moved by subconscious urges triggered by devilishly skillful propagandists. It is rather one of an electorate moved by concern about central and relevant questions of public policy, of governmental performance, and of executive personality.[34]

Later, he summarizes his principal evidence, concerning the correlates of voting turnover between elections, thus:

> It can scarcely be said that party switchers constitute a sector of the electorate significantly lower in political interest than the standpatters . . . Instead, the switchers, who (in company with "new" voters) call the turn, are persons whose peculiarity is not lack of interest but agreement on broad political issues with the standpatters toward whom they shift . . . This should be regarded as at least a modicum of evidence

33. *Public Opinion and American Democracy.*
34. *The Responsible Electorate,* pp. 7–8.

for the view that those who switch do so to support governmental policies or outlooks with which they agree, not because of subtle psychological or sociological peculiarities.[35]

What does the map contribute to the interpretation of these data
and conclusions?

For one thing, the suggestion immediately arises that voters in
the aggregate may look more rational than they do singly—if
true, a fortunate outcome for the democratic system. Such would
be the case if two conditions turn out to hold: first, that group
norms with respect to the vote reflect genuine group interests,
and, second, that the roots of voting choice in externalization and
ego defense are personally idiosyncratic and distributed unsyste-
matically through the population.

Consider the second of these specifications. If there are irrational private components in everyone's vote, *but* these vary un-
systematically across persons and candidates, their effect should
cancel out in the aggregate, leaving a residue that reflects rational choice. And perhaps this is indeed the normal, fortunate
state of affairs. The abnormal may be exemplified by episodes of
"hysteria" like McCarthyism—mass externalization running
parallel?—from which the electorate subsequently emerges with
a collective hangover. From this point of view, it is fortunate that
political choices seem not to have the standardized unconscious
meanings that lay Freudians were wont to look for. Not to every-
body was Eisenhower a father-figure.

As for the first condition, concerning the degree to which
group voting patterns represent genuine group interests, Key argues from his data that they correspond fairly closely by and
large. To the extent that they do, of course, the first two functional bases of attitudes pull together. When group norms reflect
individual interests, mediation of self–other relations yields the
same result as object appraisal.

Key's vivid rhetoric in dramatizing his point, of course, plays
up a needless conflict in interpretation. "Sociological peculiarities" or "social determinants" do not have their influence by any
mysterious process of "strait-jacketing" the electorate, and no-
body ever claimed that they do. Their influence, indeed a determining one, lies primarily in the fact that common experience
and common social position yield similar perceptions of interest,
and over time lead to the emergence of norms that reflect these

35. *Ibid.*, p. 104.

perceptions. Social determination is by no means incompatible with political rationality.

Similarly with psychological determination. Aggregate rationality is entirely compatible with "subconscious urges," so long as they are divergent. Note also that psychological determination cannot fairly be equated with the subconscious—with externalization and ego defense. Orientation toward norms and orientation toward consequences for one's interests and values are psychological too!

We must remember, finally, that presidential elections with their simplified choice, their high salience, may not be typical of other political behavior that the citizen is called upon to perform. Presidential voting may indeed be a rational performance as compared, for example, with voting on the many initiative and referendum measures on a long California ballot.

The tentative principle of aggregation suggested in our consideration of Key's analyses has interesting consequences with respect to other features of the map. One major feature that we have seen as limiting political rationality—people's informational deficiencies—will clearly *not* be distributed randomly in the electorate. Obvious correlations of informational adequacy with educational and socioeconomic level will have consequences for the degree and manner of political participation. Systematic differences in available public media and in subcultural informational habits should give rise to regional variation and persisting rural–urban differences. There should be substantial differences by topical content as well, placing a particular handicap on the rational public consideration of foreign policy issues. If we agree with Key that in the long run and on the major policy alternatives, the electorate is basically rational, it does not follow that it is homogeneously rational across social strata, regions, and issues. The heterogeneities pose challenging problems of articulation for political theory, and of organization and leadership for political practice.

By this point we perhaps have a sufficient sampling of what the map can and cannot do. As a heuristic scanning device, it summarizes the wisdom born of long traditions of research and theory by calling attention to variables and classes of relationships that are relevant to a psychologically focused perspective on political behavior. It further draws explicit attention to the boundary problems involved in articulating such a perspective with the sociologically centered perspective that is equally indispensable in the study of politics. To the extent that the map draws distinctions familiar to political scientists, it codifies what they know. If it also draws some novel ones, it may help to throw new light on old problems. At best, it can be an aid to the attainment of better research and better theory. It is, of course, a substitute for neither.

Douglas Price

Micro- and Macro-politics: Notes on Research Strategy

"Between the intentions of the governors and the will of the governed falls the shadow."

John Clive [1]

Introduction

In the years since World War II political science has managed to discover—or borrow—a wide range of techniques for studying the individual. The raw materials of political science are no longer limited to the court cases or election returns that may be found in a library. The modern student of politics, like a sort of Prometheus unbound, can design his own research instruments and capture custom-tailored data, at least within the bounds of access, funds, and historical time. In the long run these riches must surely prove of tremendous value in improving our understanding of the political order. But in the short run these innovations have also produced tensions between the more traditional study of institutions and the behavioral emphasis upon study of the individual as microcosm.

For some the study of individual behavior has become an end in itself. Given the complexities of the effort and the advantages of specialization, this is understandable and perhaps even desir-

1. *New York Times Book Review*, November 28, 1965.

able, but for the profession as a whole the task is one of integrating findings about individual behavior into a more sophisticated understanding of how political systems and subsystems operate. Gradually this has focused into an increased concern over "linkages" between individual behavior and system performance, or (viewed from the system down) analysis of the correlates of system output and performance.

But an interest in "linkages" does not guarantee that one can find them, any more than an interest in systematic theory can guarantee its development. Indeed, it is usually easiest to work with existing techniques and to hope that in some very long run they will "add up" or "spin off." Angus Campbell has recently noted this tendency in the direction of public opinion research since World War II. Despite the urging of critics such as Herbert Blumer,[2] research on "publics" and on "opinion" has, as Campbell perceptively notes, "not greatly illuminated the way in which public opinion, defined as effective influence on decision-makers, actually operates in our society." Campbell continues:

It is curious that Blumer's hopes for the functional analysis of public opinion have been so little realized. The ability to conduct effective research on the problems he would have selected seems to elude us. The direction research has actually taken has been heavily influenced by the methods available.[3]

All of which presents political science with a severe dilemma. Although the profession is committed to the search for the "big game" of politics, it has few tools for the task. Effort devoted to building a better mouse trap, or improved questionnaire, *may* lead to catching an elephant. But it also may not. In this essay I have sought to deal with four topics related to V. O. Key's persistent interest in the "big game" of politics.[4] The first two are primarily substantive and touch on the historical pattern of de-

2. For a typical statement see Blumer, "Public Opinion and Public Opinion Polling," *American Sociological Review* 23 (1948), 542–549.

3. Campbell's comments were made in reviewing a recent summary of public opinion literature in *American Sociological Review* 30 (1965), 633. On the micro-macro gap see also Stein Rokkan, "The Comparative Study of Political Participation: Notes Toward a Perspective on Current Research," in Austin Ranney (ed.), *Essays on the Behavioral Study of Politics* (Urbana, Ill., 1962), pp. 47–90.

4. Key's *Public Opinion and American Democracy* (New York: 1961) is an attempt to use Survey Research Center data to achieve some of the goals stressed by Blumer.

velopment of the party system, and the role of the electorate in influencing policy. The second two are primarily methodological and deal with the relation of individual, group, and aggregate (or "ecological") data, and with the research strategy of "reductionism." The latter two topics are doubtless rather more abstract and methodological than Key would be enthusiastic about. The former are certainly based on less data than he would want to see, but represent summaries of more extensive work in progress.

I. The Party System and Supplementary Linkages

Much of American political science has been concerned with the processes by which voters can exert leverage of one sort or another on their government. The three most obvious channels are through elections and the party system, the activities of organized interest groups, and the more recent emergence of direct public opinion polls. Obviously national leaders must also consider events outside the system (e.g., missiles in Cuba), estimates of sheer technical feasibility (e.g., in Manhattan project), and their own consciences (e.g., Hiroshima). But in the study of American politics much emphasis has been on the presumptive causal influence of parties, interest groups, and public opinion. Indeed, many political scientists can be classified by the emphasis and the evaluation that they place on alternative channels.[5]

It can be argued not only that the party system emerged first in point of time, but that its existence is necessary to insure the appropriate functioning of interest groups and public opinion more generally. These latter two can be said to gain much of their political importance because of the possibility of electoral defeat—by means of the party system—for officeholders. Thus, to borrow from the terminology of the analysis of variance, the party system is important both for its own direct effect and for its "interaction effect" in conjunction with interest groups and public opinion. Indeed, one can go beyond the presumed interaction effect and suggest that the mere existence of the party system has latent consequences for the operation of interest groups and public opinion even when it is not actively involved. Hence questions of change in the functioning of the party system and of trends in its development are of particular importance.

5. This becomes particularly obvious in the case of the debate over a "more responsible party system," to be achieved by reducing the impact of interest groups.

The development of the modern American two-party system was a lengthy and complex process, with enough misadventure along the way to suggest caution in criticism of the political immaturity of the current generation of developing areas.[6] Some degree of order can be given the process by focusing attention on (1) the extent of party identification in the electorate, and (2) the degree of strength displayed by party organization. A typical modern view would be that both are desirable, at least in moderate degree. But even a slight brush with American history alerts one to the fact that in various periods one or the other, or

Table 1. Typology of American party system based on strength of party organization and extent of voters' party identification

Extent of party identification within the electorate	Strength of Party Organization			
	High	Medium	Low	Generally absent
High	1860's–1900 (Ostrogorski)	—	—	—
Medium	—	1900–1940's (Key's text)	1940's–1960's (Campbell *et al.*)	—
Low	1850–1860 (Roy Nichols)	1830–1850 (McCormick)	1796–1815 (Chambers & Lipset)	—
Generally absent		—	1815–1830 (J. Young)	early 1790's

Note: For full identification of typical accounts of the politics of various periods see text and notes.

even both, have either been generally missing or have been present to an embarrassing degree.

In the absence of better data any classification of past degree of organizational strength or extent of party identification must be highly tentative. Table 1 presents such a tentative classification, based on these two dimensions. This suggests some eight possible stages in the evolution of party politics. Some of the dis-

6. See William N. Chambers, *Political Parties in a New Nation* (New York, 1963); Seymour M. Lipset, *The First New Nation* (New York, 1963); and James S. Young, *The Washington Community* (New York, 1966).

tinctions—such as the break at 1860—would probably command wide assent. But others are much less clear. Thus the politics of the 1850's seem to differ substantially from those of the Jacksonian period, but whether to attribute this to further growth of party organization or perhaps to decline in already weak party identification is not so clear. There is also the nagging question of *other* dimensions which may be of crucial importance. Thus the extent of sectionalism and related question of extent of two-party competition within various states could be examined.

Historians have given a great deal of attention to the development of the "first" American party system of Federalists and Jeffersonian Democratic-Republicans. And both Lipset and Chambers have suggested the analogies to present nation-building. Jefferson is much acclaimed for his organizational skill, but he was operating on a small scale, within a restricted electorate, and did not arrive at institutional solutions which were to prove stable. Although there developed much bitterness toward Federalists (when they were in power) and later toward the Jeffersonians, this did not develop into lasting party identification; nor did it always penetrate to newer sections of the country.

The disorganization and weakness of the political structure in the first quarter of the nineteenth century is well portrayed in James S. Young's recent volume, *The Washington Community: 1800–1828.*[7] And the development of organized parties at the state level has recently been analyzed by Richard McCormick in his aptly titled *The Second American Party System.*[8] He shows quite clearly the extent to which sectional ties and reactions to various presidential candidates shaped the emergence of a new two-party system. The development of significant mass party organization, based on extensive use of patronage, is commonly credited to the Jacksonians. Indeed, to achieve the major expansion of the electorate that was carried out, both a popularization of political style and a substantial political organization would seem necessary (especially in the absence of electronic media).

It is amazing how much of our institutional practice and party structure were shaped by the Jacksonian era.[9] Among the innovations customarily associated with the Jacksonians one can list:

7. See especially parts three and five.

8. McCormick, *The Second American Party System* (Chapel Hill, 1966).

9. The literature on the Jacksonians is voluminous, but see also Roy F. Nichols, *The Invention of the American Political Parties* (New York, 1967).

Spread of direct delegate convention (replacing legislative caucus)

Development of mass party organization

Extension of suffrage to virtually all adult white males

Popular style of mass politics

Systematic use of patronage on wide basis to develop organization

Rotation in office, with short terms and long ballot

Direct election of Presidential electors, as all-or-nothing units within states

Emergence of the President as "tribune of the people" and policy leader

Use of presidential veto on political as well as constitutional grounds

In some instances and in some areas the Whigs deserve part of the credit, but the overall impetus was Jacksonian. Most of the Whig efforts at innovation—as with a "collective cabinet" under Harrison, or even Clay's "American system"—were abortive. But by accepting in 1840 the logic of mass democracy, and beating the Democrats at their own game, they showed how a more conservative party could compete and win under the new rules. As with the Federalist acceptance of opposition within the system and peaceful change after the election of 1800, this was an important precedent for the system.

The party battles of the Jacksonians and Whigs also created an intense and unprecedented degree of close two-party competition within the states. As Figure 1 shows, the extent of party competition in the period 1836–1856 was vastly greater than that of the 1896–1908 period. Indeed, it was even somewhat greater than that of the 1940–1952 period. But the Jacksonian party system was not sufficiently stable to maintain this degree of competition, or ultimately even national unity, in the face of the intense sectionalism of the 1850's.

Despite their firm organizational status the pre-Civil War parties appear to have rested on a very shaky basis in terms of what we now term party identification. The Whigs were notorious for agreeing on nothing but their opposition to Jackson, and the

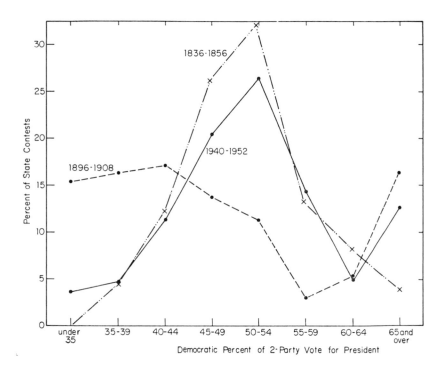

Figure 1.   Statewide competitiveness: Democratic percentage of state vote for President in three contrasting periods, (Three Free Soil states in 1848 and four Dixicrat states in 1948 are omitted.)

Jacksonian Democrats—often styled "the Jackson men"—were not much more coherent. The rapid rise of the anti-Masonic Party, the Free Soilers, the Know-Nothings, and later the Native American Party, give eloquent testimony to the seeming lack of stable party loyalty. The quick collapse of the Whig Party in the 1850's would hardly have been possible if it had enjoyed strong party identification among wide portions of the electorate.

Conclusive evidence that party identification was weak and diffuse in the United States prior to the Civil War is lacking. An alternative view is that the focusing of controversy around the slavery dimension "became at last so strong that it provided a basis for the dissolution of long-standing party loyalties in much of the electorate." [10]

In any case it is clear that the Civil War created a vast reservoir of strong party loyalty, and that this was further augmented by the tensions of Reconstruction. Moreover, this massive infusion of intense party identification was, of course, distributed on a sharp sectional pattern.[11] In a very real sense our parties still operate within a somewhat diluted carry-over of the post-Civil War loyalties. The late nineteenth-century parties thus operated in an environment of intense voter partisanship, and with extensive patronage and other organizational resources. And in most of the country they did so without the useful check of two-party competition.

The late nineteenth-century party system was strongly entrenched, but not necessarily effective as a guide to policy. The very strength of party feeling and extent of organizational resources made the system somewhat insensitive to popular demands. Writing around the turn of the century, Ostrogorski was appalled at both the "fetish-like worship of the 'party' " and the extensive use of spoils. He put great emphasis on "the feeling of loyalty to the party, diffused throughout the great mass of the

10. Donald E. Stokes, "Spatial Models of Party Competition," *American Political Science Review* 57 (1963), 368–377, at 376.

11. The study of individual party identification is, of course, a recent development associated with survey research. But the intense sectionalism of post-Civil War politics made "party identification" of states and counties the basic theme of political history and analysis (as well as of folklore such as "Iowa will go Democratic when Hell freezes over") See V. O. Key and Frank Munger, "Social Determinism and Electoral Decision: the Case of Indiana," in E. Burdick and A. Brodbeck, eds., *American Voting Behavior* (Glencoe, Ill.: 1959), chap. 15.

electorate." Indeed, he repeatedly compares loyalty to party with a religion:

After all, the name of the party is its own justification, in the eyes of millions of electors. They say . . . "I am a Democrat" (or "I am a Republican," as the case may be), just as a believer says, to explain and justify his faith, "I am a Christian!" The reader knows how, and through what political circumstances, party devotion, which is rather an unreasoning sentiment all the world over, has been intensified in the United States and raised to the level of a dogma,—the dogma of "regularity," which makes the party creed consist in voting the "straight party ticket," whatever it may be. The sins against the religion of the party are sins against the ticket." [12]

How, one might inquire, could such a party system help to influence policy in a direction preferred by the electorate so long as the bulk of the electorate responded in nonpolicy terms? A similar query, based on somewhat different conditions, rises from modern survey analysis.

In truth the ability of a two-party system to direct policy in a fashion preferred by the electorate should not be overemphasized. Even if nineteenth-century voters were not blinded by party loyalty or seduced by tangible nonpolicy rewards they would face all the complexities of the "Arrow problem" [13] in attempting to command complicated preferences by a simple choice between only two parties. If only one issue were involved then the outcome should be clear, but as soon as one admits the possibility of several issues, and these of varying intensities and often more than two alternative responses, then the situation becomes exceedingly complex. Any electoral "mandate" for future policy is hard to discern. What the parties have been able to provide is an overall vote of confidence or of no confidence in the past performance of the party in power (and since Jackson "in power" has meant control of the Presidency).

Ostrogorski's critical view of the party system circa 1900 went so far as to regard existing major parties as hopeless for any effective policy purpose, and to propose the need for a new type of organization. This was to be the "single-issue party" on the model of the British anti-Corn League. As he put it:

12. M. Ostrogorski, *Democracy and the Organization of Political Parties*, Vol. II: *The United States*, edited by Seymour M. Lipset (Chicago, 1964 paperback edition), p. 173.

13. See Kenneth J. Arrow, *Social Choice and Individual Value* (New York, 1951); and Robert A. Dahl, *A Preface to Democratic Theory* (Chicago, 1957).

"Down with 'party,'" and "Up with 'league,'" that is the cry of the political evolution which is beginning to take shape.[14]

This critique reflected typical French emphasis on accuracy of interest articulation rather than on ease of aggregation. Parties based largely on loyalties deriving from the Civil War and Reconstruction (plus Irish-Catholic conflict with Yankee Protestants) became increasingly irrelevant to the issues of an urban industrialized society. And, again as Ostrogorski noted, society was becoming more complex and marked by a much greater range and variety of issues. Ostrogorski accurately diagnosed a functional need not met by the party system.

The modern interest group has come to fulfill a very similar function, but in supplementing rather than replacing the party system. The network of groups expanded rapidly in the late nineteenth century, and so did their range of activities. In the twentieth century the individual lobbyist has been largely replaced by the institutionalized association, at least at the national level (state-level lobbying appears to be closer to the nineteenth-century national pattern, just as state legislatures now tend to resemble nineteenth-century Congress in organization, staff, membership, and turnover).

So long as groups are not in a position to manipulate their members or followers and have long-term interests in survival they can become a valuable means of organizing interest around particular issues and giving more explicit evidence of the size and depth of concern. At least this is the argument if one assumes that the ability and resources to organize are widely distributed. In fact, however, organizational ability itself is by no means uniformly distributed. There is both a class bias in general, and a heavy weighting of advantages on the side of the "leaders" as compared with the rank-and-file. The latter point has received renewed attention on the basis of survey data over the past decade,[15] but it is crucial to Michel's theory of organization (the terms "leaders" or "leadership" occur in the titles of five of the six major parts of Michel's *Political Parties*).[16]

14. Ostrogorski, fn. 12 above, pp. 366–367.

15. The basic source is, of course, Samuel A. Stouffer. *Communism, Conformity, and Civil Liberties* (New York, 1955).

16. Since Michel's conclusions about "oligarchy" have attracted considerable attention it is strange that his more basic assumptions about differences between "leaders" and "followers" attracted so little attention. See Robert Michels, *Political Parties* (Glencoe, Ill.: 1949).

After a generation of muckraking, social scientists have come to describe and evaluate the interest group system in a somewhat more favorable light. If *all* possible interests were organized, then much of the competitive advantage coming from organization would be canceled out, though the total system might be a marvel of information provision for politicians. But many political scientists were more struck by the *disparity* in degree of organization. Thus E. E. Schattschneider is typical of those who saw "interest group politics" as inherently small-scale politics,[17] favoring the already privileged groups, in contrast to wide-scale "party (electoral) politics" which gave greater advantage to sheer numbers.

For dealing with a broad crisis, such as a depression, or for giving some general indication of a preferred overall direction for policy, the party system might well be ideal. But as the tasks of government and the range of interests in society both increased, the ability of a single general election clearly to indicate voter preferences on a myriad of issues is hard to accept. Indeed, much of the enthusiasm for "more responsible" parties seems to have rested on the assumption (probably erroneous) that a majority preference for a variety of liberal programs still existed in the 1940's or 1950's, and was only frustrated by the institutional mechanisms of Congress or the party system. The alternative view would be that the magnitude of Roosevelt's electoral victories never could be read as reliable indicators of popular enthusiasm for each and every aspect of the New Deal (thus Mississippi whites voted overwhelmingly for Roosevelt, but surely did not favor civil rights legislation). It was easy to assume that "the people" were with the liberal cause and that it was the evil organized interests which were able to short-circuit the ineffective party system.

In analyzing the impact of both elections and of interest group activity it is customary to consider how politicians anticipate that people will react as well as to look for actual responses. To the extent that electoral and interest group reaction is successfully anticipated and accounted for, then actual turnover of incumbents is less likely. Two further supplemental sources of cues are also of considerable consequence. First, formal polling procedures offer something of an outside check on performance be-

---

17. E. E. Schattschneider, *The Semi-Sovereign People* (New York, 1960).

tween elections, and a possible deflator of interest groups claims. Here the polls are probably more useful in giving generalized approval or disapproval than in tapping public sentiment on specifics. Particular issues usually are of great concern only to particular sub-sets of the public, and the full range of alternatives and issues is not well accommodated by usual polling procedures. But the polls can serve to indicate more clearly whether an issue has become a "must" item on the agenda of public concern.

The range of channels by which individuals can seek to influence government is impressive. They extend far beyond the formal ballot, as Paul Appleby indicated in a fascinating description published in 1949:

Citizens vote, then, by adding their names and energies to membership rolls. They vote by swelling, or failing to swell, the circulations of particular newspapers or periodicals. They vote by contributing to the popularity of particular radio or newspaper commentators. They vote by writing "letters to the editor." They vote much more potently than they know when they write or talk to members of legislative bodies and to administrative officials. They vote as they express themselves in labor unions, farm organizations, business and professional bodies. They vote in every contribution they make to the climate of opinion in a thoroughly political society. They vote more effectively still as they organize to exert influence. They vote effectively in proportion to the persistence of their efforts, for persistence is an index to intensity of feeling.[18]

In addition, much agitation for action now comes from *within* government itself. On domestic issues, at least, this is usually within the context of anticipating the needs or approval of some segment of the public, and is often carried on in close collaboration with interest group activity. Indeed, one reason for the generally lessened concern with the impact of interest groups may well be the fact that as more and more programs have been built into government the spur for policy development has increasingly come from the agencies themselves, with interest groups in a supporting role. Conceivably this could be regarded as a fourth separate type of linkage, but since the direction of causal influence is ambiguous I shall not attempt to deal with it here.

Any overall evaluation of the effectiveness of the three mechanisms will depend rather heavily on one's evaluation of their re-

18. Paul H. Appleby, *Policy and Administration* (University, Alabama, 1949), chap. VII.

spective importance and legitimacy. In a pessimistic vein one can regard elections and the party system as offering no real alternative, while special interests dominate policy-making, mass media manipulate public opinion, and most vital decisions are arrived at by bargaining among governmental agencies and elites. This view has been forcefully expressed by C. Wright Mills and others. It would appear that any evaluation also must be some sort of composite judgment of a variety of different policy areas. So even if there were approximate agreement on the pattern of influence within various policy areas (perhaps elites having broader discretion in military policy; much less in agricultural policy), the overall rating would necessarily depend upon the weight one attaches to different policy areas.

Few would deny that in modern America there are powerful linkages between government and the populace. Obviously there are feedback effects on the populace even when it exerts leverage on government. But the question of concern here is whether and to what extent one could say that the government's actions are indeed in accord with popular preferences, either expressed prior, or by subsequent approval, to leaders' anticipations. In particular, are popular elections under American conditions an effective means of exercising control by followers over leaders? If so, then the system would seem to rest on a very powerful base since the other modes each assume recourse to elections as the ultimate sanction. But, if not, then the whole structure is called into question. And as the study of electoral behavior has added large-scale individual data to what was previously surmised on the basis of aggregate data of election returns, the picture is by no means clearly reassuring. It is to questions about the role of the electorate that we now turn.

II. Role of the Electorate

The existence of contested elections and organized parties may be essential for effective voter influence on government. But they do not guarantee such control. Survey research of the past two decades has documented the continuing importance of party loyalty and demonstrated the seeming thinness—at least in the total electorate—of knowledge and concern about issues. Grounds for pessimism abound. On the one hand electoral participation and sense of party identification are far below the levels of late nineteenth century. On the other hand, knowledge of and interest in issues appear to be quite limited. By such innocuous seeming criteria the voters are not performing their necessary role in the system. But seemingly innocuous criteria may in fact be far too strong—as the history of mathematics and logic clearly demonstrates.

Perhaps the electorate still manages to "muddle through" in an appropriate manner. Moreover, the twin criticisms cited above run somewhat counter to each other. Hence it may be useful to re-examine the criteria for evaluating the role of the electorate. In a thoughtful and important article Walter Dean Burnham has presented long-run data on participation which lead him to pessimistic conclusions:

> In the United States these transformations over the past century have involved devolution, a dissociation from politics as such among a growing segment of the eligible electorate and an apparent deterioration of the bonds of party linkage between electorate and government.[19]

His pessimism rests in part on the assumption that a long-run decline in turnout means that the electorate is "decomposing as a relative increase in its component of peripherally involved voters occurs." [20] An innocuous assumption, perhaps, but turnout may be a much more ambiguous indicator.

Many commentators have suggested that the ranks of the nonvoters include substantial numbers of those who are reasonably content, have no strong policy complaints, and therefore act rationally (and one might argue, properly) in abstaining. Anthony Downs has stated the logic quite clearly.[21] But other critics suggest that substantial numbers of voters are "alienated" and see politics as hopeless or meaningless, and therefore the number of nonvoters is taken as an indicator—as Burnham suggests—of a bad situation. Data on turnout permit no easy distinction between the motivations or circumstances of nonvoters, or of voters. Hence if one wants to consider criteria of "good" or "bad" reasons for voting and nonvoting, changes in the level of participation are inherently ambiguous: an increase in nonvoting may mean more apathy based on satisfaction, or it may indicate more alienation. Equally difficult is the task of evaluating the voters. If one hopes for policy preferences to be the chief moti-

19. Burnham, "The Changing Shape of the American Political Universe," *American Political Science Review* 59 (1965), 7–28, at 10.

20. *Ibid.*

21. Anthony Downs, *An Economic Theory of Democracy* (New York, 1957).

vating force, then voters may be voting for either "good" or "bad" reasons. And in the nineteenth century the component of voters who followed a blind party loyalty or who supported a local urban machine for tangible or primary group reasons was substantial. Thus the size of the component of voters is also ambiguous; without some means of subdividing the categories of voters and nonvoters each into subcategories, sheer change in the level of participation remains ambiguous on both sides of the ledger.

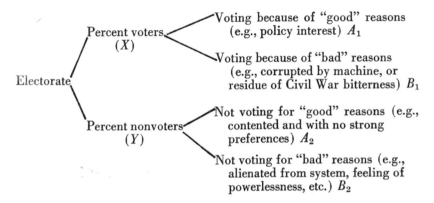

Figure 2. Electoral turnout: an ambiguous indicator as to reasons for voting.

Thus, as Figure 2 suggests, knowing the percentage of voters (X) or nonvoters (Y) does not guarantee direct insight into changes in level of $A_1 + A_2$ (or of $B_1 + B_2$). Indeed, the problem is even more intractable than the usual analysis of aggregate data, in which one has only the marginal distributions. Here we know only one of the two marginal distributions, and none of the individual cell entries.

The high participation and strong party zealotry of the late nineteenth century need not be taken as a "golden age" for all criteria. And inferences from aggregate data are tricky, whether in a statistical or qualitative sense. Hence it may be useful to consider some alternative interpretations for other of the criteria which Burnham has examined. Interest in the systematic analysis of historical election data is growing, and any hints or warning posts in regard to general interpretations may be helpful as political science undertakes the massive job of analysis in historical depth.

(1) Estimated turnout. Here all agree on a substantial decline, and most agree that enfranchisement of women is the most obvious single factor. But, as indicated above, there are substantial reasons for not regarding all voters (including the corrupt, the graveyard vote, the pathological partisans) as evidence of "health" of the party system and all nonvoters (including the satisfied and the indifferent) as evidence of pathology. As suggested previously, the ratio of people with "good" reasons for voting or not voting to those with "bad" reasons for voting or not voting is much more complex than that of voters to nonvoters. And there is a good deal of impressionistic evidence (see Ostrogorski, plus any book on the Tweed machine) that "bad" reasons were common circa 1900.

(2) Drop-off, between presidential and nonpresidential years, is a common twentieth-century phenomenon. Although it could rest entirely on an enlarged number of "peripheral" voters, many of the same considerations apply here as to turnout. That is, high mobilization of the off-year vote in the nineteenth century may have rested on "bad" reasons (tangible resources of machines plus unthinking party zealotry). But an increased emphasis on presidential elections would be rational if—as certainly seems the case—the president is seen as playing a more central role in American politics. Thus the differentiation accompanies the rise of strong presidents (usually dated from T.R.), and the presumed decline in importance (at least relatively) of Congress. Indeed, since Congress has become a very intricate internal system, shifts at a single off-year election may have little policy impact. The institution is more yielding to the effects of presidential landslides, especially if repeated.

(3) Roll-off, or decline in voting for lesser offices on ballot than for top offices, has also increased. Here ballot form—which began to change in the 1890's—is probably of crucial importance. We know from survey data that an office-bloc type ballot may have little effect on highly interested and educated voters, but that it does make a difference to the less involved. But in the absence of such ballots—and Massachusetts was the first to adopt one in 1889—all voters were likely to cast a complete ballot (since it usually took positive action to "scratch" a candidate). Of the two inferences of increased peripherality or of the ballot making possible the differential behavior of the less involved, I see no strong reason for preferring the first, at least until the impact of the substantial ballot changes of the late nine-

teenth century are explored. Here is some evidence presented by Key on the effect of the ballot change in Massachusetts:

In an attempt to measure the effect of ballot form, my research assistant, Mr. H. D. Price, hit upon an interesting incidental consequence of ballot form. The office-bloc ballot evidently handicaps the minor-office candidates of the party whose adherents include the larger proportion of poorly educated voters. Massachusetts in 1888 adopted the Australian ballot in the office-bloc form to replace, effective with the election of 1889, ballots provided privately by parties.—*Acts and Resolves*, 1888, ch. 436. With the election of 1889 the Democratic minor-office vote dropped sharply in relation to the Democratic gubernatorial vote, whereas the Republican minor candidates continued to poll about as large a vote as the head of their ticket. The average minor-office vote as a percentage of the gubernatorial vote for each of the parties follows for a series of elections:

Year	1885	1886	1887	1888	1889	1890	1891
Republican	100.2	100.2	102.4	103.0	103.4	99.8	101.1
Democratic	100.7	100.0	97.3	97.6	89.2	90.0	88.6

While factors other than ballot form doubtless contributed to this spread between the vote on minor office and on governor, the timing of the appearance of the spread strongly points to the ballot reform as differential in its partisan incidence over the short-run at least.[22]

One might add that it is hard to believe that the Massachusetts voters became alienated and peripheral between the 1888 and 1889 annual elections.

(4) Split-ticket voting. Here again we have an ambiguous measure, since even party loyalty can have too high a price. Voters may prefer a split ticket, again, for either "good" reasons (e.g., candidate of their party may be outright criminal) or "bad" reasons (presumably an excessive emphasis on pure personality or glamor). We know that split-ticket voting has increased, but has it been mostly because of "bad" reasons? Some increase doubtless may be attributed to "bad" reasons, but a goodly part of the variance may well be attributed to good, or at least neutral, reasons. Again, changes in ballot form are probably of crucial importance, at least for the less involved (and the "less involved," like the poor, have always been with us). The decline of excessive partisanship (Civil War and Reconstruction type) probably has increased the percentage of non-strong party identifiers. But among the potential "good" reasons for split-ticket voting one might consider the legitimate desire of ethnic

22. V. O. Key, *American State Politics* (New York, 1956), p. 212.

groups for recognition, leading to much split-ticket voting (as in the Northeast). Here the drive of Irish- or Italo-American voters for "recognition" is an indicator *of involvement* and legitimacy for the system, rather than the opposite. Far from being "peripheral," they are passionately concerned about who wins. So long as the ethnic candidate is not an utter scoundrel (and the same test might be required of nineteenth-century "party" candidates) this would seem desirable. And certainly the complexity of the ethnic mixture has increased markedly since the late nineteenth century. The same can be said for the range of issues at stake. Indeed, one might well say that in the absence of an increased flexibility of voting (to accommodate the greater range of issues and the complexity of ethnic demands) the party system would be in grave trouble.

(5) Mean partisan swing in average party vote between elections has also increased. Again one wonders about the components of variance. Obviously nonpresidential year drop-off increases likelihood of partisan swings, and any regional party realignment—as of the South—requires a party swing. Indeed, without partisan swing we would be frozen in an increasingly irrelevant politics of the past. At any rate, not all the blame need be laid on tendency toward uninvolved or image-oriented voters.

In gross outline the trend of the historical data is clear. But the inferences to be drawn from it are not so clear, and depend substantially upon one's assumptions and criteria. For recent elections more direct evidence is available from survey studies. But even here there is room for substantial difference of opinion in interpretation. Key put great emphasis on party, but did not see either party identification or candidate image as excluding a role for voter reaction to government performance:

All these patterns of behavior are consistent with the supposition that voters, or at least a large number of them, are moved by their perceptions and appraisals of policy and performance. They like or don't like the performance of government.[23]

Even the collection of the data is likely to skew the enterprise in one direction or another. Thus in many situations respondents appear all too ready to volunteer responses on subjects about which they literally know nothing, or to use classification schemes (such as upper, middle, lower class) which many of

---

23. V. O. Key, *The Responsible Electorate* (Cambridge, Mass., 1966), p. 150.

them would not volunteer. An alternative, used by SRC, is to rely on more open-ended questions and subsequently classify the various spontaneous responses. But this also may skew things, since in the long run politics comes to the voter and does not have to be defined by him. Moreover, many people of modest educational background find it difficult to put into words anything other than the most cliché-ridden response. Does the awkwardly formulated response, or the lack of a response, in the interview situation really indicate that the individual cannot respond to given political stimuli in a more coherent way? Much electoral behavior seems to be more coherent than the public's banal comments would suggest. This would be a useful area for some experimental work, since the adequacy of the data is *basic* to any analysis of its implications.

Even beyond the difficulties of open-ended questions it would be possible for many voters to perform responsibly *if* they are so situated as to get appropriate policy-oriented cues, even though their understanding or verbalization of the subject is poor. Thus, if union members hear predominantly that Goldwater is "a bad egg," they may come to a policy conclusion appropriate to their position even in the absence of more specific information.

Finally there is the question of the relation of issues and of party. This was Ostrogorski's great area of complaint, and in some recent elections it would appear that party loyalty does account for more than do the issues. Indeed, the Elmira study neatly documented how party identifiers tended to distort or screen out information about issues that ran counter to their party. Obviously, then, party loyalty is a potent factor—a point evident to anyone who has worked with aggregate time series,[24] as well as to recent survey data. But we have not had much opportunity to study the processes of creation of new party loyalties in times of unusual stress. Socialization presumably is the major mechanism under routine circumstances. But the American party system has been heavily influenced by special major crises, which managed to shake the usually stable party loyalties of millions of voters. Thus the Civil War and Reconstruction was a major watershed, which was somewhat modified in the North by the election of 1896. The emergence of Al Smith was catalytic in much of the Northeast in 1928, and the experience of de-

24. See note 11, above.

pression and the early New Deal was the most drastic change since the Civil War.

Party loyalties can be created or changed by major disasters such as civil war, major economic depression, and perhaps large-scale foreign policy defeats. In accounting for the total elector-ate at a given time the largest component of influence is usually that of traditional party loyalty (a concept which SRC has used to create a "normal vote,"[25] if one can imagine an election with-out candidates and without any attempt even at issues). In a rel-atively "steady state" politics, party loyalty is a highly potent predictive device. But in a period or region of rapid change in basic loyalties (such as the post-1929 era or the recent South) it provides little guidance. Indeed, one might surmise that virtually every *other* indicator of change would shift first, so that those re-lying on party loyalty would be the last to perceive what was happening.[26]

In looking at the total electorate, then, in a stable period the single largest relation is usually between traditional party at-tachment and vote. Is this reasonable in terms of the functioning of the party system, or not? If party loyalties encapsulate the de-cisive crises of the past, then voting by party may be reasonable for people who have no more compelling criteria to consider. To the extent that American politics differs on a modified left–right dimension, socialization within the family will more often than not transmit the "appropriate" party identification for the next generation provided (1) that the off-spring do not sharply change status without a shift of party, and (2) that parents were indeed already in the appropriate category. Over the long run the force of party might then be considered as mildly "conserva-tive," not in a partisan sense but in the sense of conserving the patterns of conflict that existed in the past. This is hardly a prime requirement for a rational politics, but in a system that puts a great deal of emphasis on stability and that generally in-clines to make action difficult and inaction easy (a tendency much commented on in most American institutions), it is at least

25. See Philip E. Converse, "The Concept of a Normal Vote," in Angus Campbell *et al.*, *Elections and the Political Order* (New York, 1966), chap. 2.

26. Compare, for example, Donald S. Strong, "Durable Republicanism in the South," and Philip E. Converse, "A Major Political Realignment in the South?", both reprinted in Allan P. Sindler, ed., *Change in the Contemporary South* (Durham, N.C., 1963).

in accord with the general tendency of American politics. If this tendency itself is overdone then it needs to be dealt with in *many* aspects of American politics other than the party system.

What, then, of political issues? If one asks that the generality of the electorate be familiar with them, and with the respective stands of the parties on them, then the situation appears dim indeed. But most "issues" of post-World War II have not been of the crisis sort that shake up whole electorates. Indeed, the decade of the 1950's was generally thought to have been particularly nonpolitical. Perhaps only the question of the position of the Negro in the South had the salience to command general interest and a high sense of concern.

The impact of issues is most potent in specific subgroups of the electorate who are concerned, and *not* across the total electorate. Given that the total electorate is divided in a competitive fashion between the two major parties, then the marginal shifts of those who *are* issue-oriented may decide elections.[27] And the reasonableness of the party system can be evaluated in terms of its flexibility in electing or defeating candidates without requiring that all the supporters of each side be issue-oriented. Since it is generally realized that the substantial Democratic lead in party loyalty is nearly balanced out by higher Republican turnout, the party identification of the electorate produces a "normal" vote, or party preference division, of close to 50-50. In this situation the ability of particular issues to attract a self-defined segment of the public can be of importance. There is considerable evidence to suggest that indeed it is. But note that these issues are low-temperature or specialized ones, not the sort to command the attention of the entire electorate.

It may be useful to provide an example of the way in which issue involvement within a particular subgroup can reverse ordinary relations of party identification or attitude toward a candidate. Peter B. Natchez has done this, using Survey Research Center data, for a number of issues and elections. Table 2 contrasts the relation between 1964 presidential vote and attitude toward Goldwater (based on an index of candidate image)

27. For a detailed examination of the voting behavior of various issue-publics see the forthcoming doctoral dissertation of Peter B. Natchez (Harvard University, 1968). For an analysis of objectively defined subgroups see Eva L. Mueller, "Public Attitudes toward Fiscal Programs," *Quarterly Journal of Economics* 77 (1963), 210–235, especially Table XI at p. 231.

among those voters not concerned with the civil rights issue and voters who mentioned civil rights (pro-integration response) as their issue of greatest concern. Seven out of every ten pro-Goldwater voters who were not concerned about civil rights voted Republican, but among self-defined civil rights supporters the relationship was exactly reversed, with seven out of ten pro-Goldwater voters voting Democratic.

Table 2. Issue involvement, attitude toward Goldwater, and 1964 presidential vote: civil rights issue public

		VOTERS NOT A MEMBER OF CIVIL RIGHT ISSUE PUBLIC		VOTERS MENTIONING CIVIL RIGHTS (PRO-INTEGRA-TION) AS FIRST CONCERN	
		Attitude toward Goldwater (N = 939)		Attitude toward Goldwater (N = 76)	
		Pro	Con	Pro	Con
1964 VOTE	Rep.	69.3 (307)	6.0 (30)	30.4 (7)	1.9 (1)
	Dem.	30.7 (136)	94.0 (466)	69.6 (16)	98.1 (52)
		Somer's D = .633		Somer's D = .285	

In his fine study of the appropriations process, Fenno notes the use of committee hearings to communicate program information to particular clientele publics:

Every program has its interested supporters and a clientele outside the government. And agency officials view the hearings as a way of keeping them informed, of stimulating their interest, and of maintaining their support. They view the hearings record as serving this vital function:
I'll admit it's only a small but special segment of the public that reads it and that's important. We prepare our opening statement with that in mind. It's not to be read by the Committee, but by the interested people outside.[28]

Yet a national sample might well turn up no one who had ever had occasion to read the reports of appropriations committee hearings.

If one accepts party voting as reasonable enough in the absence of a contrary issue concern, then the voters' performance

28. Richard F. Fenno, *The Power of the Purse* (Boston, 1966), p. 281.

in the American system can be rated much higher. Among those who are concerned about a specific issue an appropriate shift of voting behavior is quite likely. But the adequacy of the system is still open to some question. If elections turn not on the massive impact of decisive issues on the greater part of the electorate, but on the shifts of various small issue publics, how can one be sure that these policy preferences will indeed be reflected. Or should they be? This is a problem of impact, or of representation. And here it is clear that the ability of the party system to command specific responses is limited. Thus if voters favored Eisenhower for reasons both of foreign policy and domestic policy, but mostly the former, they got an administration equally committed to both.

The fineness of response of the party system should not be overemphasized. But it is supplemented by the more complex and more sensitive system of interest group activity, as well as congressional representation. By decentralizing policy into a variety of arenas the ability of a relatively small issue public to play a decisive role is increased. And the party system remains as the most efficient way to give a general across-the-board nudge for greater spending and more government activity (with the Democrats) or for less (with the Republicans). Thus the two systems dovetail in a rather neat fashion to provide a complex system of representation for particular concerns while also permitting a broad shift of emphasis for the whole system.

III. Relationship of Individual and Aggregate Data

A clarification of the relation between individual and aggregate data promises to increase the sophistication of analysis of past election returns and may help give greater political relevance to survey research. The problems involved are not particularly esoteric, and were duly noted in the 1930's. But the issue has too often been oversimplified into discussion of the so-called "fallacy of ecological correlation." Too many political scientists have jumped to the hasty—and erroneous—conclusion that analysis of aggregate data can only lead to spurious findings.

Within political science the analysis of aggregate voting data made almost no technical advance from the initial probes of the turn of the century to the 1940's. It remained a craft-oriented skill, usually involving neither modern statistics nor automatic data processing. Users of aggregate data seldom distinguished clearly between analysis of characteristics of the aggregate units themselves and the desire to obtain insight into the behavior of types of individual voters. For the latter, aggregate data provide a large volume of highly valuable clues, but they need to be handled with care. This was duly noted in the 1930's by Herbert Tingsten, whose statistical consultant was no less than Herman Wold.[29] They carefully noted, in a footnote that few seem to have noticed, that correlations based on aggregate data were affected by the size of the units. Hence correlations from different-sized units could not be directly compared, and obviously they did not exactly correspond to individual correlations.

I wish to stress, that in the case of time and spatial series all correlation indices are conditioned by the size (delimitation) of the statistical units to which the data are referring. It is, for instance, incorrect to compare directly the coefficients referring to different countries when correlating two social phenomena. This fundamental fact has been pointed out by Mr. H. WOLD in a preliminary note, "On Quantitative Statistical Analysis," *Skandinvask Aktuarietidkrift* (1936), pp. 281–284.[30]

In 1950 two important clarifications were made, but only one of the two received much attention. This was W. S. Robinson's famous article on "the ecological fallacy."[31] After listing a long collection of substantive articles by sociologists and some political scientists in which correlations based on percentages for an aggregate area were used, Robinson showed that such correlations were not necessarily good substitutes for correlations on the individual data. In fact, with increasing size of the aggregate unit the correlation is likely to exaggerate the extent of the relationship—as Wold had pointed out in the 1930's.

Now this was a useful point, and something that had been pointed out in psychology and statistics and that economists have been aware of. But the Robinson article amounted to academic

29. See Edward L. Thorndike, "On the Fallacy of Imputing the Correlations Found for Groups to the Individuals or Smaller Groups Composing Them," *American Journal of Psychology* 42 (1929), 122–124; and G. Udny Yule and Maurice G. Kendall, *An Introduction to the Theory of Statistics,* 14th ed. (New York, 1950), pp. 310–315.

30. Herbert Tingsten, *Political Behavior* (Stockholm, 1937), footnote 37a, at p. 77.

31. "Ecological Correlations and the Behavior of Individuals," *American Sociological Review* 15 (1950), 351–357. See also the "Comment" by Herbert Menzel, *ibid.,* p. 674.

"overkill." The author went on to suggest that the *only* purpose of analyzing aggregate data was as a (poor) means of estimating individual correlations. Nor did he suggest that aggregate data could be used to approximate individual correlations, as it often can. The early 1950's were marked by an excessive desire for rigor in regard to a number of procedures. S. S. Stevens laid down strict criteria for differing levels of measurement; need for nonparametric statistics in the absence of "strong" measurement was emphasized; and a hard line against correlation of aggregate data was thus quite in order (though the chief villain was correlation—which Stouffer had warned against in the 1930's [32] —and not necessarily aggregate data). A decade later a more thorough understanding of the problems led to an interesting reversal on all of these fronts. There was more willingness to use parametric methods even where the conditions of "strong" measurement were not fully met, and there was a greater awareness of the possible misuses of X^2 tests. By 1959 Abelson and Tukey noted that "when we say we only know rank order, we actually know more than this, but don't know how to express what else it is that we know." [33] Something of the same can be said for aggregate data—when we say we know only the marginal distribution, we actually know more than this, but don't know how to express what else it is that we know.

In the first place, it should be made clear that aggregate data which involve very high percentages (what we might call "test-tube" purity) *do* very definitely impose close restrictions on the possible individual correlations. Consider the accompanying table showing the marginal distribution of 100 voters by race and by party identification.

	Dem	Rep	
Negro	?		99
White			1
	99	1	100

32. See Samuel A. Stouffer, "Problems in the Application of Correlation to Sociology," *Journal of the American Statistical Association* (1934), supplement, pp. 52–58; reprinted in Stouffer, *Social Research to Test Ideas* (New York, 1962), pp. 262–270.

33. R. P. Abelson and J. W. Tukey, "Efficient Conversion of Nonmetric Information into Metric Information," *Proceedings of American Statistical Association Meetings, Social Statistics Section* (1959), 226–230.

We have no idea whether the one white is Republican or Democratic, or whether the one Republican is white or Negro. But we very well *do* know that at least 98 (and perhaps all 99) of the Negro registrants are Democrats, and we know that at least 98 (and perhaps all 99) of the Democrats are Negroes. The marginal distributions *do,* at sufficiently high levels of percentage, impose limits on the possible cell distributions. The point has been made in full detail by Hanan Selvin, and any doubters are referred to his excellent re-analysis of Durkheim's procedures.[34]

This loophole to the Robinson argument is, however, of limited practical utility. Not many variables are found in such convenient situations of very high concentration, although percentage of nonwhite population often does in areal units below the county level. Even when such a variable is located it is likely to be subject to two other limitations. First, there is the obvious problem that the particular variable one is interested in may be closely related to a number of other variables (economists' multicollinearity problem). In such cases one might infer cell entries that would be approximately correct in a descriptive sense, but would be spurious due to the effect of the third variable for which the aggregate data would not provide a clear test. Second, there is the more subtle problem that the very feature of high concentration itself may be self-defeating for the analyst; that is, it may make individuals in such situations subject to a somewhat different environment from those who are not. Propositions about the last point date back at least as far as Tingsten's work,[35] and they suggest an additional important perspective on the problem of relating individual and aggregate data.

Where one is not operating at high percentages, the problem of inferring cell entries (this is, individual correlations) from marginal distributions is more complicated. As Hayward Alker has neatly shown, the whole matter can be summarized mathematically in terms of the covariance theorem.[36] This emphasizes

34. Hanan C. Selvin, "Durkheim's *Suicide:* Further Thoughts on a Methodological Classic," in Robert A. Nisbet (ed.), *Emile Durkheim* (Englewood Cliffs, N.J., 1965), 113–136.

35. Thus Tingsten writes (*Political Behavior,* p. 230): "In regard to the social groups there is evidence from various quarters that the electoral participation within a group rises with the relative strength of the group in the electoral district."

36. See Hayward R. Alker, "A Typology of Ecological Fallacies," paper presented at International Social Science Council (Evian, France, September 1966); and Alker, *Mathematics and Politics* (New York, 1965), pp. 96–106.

the useful point that there are really *three* levels of concern, and not just the two of individual and ecological. The third, which is of great but neglected importance for political analysis, is the question of individual correlation within various subgroups. Alker has spelled out the mathematics, but for those who might prefer a simplified (and less complete) visual presentation the following may be useful.

In each of the accompanying charts (see Figure 3), subgroup means are indicated by an "X" and the distribution of individual scores around each mean are delimited by a circle. Below each chart we have indicated three summary statistics: 1) the level of association within the subgroups; 2) the overall individual association for the total population (which in politics is usually a system of subsystems); 3) the aggregate (ecological) association as measured by the subgroup means. What do these charts show? For one thing, they make clear that the ecological correlation may or may not be of the same general magnitude as the total individual association; but they also emphasize the need to look at individual associations *within* politically meaningful subunits. This has seldom been done, and the charts should remind us that the overall individual association may *also* be misleading with respect to the individual associations within particular subunits.

In the same year that the Robinson article appeared, Paul Lazarsfeld and Patricia Kendall presented a detailed analysis of the use of both individual and aggregate data in the massive study of *The American Soldier*.[37] Lazarsfeld and Kendall distinguished five types of data, all but one of which had both individual and aggregate forms. Their clarification has received little attention from political scientists, but has some very useful properties. At the individual level one may note the presence or absence of an attribute; at the aggregate level one has the *rate* of its presence (type I data). When an individual is characterized

<hr/>

37. See Patricia L. Kendall and Paul F. Lazarsfeld, "Problems of Survey Analysis," in Robert K. Merton and Paul F. Lazarsfeld, eds., *Continuities in Social Research: Studies in the Scope and Method of "The American Soldier"* (Glencoe, Ill., 1950), pp. 133–196, and especially the section on "The correspondence between personal and unit data," pp. 187–195. It is unfortunate that the Robinson article and the Lazarsfeld study were in press at the same time, so that Robinson was not alerted to the uses of unit and relational indicators nor Lazarsfeld to the problems of ecological correlation (which, it should be noted, was *not* the procedure used by Stouffer in *The American Soldier*).

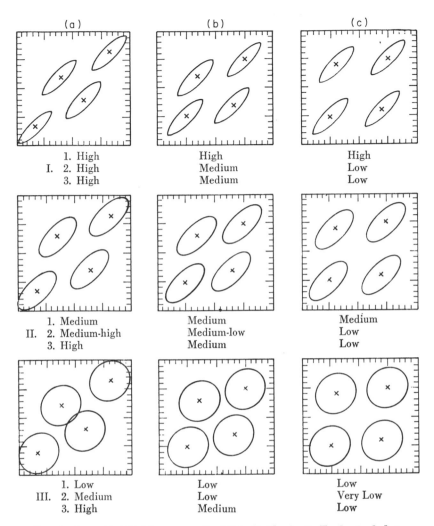

Correlations: 1. Within group. 2. All individuals. 3. Ecological data.

Figure 3.   Varying patterns of association: schematic comparison of association between grouped means, among individuals within groups, and for all individuals in total population. (The ecological correlation is held constant in each of the three columns; the extent of within-group association is held constant across each of the three rows. The over-all individual association varies as a function of *both* of these, but need not coincide with either one.)

by a variable, such as age, the corresponding aggregate measure is an *average* for that variable (type II). But a variable can also yield various *parameters* of its distribution, such as the standard deviation for age in a group (type III data). Ordinary survey research provides data from which one can estimate rates, averages, and various parameters of the population. But there are two further types of data which are often ignored in survey analysis. Thus Kendall and Lazarsfeld point to the importance of *relational* measures which characterize an individual by reference either to other individuals within the group or to aspects of the aggregate unit itself—this they term type IV data. Finally, there are purely unit or *aggregate characteristics*—such as whether a nation has a king or not—for which there is no individual level equivalent (although the characteristic may enter into a relational measure of the previous type, as with persons living in a country with a king). This they label type V.

Over a twenty-year period a variety of different terms have been used in regard to data similar to what Kendall and Lazarsfeld label as types IV and V. Table 3 presents a summary of some of the leading explications. It is strange that political science has been so slow to make more use of such data. Key's *Southern Politics* made extensive use both of ecological data (though not of correlations) and of Lazarsfeld's type IV relational data. Thus the behavior of whites living in areas with a very large percentage of Negroes was of crucial importance. But note that this is not a purely individual characteristic; it depends upon the context in which the individual is placed. Indeed, it turns out that individuals with given characteristics often behave quite differently, depending upon the context in which they are located. Even the percentage distribution of a variable distinguishing an individual may have a substantial effect on the way that variable is related to the individual's behavior. This highly promising line of analysis descended from Lazarsfeld's distinctions and was elaborated by Peter Blau as "structural effects" and subsequently codified by Davis *et al.*[38] But this has put it more in the research tradition of Lazarsfeld and more recently

38. Peter Blau, "Structural Effects," *American Sociological Review* 25 (1960), 178–193; James A. Davis *et al.*, "A Technique for Analyzing the Effects of Group Composition," *American Sociological Review* 26 (1961), 215–225. The process had been explicitly noted by Kendall and Lazarsfeld, "Problems of Survey Analysis," pp. 195–196.

of the NORC, and political science has relied almost exclusively on the interests of SRC, which have been in a quite different direction.

Table 3. Alternative classifications of individual, relational, and group characteristics

Description of data	Terminology Suggested by			
	R. B. Cattell [a]	Lazarsfeld & Menzel [b]	Selvin & Hagstrom [c]	P. Blau [d] & J. Davies *et al.* [e]
Attribute or variable of individual member	population variable	analytical property	aggregative property	—
Relation of individual member to other members	structural variable	structural property	contextual property	"structural effect"—Blau or "composition effect"—Davies
Characteristic of aggregate itself, not based on data about individual members	syntality variable	global property	integral property	—

[a] R. B. Cattell, "Concepts and Methods in the Measurement of Group Syntality," *Psychological Review* (1949), 48–63.

[b] Paul F. Lazarsfeld and Herbert Menzel, "On the Relation between Individual and Group Properties," in Amitai Etzioni (ed.), *Complex Organizations* (New York, 1961).

[c] Hanan C. Selvin and Warren O. Hagstrom, "The Empirical Classification of Formal Groups," *American Sociological Review* (1963), 399–411.

[d] Peter Blau, "Structural Effects," *American Sociological Review* (1960), 178–193.

[e] James A. Davis *et al.*, "A Technique for Analyzing the Effects of Group Composition," *American Sociological Review* (1961), 215–225.

Lazarsfeld had opened the way to the systematic use of both individual and aggregate data, and to the need for their combination. But political science was to take a fifteen-year detour in which aggregate data were first denounced as leading only to "fallacy" and then eventually reinstated as it became clear that procedures *other* than correlation could be usefully applied (largely the work of Leo Goodman [39]), that areal data were

39. Leo A. Goodman, "Some Alternatives to Ecological Correlation," *American Journal of Sociology* 65 (1959), 610–625.

useful for other purposes (e.g., O. D. Duncan, *Statistical Geography* [40]), and finally that even in regard to individual behavior, in certain cases aggregate data *could* provide bounds within which the individual behavior must fall (Hanan Selvin [41]). But the immediate impact in the 1950's was a loss in the ability to use aggregate data either to supplement, guide, or in combination with, survey data. And survey material too often was not related to any structural or contextual data.

Even the comparison of pure aggregate characteristics fell into limbo. It was only after the emergence of cross-national macro studies (Banks & Textor, and so on) that interest perked up in collecting systematic data on American states as units (or on cities).

Thus the older tradition of aggregate analysis provided an imperfect guide to individual associations within specific politically relevant subgroups, which was even more imperfect for analyzing total individual associations. This was so both because of the severe statistical limitations and because of the importance of the structural effects present in the units most likely to be analyzed. Modern survey research has opened up a whole new range of possible variables and permitted much more accurate inference about total individual association across "the nation." But it has generally not provided acceptable subsamples of the politically crucial subunits. If there were no variance at this level there might be no cause for alarm. But when Stokes analyzed the components of variance in direction of party vote by congressional districts he found the national component to account for only 32 percent of the variance. The statewide and district components accounted for 68 percent. [42] It would appear that the country is not quite of a single piece, and hence that survey analysis eventually will have to expand its horizons to deal with something more than the total national component. [43]

40. Otis Dudley Duncan *et al.*, *Statistical Geography* (Glencoe, Ill., 1961), esp. pp. 62–80.

41. See fn. 34 above.

42. See Donald E. Stokes, "A Variance Components Model of Political Effects," in *Mathematical Applications in Political Science*, Vol. I, John M. Claunch (ed.), The Arnold Foundation (Dallas, Texas, 1965), 61–85, at 76.

43. For an interesting contrast compare Werner Z. Hirsch, "About State and Regional Data Needs," and Donald E. Stokes, "The Electoral Series of the Survey Research Center," both in *Proceedings of the Social Statistics Section, American Statistical Association*, 1966 meetings (Washington, 1966), pp. 7–10 and 362–367 respectively.

The simple fact is that *neither* total individual association nor the aggregate (ecological) association guarantees discovery of the politically important question, which is of within-group individual association. From data on within-group individual behavior one can easily determine both total individual association (a simple matter of pooling the data) and the ecological association (by computing the group means, and comparing them). But there is no necessity for within-group individual associations to accord with ecological association, or with the overall individual association.

The practical difficulty is that ecological data are the cheapest and most readily available—indeed the *only* type of data for most questions up to World War II. And overall national samples have a public and commercial appeal which makes them feasible. But to require a sample of various states, or a national sample consisting of state subsamples, is a much more complex and costly matter. It is an important step, however, if survey analysis is to move beyond studying individuals in terms of purely individual characteristics and begin to explore the effects of structural characteristics and the specific linkages to office-holders.

The "conventional wisdom" of the early 1960's has been that the explanation of political phenomena was to be found in individual data from an overall sample, and that ecological data were necessarily misleading as to such individual associations. The attempt to explain group or national phenomena in terms of purely individual characteristics raises the question of "reductionism," to which I turn in the next section. Here I would like to summarize the argument that the whole complex interplay of system attributes (for which there is no individual counterpart), contextual effects, and relation of group and individual association is much more complex. Individual data from an overall sample are not the final answer, and aggregate (ecological) data are by no means useless. Since aggregate data are the only data we have for most politically relevant subunits and for most of history, it is vital that we make the best possible use of it.

1. Aggregate (ecological) data may closely approximate individual data for both sub-groups and for total population.
   a. Where two properties are present in very high degree (each over 75 percent) there frequent joint occurrence is a logical and necessary result—as Selvin has shown. Such homogeneity is more likely with small units, as shown by Dun-

       can and—in reverse—by Robinson's regional analysis.

   b. At lower levels of two properties, simple correlation is likely to be misleading (as Robinson, Wold, and others have shown), but other techniques may prove of value—see Goodman on use of regression.

2. The shape of the distribution of individuals within a group may have a marked effect on the behavior of specific individuals. See Blau on "structural effects" and Davies *et al.* on "compositional effects."

3. Within-group individual associations may differ greatly from total individual association—see Alker on covariance analysis. In extreme, as with third variable analysis, a lack of association may rest on strong positive association in half the groups and strong negative association in the other half.

4. Pure group characteristics (integral or syntality properties, such as having a royal family) may effect individual behavior, and may also be a matter of great importance in explaining behavior of the system (the system need not be entirely reducible to characteristics of an individual sample).

In the best of all possible worlds the social scientist would have data on various aggregate units, data on individuals from that total population, and data on individuals in each of the units making up the population. In sad fact, however, most historical election data are limited to those of units only, and most national surveys are limited to individuals in the total population. There are few opportunities to analyze political subgroups (though regional controls are usually possible), but the largest unit within which an election is held in the United States is the state—the presidential election being the result of counting the state electoral votes (as a reading of the Constitution will make evident). It is not surprising that commercial polls have operated on the basis of a simple atomistic national sample. But those with a concern for the realities of electoral politics, which is conducted within more specific jurisdictions, might be expected to have developed more sophisticated sampling procedures.

IV. The Strategy of Reductionism

If there is a single basic underlying dimension to differences in approach to the use of survey data it probably relates to the question of "reductionism." Though not much discussed in political science, orientations toward reductionism in general and "methodological individualism" in particular seem to have a lot to do with the questions that a researcher poses. And our questions certainly have a substantial share—along with such data as can be obtained—in determining the findings that constitute our discipline. Enthusiasm for "reductionism" is both an aspect of the "new look" in political science and one of the most ancient themes of Greek political thought.

Here we shall mean not an organic analogy between man and society, but rather the possibility (or logical necessity) of explaining macro-level characteristics of society entirely in terms of individual behavior. Or, as Ernest Nagel puts it: "Reduction, in the sense in which the word is here employed, is the explanation of a theory or a set of experimental laws established in one area of inquiry, by a theory usually though not invariably formulated for some other domain." [44] Survey analysis of national samples is well adapted to a strategy of "reduction," but there may be limits to the extent that the reductionist strategy is well adapted to dealing with politics.

Among the social sciences, psychology is far and away the most "reductionist"-oriented, and modern economics perhaps the least so. Thus the Keynesian interpretation of various national aggregates has generally withstood the criticism of the older "marginalist" school (Hayek and von Mises) as well as the effort of modern survey work on consumer behavior. Far from worrying about "fallacies," the economists happily talk of the *advantages* of aggregation. [45]

The necessity of reducing all macro (or system) phenomenon to micro (individual) terms is questionable. Thus both Abraham Kaplan and Ernest Nagel—two of the most influential philosophers of science in the Western world—have recently denied the thesis; thus Kaplan writes:

Many behavioral scientists, especially psychologists, believe that a satisfactory theory of human behavior must "ultimately" be a micro theory . . . That large-scale phenomena must be understood in terms of what is happening in the small has a certain plausibility, but I believe that the necessity is spurious." [46]

And Nagel says:

We therefore conclude that, although it is a sound methodological assumption to interpret collective terms in social science as designations

44. Ernest Nagel, *The Structure of Science* (New York, 1961), p. 338.
45. See, for example, Yehuda Grunfeld and Zvi Griliches, "Is Aggregation Necessarily Bad?", *Review of Economics and Statistics* 42 (1960), pp. 1–13.
46. Abraham Kaplan, *The Conduct of Inquiry* (New York, 1963), p. 322.

for groups of human beings or their modes of behavior, these terms are not in fact invariably defined by way of individual terms, nor does the assumption necessitate that collective terms must in principle be so defined.[47]

Granted that "reduction" is not absolutely required in each and every research effort, we are still left with major strategic choices as to the extent to which we shall emphasize a reductionist-oriented strategy, and tactical choices about alternatives within such a strategy. Thus cross-national research might be pursued solely in terms of macro-level data (such as figure prominently in the Banks and Textor or Deutsch *et al.* collections), or by pursuit of cross-national survey data (as used by Almond and Verba). Fortunately, in this particular instance both types of analysis are being pursued.

There are a number of sound reasons for supplementing survey data with other types of information. Herbert Simon pointed to one of these fifteen years ago when he emphasized that the processes involved in a large-scale organization (and modern government falls in this category) are *not* a mere extension of small-group characteristics.[48] Thus, to explain the behavior of the large-scale organization one need be sensitive to features other than micro-level or even small group.

A related point is the rediscovery that leaders differ in many ways from the rank and file. Interestingly, in its modern form this proposition dates from Stouffer's survey of attitudes toward communism and conformity which gave explicit attention to leaders as well as to a national sample. But the point is basic to Michel's well-known theory of bureaucracy. Indeed, he saw the reason for an "iron-law" of oligarchy in the necessity for leaders to have both prior skills and subsequent opportunities not generally available to the rank and file.

Any moderately complex political system involves elements of structure, formal or informal. This creates processes which elude the net of modern probability sampling, and which render the cross-tabulation procedures of survey research of limited value. No one has stated this more clearly than Warren Weaver, a distinguished mathematician and former Director for the Natural

47. Nagel, *The Structure of Science*, p. 540.

48. Herbert A. Simon, "Comments on the Theory of Organization," *American Political Science Review* 46 (1952), 1130–1139.

Sciences of the Rockefeller Foundation.[49] Writing in 1958, he distinguished three types of problems—those of simplicity (involving only two variables), of disorganized complexity (where probability theory reigns), and finally of organized complexity.

Modern survey analysis works well with questions of *simplicity*:

Speaking roughly, one may say that the seventeenth, eighteenth, and nineteenth centuries formed the period in which physical science learned how to analyze two-variable problems . . . The essential character of these problems rests in the fact that, at least under a significant range of circumstances, the first quantity depends wholly upon the second quantity, and not upon a large number of other factors . . .

These two-variable problems are essentially simple in structure, this simplicity resulting largely from the fact that the theories or the experiments need deal with only two quantities, changes in one of which cause changes in the other.[50]

The logic of such analysis was made explicit in the early chapter of Yule and Kendall's classic statistics text and was brought to attention in the United States by the restatements of Lazarsfeld, Kendall, and Hyman.[51] Where a reasonably self-contained system of a few variables seems appropriate, further developments have been made by Wold, Simon, and econometricians whose work has been brought to political science attention by Blalock and Alker.[52]

But such an approach is no universal research solution; it requires an extremely large number of cases, and proceeds best if the effects of other factors can be ignored. Proper handling of the "third variable" involves very considerable problems in itself, and in the social sciences many problems seem to involve far more variables.

At the opposite extreme the physical sciences have succeeded brilliantly in developing probability techniques to deal with statistical regularities in the behavior of very large numbers of variables.

49. Warren Weaver, "A Quarter Century in the Natural Sciences," in *Rockefeller Foundation Annual Report* (1958), pp. 7–8.

50. *Ibid.*, p. 8.

51. In the absence of experimental control, the tradition of survey research has had to emphasize the need for "controls" and subgroup comparisons as a check against spuriousness.

52. Hubert M. Blalock, Jr., *Causal Inferences in Nonexperimental Research* (Chapel Hill, N.C., 1964).

It is a problem in which the number of variables is very large, and one in which each of the many variables has a behavior which is individually erratic, and may be totally unknown. But in spite of this helter-skelter or unknown behavior of all the individual variables, the system as a whole possesses certain orderly and analyzable average properties.[53]

Demography, sampling, and study of information theory can draw on this tradition. But most of the interesting aspects of political systems relate to yet a *third* range of activity.

In this third, or middle, region the number of variables is moderate, but the crucial thing is that they display *structure* of a complex sort. As Weaver puts it:

The problems in this middle region will, in fact, often involve a considerable number of variables; but much more important than the mere number of variables is the fact that these variables are all interrelated. That is to say, the really important characteristic of the problems of this middle region which science has as yet little explored or conquered lies in the fact that these problems, as contrasted with the disorganized situations with which statistics can cope, show the essential feature of organization. We will therefore refer to this group of problems as those of *organized complexity*.[54]

Here social science, like biology, faces a severe challenge. Something of this structure may be gleaned by advanced multivariate techniques. And, as Herbert Simon has noted, in many cases the structure is such that *hierarchy* is of great importance, and many subsystems are relatively insulated.[55] Thus the situation is by no means hopeless, but it suggests that a good deal will be left unexplained even by a vast expansion in our understanding of micro-processes in the total population.

Political outcomes depend heavily upon what happens in such highly specialized substructures as the House Appropriations Committee or Rules Committee. Thus the landslide of 1958 indicated general voter approval of programs backed by liberal Democrats in Congress. But a change in House Republican leadership (Charles Halleck upsetting Joe Martin as leader) brought a shift in the conservative direction within the crucial Rules Committee. And this ultimately brought on the 1961 showdown over "packing"—or "unpacking"—the committee. The balance within such elite arenas can, on occasion, move in the

53. Weaver, *Rockefeller Foundation Report*, p. 11.

54. *Ibid.*, p. 13.

55. Simon, "The Architecture of Complexity," *Proceedings of the American Philosophical Society* (1962), 467–482.

opposite direction from that suggested by the general disposition of the electorate.[56]

This also involves a question of whether mass attitudes, such as those studied by Almond and Verba in *The Civic Culture,* are the crucial causal factors in determining whether a nation has a democratic form of government or not. Clearly such basic attitudes are relevant, but the manner or extent to which they may be determining is a more difficult question. In elections sampling is appropriate, access is easy, and electoral responses are limited to a narrow range of choice, with all votes counting equally. But in the complex operation of government the number of crucial individuals may be quite small, access is difficult or even impossible, the range of possible responses is vast, and individual importance varies widely among individuals and even fluctuates over time for a given person.

For particular political subsystems, such as the Rules Committee or Appropriations Committee of the House of Representatives, an understanding of the norms by which the system operates is of vital significance. But the counting of frequencies by means of samples is by no means necessarily efficient or even sufficient to obtain the type of information we want. Morris Zelditch pointed this out in a very useful article in which he stressed that participant-observation was the best method of obtaining information about particular incidents or histories, and that interviewing informants was most efficient in dealing with institutionalized norms and statuses.[57]

It would help, obviously, to have more academic survey work on samples from populations which are in fact electoral constituencies. Public interest in overall national trends insures that considerable commercial polling will always be done on total na-

---

56. The situation in the U. S. House of Representatives after the 1958 elections is an interesting case in point. The election resulted in a near-landslide for liberal Democratic candidates. But, after a change in the Republican leadership, vacancies on the crucial Rules Committee were filled in such a way that highly conservative Republicans replaced moderate Republicans (such as Hugh Scott of Pennsylvania, who had been elected to the Senate). As a result, a six-man coalition of Republicans and Southern Democrats on the Committee was able to hold up a variety of measures passed by the increased liberal majority. After the 1960 election, Speaker Rayburn found it necessary to wage a bitter floor fight to expand the membership of the Rules Committee.

57. Morris Zelditch, "Some Methodological Problems of Field Studies;" *American Journal of Sociology* 67 (1962), 566–576.

tional samples. And the strictly local survey is within the resources of the individual scholar with only modest financial assistance. What has been strangely lacking is attention to *state* electorates, which are the basic units of the presidential contest as well as the constituencies for state executives, Unites States senators, and the areas within which all House seats are defined.

If we were sure that there are no differences among the states, except as a result of differences in distribution of various individual characteristics (Cattel's type I variable), then little would be lost. But there is a good deal of evidence that states and regions do differ significantly, especially in contests other than the presidency (which is conducted nation-wide, and with an eye to repercussions in all parts of the country). Without specific state samples there is no way even to check for possible contextual or structural effects within states (Cattel's type II), or to make comparisons among varying unit characteristics (type III). Since American politicians, including the president, are elected *exclusively* by the result of subnational constituencies, it would seem highly advantageous to pursue surveys based on these constituencies. With all its emphasis on intervening variables it is strange that so much survey work has been concentrated on a national public, far removed from policy-making and without any direct constituency function.

To summarize, a strategy of "reductionism" may be ideal for those interested in psychological variables to begin with, and in the individual voting decision as a final dependant variable. A reductionist strategy is *not* ideal for all aspects of politics, and may so skew the range of questions asked and data collected as to inhibit research on the impact that elections and electorates have on governments. In any event, it is important to keep in mind that the relevant micro-level data for the United States does not lie in a simple national sample. The politically relevant populations are those that make up politically organized constituencies, both electoral (e.g., states) and functional (such as organized interest groups), plus the more elite members of the political institutions themselves.

Part Three

On Party

Austin Ranney

The Concept of "Party"

In the last edition of his magisterial textbook on American parties and politics, V. O. Key, Jr., wrote:

According to literary convention a discussion should be introduced by a definition of its subject. Pat definitions may simplify discussion but they do not necessarily promote understanding. A search for the fundamental nature of party is complicated by the fact that "party" is a word of many meanings. Indeed, the genus party comprehends many species. To define sharply one party may be to exclude another, for the role of party may differ from country to country. Moreover, even within the same political order the term "party" may be applied to different elements of the governing system. An approach more indirect than the proposal of a two-sentence definition may lead toward a comprehension of the basic nature of party in the American system: the nature of parties must be sought through an appreciation of their role in the process of governance.[1]

At first glance this seems a counsel of despair. Scholars, like anyone else, cannot think about everything at once. From the infinite universe of data they perforce select some and reject others as more and less relevant for the particular slice of reality they want to understand—in this case the persons, interrelations,

1. *Politics, Parties, and Pressure Groups,* 5th ed. (New York: Crowell, 1964), p. 200.

activities, and functions which together comprise something called "political parties" and something called "party systems." Students of party, consciously or otherwise, make their selections on the basis of some concept, explicit or tacit, of what a party *is*. Surely it would be helpful if we could put our findings together in an additive way. And surely it would be good if we had a straightforward, clear, and explicit concept—a "pat definition" if you like—to guide our inquiry and exposition.

In accordance with some such notion, a number of Key's colleagues have felt obliged to set forth short definitions: for example, "political parties are autonomous organized groups that make nominations and contest elections in the hope of eventually gaining and exercising control of the personnel and policies of government;" [2] "the political party may be defined as an agency for the organization of political power characterized by exclusively political functions, by a stable structure and inclusive membership, and by the ability to dominate the contesting of elections." [3]

The trouble is that neatness and clarity in a concept are not enough. In Abraham Kaplan's words:

What makes a concept significant is that the classification it institutes is one into which things fall, as it were, of themselves. It carves at the joints, Plato said. Less metaphorically, a significant concept so groups or divides its subject-matter that it can enter into many and important true propositions about the subject-matter other than those which state the classification itself . . .

Every taxonomy is a provisional and implicit theory (or family of theories). As knowledge of a particular subject-matter grows, our conception of that subject-matter changes; as our concepts become more fitting, we learn more and more.[4]

Ideally, then, the study of political parties should proceed from a concept of party that is (a) clear enough to serve as an unequivocal guide for the selection of data; (b) viable for distinguishing parties from other forms of political organization so that the kinds of observations yielded by current empirical methods fall easily and cleanly into the taxonomy's various categories; (c) general enough to stimulate the development of

2. Austin Ranney and Willmoore Kendall, *Democracy and the American Party System* (New York: Harcourt, Brace, and World, 1956), p. 85.

3. Frank J. Sorauf, *Political Parties in the American System* (Boston, Mass.: Little, Brown, 1964), p. 13.

4. *The Conduct of Inquiry* (San Francisco: Chandler, 1964), pp. 50, 53–54.

theory not bound to particular nations, cultures, or times; and (d) agreed upon by all scholars working on the subject.

No such Utopia is at hand, however. It is the contention of this essay that several different concepts underlie various studies of party today and that these competing concepts need to be both syncretized and enlarged if this segment of political science is to advance very far beyond where Key left it. But before I present my case, let me review our present conceptual confusion.

I. Evolution of the Concept

The term "party" is one of the oldest in political discourse. It was used as early as the Roman Republic to denote fluid and indeterminate aggregations of nobles and their followers (e.g., the *Optimates* and *Populares*) contending for the honors, emoluments, and preferments controlled by the Senate.[5] From then until the seventeenth century the word was used interchangeably with several others—e.g., "faction" and "interest." Sometimes they referred to prominent though unorganized and diffuse currents of opinion, such as a belief in the ascendancy of the Popes over the Holy Roman Emperors (the Guelphs) or the reverse (the Ghibellines). At other times they referred to coalitions of courtiers seeking the favor of the Pope, Emperor, or king (e.g., the Cabal).[6]

Some historians have argued that the first parties fitting the modern meaning of the term were the Whigs and Tories of England between the Restoration of 1660 and the Reform Act of 1832. But Sir Lewis Namier's meticulous investigations have convinced most that these labels denoted, not "parties in the modern sense," but "names and needs moulded by deeply ingrained differences in temperament and outlook."[7] Among the most striking bits of evidence for his thesis is the fact that there was a good deal of dispute at the time over whether certain prominent political leaders—Lord North is a famous example—were Whigs *or* Tories! (We at least do not have to argue whether Richard Nixon is a Republican or Charles de Gaulle a Communist.) The division between "Patriots" and "Loyalists" in

---

5. Cf. F. E. Adcock, *Roman Ideas and Political Practice* (Ann Arbor, Mich.: University of Michigan Press, 1959), pp. 61–62.

6. Cf. James A. H. Murray (ed.), *A New English Dictionary on Historical Principles* (Oxford: Clarendon Press, 1905), VII, p. 515.

7. *Personalities and Powers* (London: Hamish Hamilton, 1955), pp. 32–34.

colonial America was of the same general character, and even from 1776 to the early 1790's American politics was "a swirling confusion of interests, issues, leaders, opinions, shifting factions or factionlike formations, and loose alignments, marked by extremes of particularism and localism." [8]

Until well into the nineteenth century, then, the terms "party," "faction," and "interest" were used interchangeably to mean any kind of identifiable current of opinion or set of common goals, organized or unorganized (the distinction was not considered important), bearing on public authorities. Hence the politician-commentators who inveighed against the disruptive and subversive influence of "party spirit" were, in effect, deploring the political quarrelsomeness of their times and longing to return to a Golden Age when Patriots stood together to fight as one for the general weal.[9] And those who regarded "party" as an unfortunate but unavoidable by-product of freedom of expression and organization were also talking about political contentiousness in general rather than any particular form of political organization.[10]

Even Edmund Burke's defense of parties, resting as it did upon his much-quoted (but little-followed) definition,[11] was a brief for the general desirability of political organization to promote principles and programs, not for "party" as opposed to "faction" or "interest." So too was the argument of Burke's German-American follower, Francis Lieber, who defined "party" as "a number of citizens who, for some period and not momentarily, act in unison respecting some principles, interest, or measure, by lawful means . . . for the real or supposed common good of the whole commonwealth"—as opposed to a "faction," which Lieber defined as a body of citizens acting "by unlawful

---

8. William Nisbet Chambers, *Political Parties in a New Nation: The American Experience, 1776–1809* (New York: Oxford, 1963), p. 21. See also William Nisbet Chambers and Walter Dean Burnham (eds.), *The American Party Systems* (New York: Oxford, 1967).

9. For example, such writers as Halifax, Bolingbroke, Washington, and Taylor. For an exposition of their views, see Ranney and Kendall, *Democracy and the American Party System*, pp. 118–123.

10. For example, Hume, Madison, and de Tocqueville, *ibid.*, pp. 129–136.

11. "A body of men united, for promoting by their joint endeavours the national interest, upon some particular principle in which they are all agreed": "Thoughts on the Cause of Present Discontents," in *Works* (Boston, Mass.: Little, Brown, 1871).

means or for sordid, selfish ends, or striv[ing] secretly or openly, beyond the fundamental law." [12]

Indeed, of all the early writers on party, only the little-noted and long-forgotten Philip Friese conceptualized party as a particular structural form of political organization: it is, he said,

a union of citizens agreed in opinion and design concerning government, and organized for the double purpose of propagating those opinions and designs by discussion, and of personifying them *by the election and appointment of persons strongly entertaining them* to fill the leading positions of the state.[13]

Not until political science emerged as a separate discipline in the last third of the nineteenth century did party come to be widely conceived in Friese's terms.

II. Concepts of "Party" in Modern Political Science

The most comprehensive analysis of modern scholarly concepts of party yet written is the short study published by Neil A. McDonald in 1955.[14] He reviews the principal literature on parties in the United States and Great Britain, and concludes that the authors' concepts of party differ most markedly in their notions of its essential structural characteristics. Some, he notes, see party primarily as a *sociopsychological group*—an aggregate of persons in the electorate who share certain attitudes evoked by the party label. This, he declares, is the notion held by the Survey Research Center of the University of Michigan. Others, such as Maurice Duverger and David Truman in their different ways, think of party as an *association*—a network of interpersonal relations. And still others, Ostrogorski, Michels, and Schattschneider, for example, conceptualize party as an *organization,* and stress formality, explicitness, determinate location of authority, and the like.[15] McDonald describes the many different activities scholars say parties engage in and the many different functions they are said to perform in society. He analyzes what has been written about the socioeconomic group structure of the American major parties' electoral support, and

12. *Manual of Political Ethics,* 2nd ed. (Philadelphia: Lippincott, 1876), II, 253. The first edition was published in 1838.

13. *An Essay on Party, Showing Its Uses, Abuses, and Natural Dissolution* (New York: Fowler and Wells, 1856), p. 7, emphasis added.

14. *The Study of Political Science* (New York: Random House, 1955).

15. *Ibid.,* pp. 11–19.

about the parties' influence on the electorate and on public officials. And he concludes with a plea for reuniting the empirical studies of party with the broader concerns of political theory, mainly by viewing parties "as performing a unique role in reconciling and making congruent the impulsive and uncalculated elements in a society in order that calculated control be made possible." [16]

Whatever else may be said of McDonald's analysis, it seems to have had little impact on research and writing in the field: for instance, of the eleven principal studies of American national parties published between 1957 and 1966, only four cite the book at all, and none take his analysis into account when formulating their own concepts of party. But whether or not McDonald has had his due, even more striking is the fact that those writing on American and Western European parties in the past decade [17] have made no effort to incorporate in their theoretical structures the burgeoning literature on politics and parties in the developing nations.

This, I have come to believe, is a major mistake. Most political scientists writing on the new nations have not been content to describe the uniquenesses of particular nations; they have sought, rather, to help build a universal political science. To that end they have tried to orient their research in and relate their findings to theoretical frameworks of sufficient generality that their work can be combined with work on the "developed" nations. One leading example is Gabriel Almond's introduction to *The Politics of Developing Areas*,[18] which is one of the most influential essays in post-war political science. Even most critics of his particular functional approach have operated at comparable levels of generality.

Significantly, many students of developing nations have found party as useful and central an organizing concept as did Woodrow Wilson, A. Lawrence Lowell, James Bryce, and the other pioneers of the new political science in the late nineteenth century.[19] Of course, many of the parties they describe—e.g.,

16. *Ibid.*, pp. 84–88.

17. Including, let it be confessed, the present writer.

18. *The Politics of Developing Areas* (Princeton, N. J.: Princeton University Press, 1960), pp. 3–64.

19. For general reviews of parties in developing nations, see: Joseph LaPalombara and Myron Weiner, *Political Parties and Political Development* (Prince-

the *Néo-Destour* of Tunisia, the Burmese Anti-Fascist Peoples'
Freedom League, the Convention People's Party of Ghana, the
Partido Revolucionario Institucional of Mexico—seem very far
indeed from the reassuringly familiar Democrats and Republicans or Conservatives and Labour. Yet, if political science is to
comprehend both Western and non-Western governments, as
surely as it should, then students of party must conceptualize
their concerns so as to include both Western and non-Western phenomena.

But *can* we? Stretching the concept of party enough to include
the *Néo-Destour,* the Republicans, the *Union Soudanaise,* the
Socialist Labor Party, and the Mapai may leave it so broad and
porous that it will lose all utility as a criterion of relevance. If
so, we must either abandon the dream of a universal political
science or at least conclude that party is not a useful concept for
helping achieve it.

Before we do either, however, it might be useful to survey the
contemporary literature on parties, in developing as well as developed nations, and try to identify the principal areas of agreement and disagreement about what parties are. The agreements
will show us what we have to build on, and the disagreements
will warn us of the problems we face.

My reading of the literature indicates that students of the subject are generally agreed upon a number of differentiae distinguishing parties from other forms of political organization. The
most prominent may be summarized as follows.

(1) A political party is an aggregation of persons to
whom a certain identifying label is generally applied, in-

---

ton, N.J.: Princeton University Press, 1966); David E. Apter, *The Politics of
Modernization* (Chicago, Ill.: University of Chicago Press, 1965), pp. 181ff; and
Fred R. von der Mehden, *Politics of the Developing Areas* (Englewood Cliffs,
N.J.: Prentice-Hall, 1964), chap. IV. Some of the leading special studies in-
clude: Aristide R. Zolberg, *Creating Political Order: The Party-States of West
Africa* (Chicago, Ill.: Rand McNally, 1966); Gwendolen M. Carter (ed.), *Afri-
can One-Party States* (Ithaca, N.Y.: Cornell University Press, 1964); Thomas
Hodgkin, *African Political Parties* (Baltimore, Md.: Penguin Books, 1961); Ruth
Schachter Morgenthau, *Political Parties in French-Speaking West Africa* (Ox-
ford: Clarendon Press, 1964); Robert E. Scott, *Mexican Government in Transition* (Urbana, Ill.: University of Illinois Press, 1957); Robert W. Anderson,
Party Politics in Puerto Rico (Stanford, Calif.: Stanford University Press,
1965); and Myron Weiner, *Party Politics in India* (Princeton, N.J.: Princeton
University Press, 1957).

dividually and collectively, by themselves and by others: e.g., "Democrats," "the Labour party," and so on.

(2) At least some of these persons are organized, and deliberately and openly act in concert to achieve the party's goals—whatever they may be [20]—either outside the government or inside or both.

(3) Their right to organize and work for party goals is legitimized; hence, where all parties are formally prohibited, as in Ethiopia, Libya, and Yemen,[21] the contending groups are clandestine and are more appropriately called "juntos" or "cabals."

(4) The party is involved with the mechanisms (if not the spirit) of representative government, and uses them, including making nominations and appealing to the voters for support of candidates and programs, as part of its strategy. Hence, where there are no elections, as in Saudi Arabia, there can be no parties.

These propositions add up to a considerable area of agreement, but the disagreements are sufficiently widespread and on sufficiently important issues to constitute major barriers to the development of a universally accepted concept of party. Most of the disputes center on one or both of the following two issues.

First, is the single legally tolerated official party in an authoritarian one-party regime a "party" in enough significant respects that it may appropriately be included in the same genus with parties that face legitimized competition from other parties? Some students of American parties clearly answer in the negative. Charles E. Merriam and Harold F. Gosnell, for example, briefly describe the one-party regimes of Fascist Italy and Nazi Germany, and conclude: "All this constitutes a form of organization of political power, but in no sense a party as the term is generally employed." [22] In the first three editions of his text-

20. Until recently a number of writers wrangled over the question of whether parties seek to control the personnel *and* policies of government or only the former. Happily, however, little is heard on this issue in recent works, and most writers seem to agree that parties are, in varying measures, concerned with *both* personnel and policy.

21. And as some nineteenth-century commentators argued, they should be in the United States: cf., Charles C. P. Clark, *The "Machine" Abolished and the People Restored to Power* (New York: Putnam's, 1900); and Albert Stickney, *A True Republic* (New York: Harper, 1879) and *The Political Problem* (New York: Harper, 1890).

22. *The American Party System*, 4th ed. (New York: Macmillan, 1949), p. 8.

book, V. O. Key wrote: "[Parties] compete by electoral means for control of the government apparatus. (This means, of course, that the 'parties' of one-party states that brook no opposition are not parties in the western democratic sense.)" [23] However, he abandoned the distinction in the fourth and fifth editions.

The argument for this position seems to be essentially this: by definition, a party is a *part* of a society—a "side" in competition with other sides/parts/parties. Therefore, where only one party is permitted to exist there is no side, no part, no competition, but only the whole; and so the official "party" is not really a party at all. This argument is *not*, however, extended to include systems (e.g., the one-party systems in various American localities) in which any number of parties are legally tolerated but one regularly wins overwhelming shares of the votes, offices, and power, with little or no opposition from other parties.

Understandably, no student of politics in the developing areas takes this position. A significant proportion of the nations they study have only one legally permitted party,[24] and in others, while party opposition is permitted so long as it does not get out of hand, there is one perennially dominant party closely associated with the structure of the government. Moreover, the distinctions between the "one-party," "one-party-dominant," and "competitive" regimes seem to be matters of degree, not of kind; hence, these scholars feel, it is both pointless and stultifying to exclude by definition party systems that play significant roles in the governing structures of so many nations.[25]

The second, and more divisive issue is the question of the proper criteria for determining which persons in a society should and should not be included as "members" of parties. Although terminologies differ somewhat, most scholars agree that the following different (but often overlapping) levels of participation in party affairs can be distinguished:

(1) *Leaders:* persons who exercise significant influence over such party affairs as the selection of candidates, formulation of programs, raising and expending funds, determining and executing campaign strategy, and the like.

23. *Politics, Parties, and Pressure Groups*, 3rd ed. (1952), p. 216.

24. Von der Mehden notes eighteen instances of such systems in the eighty-four nations he covers: *Politics of the Developing Areas*, pp. 56–59.

25. Cf. Gwendolen Carter's argument in Carter, ed., *African One-Party States*, pp. 1–2; Hodgkin, *African Political Parties*, pp. 15–16; and Apter, *Politics of Modernization*, pp. 181–185.

Some may hold party and public office and some may not. What distinguishes them is not their formal titles but their actual influence.

(2) *Activists* (or "militants"): persons who exercise little significant influence in party decision-making but contribute substantial time and effort to party affairs by such activities as canvassing, working in party headquarters, poll watching, soliciting funds, and so on. They too may or may not hold party or public office.

(3) *Party Members:* persons who formally join a party by, e.g., applying for membership, being formally accepted by the party leaders, formally subscribing to party principles, paying dues, and the like.

(4) *Primary Voters* (in the United States only): persons who vote in a party's primary elections and thereby have the final word in the selection of its candidates.

(5) *Supporters:* persons who support the party's candidates and cause by, e.g., making financial contributions, displaying lapel buttons or bumper stickers, trying to persuade others to support the party's candidates, and/or—at the margin—voting for all, or almost all, of the party's ticket.

(6) *Identifiers:* persons who "identify" with the party in that they have some degree of preference, some degree of psychological attachment, for the party over other parties, but who may or may not vote for its candidates or support it in any other way.[26]

All students of parties, European and American, Western and non-Western, agree that the activities, attitudes, and interrelations of persons in the first three categories should be included in the phenomena which constitute political parties. The quarreling begins when the inclusion of persons in any or all of the last three categories is at issue.

The United States is the only nation that uses direct primaries, in the strict sense of that term. It is also the only nation in which only a few party organizations—and those quite distinct from the party organizations established by statute—have formal dues-

26. For somewhat different "hierarchies of political involvement" not necessarily attached to support of a particular party, see Robert E. Lane, *Political Life* (Glencoe, Ill.: The Free Press, 1959), chap. 4; and Lester H. Milbrath, *Political Participation* (Chicago: Rand McNally, 1965), pp. 16–29.

paying members.[27] Accordingly, students of European parties generally include the first three categories in their conceptions of party, say nothing about primary voters, and exclude the fifth and sixth groups.[28]

Students of American parties, on the other hand, disagree about whether the fourth, fifth, and sixth groups should be included. Many take the position best articulated by E. E. Schattschneider:

> Whatever else the parties may be, they are not associations of the voters who support the party candidates . . .
>
> If the party is described as a political enterprise conducted by a group of working politicians *supported* by partisan voters who approve of the party but are merely partisans (not members of a fictitious association), the parties would seem less wicked. After all, we support many organizations without belonging to them and without asserting a right to control them.[29]

Others have argued that since direct primary laws give primary voters the ultimate power to control the selection of most party candidates and officers, those voters must be included in any conceptualization of American parties, whether one approves the laws or not. Samuel J. Eldersveld, for example, argues:

> The party is more than its executive elite, or campaign workers, or precinct activists, analyzed in isolation. It is a meaningful organizational system of interpersonal relationships. Concentration on those "in power," or the "inner circle," or the "activist cadre," while helpful and suggestive, cannot by itself lead to comprehension of the structure as a

27. Mainly in California, New York, and Wisconsin: see James Q. Wilson, *The Amateur Democrats* (Chicago, Ill.: University of Chicago Press, 1962); R. S. Hirschfield, B. E. Swanson, and B. D. Blank, "A Profile of Political Activists in Manhattan," *Western Political Quarterly*, 15 (1962), 489–506; and Leon D. Epstein, *Politics in Wisconsin* (Madison: University of Wisconsin Press, 1958), chap. 5.

28. Cf. Maurice Duverger, *Political Parties*, trans. Barbara and Robert North, rev. ed. (New York: Wiley, 1959), pp. xv, 61–62; Henry Valen and Daniel Katz, *Political Parties in Norway* (London: Tavistock, 1964), pp. 67–68; and R. T. McKenzie, *British Political Parties*, 2nd ed. (London: Mercury, 1963), chaps. IV and VIII.

29. *Party Government* (New York: Holt, Rinehart, and Winston, 1942), pp. 53, 59; emphasis in the original. Other advocates of this position include: Robert C. Brooks, *Political Parties and Electoral Problems* (New York: Harper, 1923), p. 14; Edgar E. Robinson, *The Evolution of American Political Parties* (New York: Harcourt, Brace, and World, 1924), pp. vii, 3–4; and Hugh A. Bone, *American Politics and the Party System*, 3rd ed. (New York: McGraw-Hill, 1965), pp. 648–649.

whole. Too much party research in America has had to settle for partial images of political reality.[30]

Some of the early writers on American parties went considerably further and included all six groups (and more!). For example, one wrote, "men join a party by voting with it; men retire from it by refusing to vote with it"; [31] and another offered the broadest conceptualization of all:

> Political parties, popular notions to the contrary, are any two or more individuals acting with a common purpose . . . If an individual insists that he is not a member of either the democratic or republican party, he is then a member of the party made up of all the people who do not believe in the principles of either of these two, he is opposed to them, and as there is more than one such in opposition, it makes another party.[32]

V. O. Key tackled the conceptual problem in a characteristically shrewd and common-sense manner. In the first two editions of his textbook (1942 and 1947) he offered only the skeptical comments on the utility of formal definitions quoted at the beginning of this paper. In the last three editions (1952, 1958, and 1964) he went much further. First, he pointed out that "the term 'political party' is . . . applied without discrimination to many types of groups and near-groups. Discussion may be facilitated by some preliminary differentiations of the usages of the word 'party.' " Next, he noted four such usages: (1) "party-in-the-electorate"—groups of persons who regard themselves as party members; (2) the "more or less professional workers" —persons who man the party organizations and do their work; (3) "party-in-the-government"—persons holding public legislative and executive offices who sometimes act with solidarity on certain matters ("we tend always to speak as if there were such a group which could be held accountable for the conduct of government"); and (4) "an entity which rolls into one" the other three meanings. Finally, he suggested:

30. *Political Parties: A Behavioral Analysis* (Chicago: Rand McNally, 1964), p. 2. For similar conceptualizations, see James Bryce, *The American Commonwealth* (London: Macmillan, 1889), II, pp. 10ff; Charles E. Merriam, *The American Party System* (New York: Macmillan, 1923), chap. II; and Dayton D. McKean, *Party and Pressure Politics* (Boston: Houghton Mifflin, 1949), pp. 15–16.

31. Albert Bushnell Hart, *Actual Government*, 2nd ed. (New York: Longmans, Green, 1904), p. 12.

32. Job E. Hedges, *Common Sense in Politics* (New York: Moffat, Yard, 1912), p. 76.

In truth, this all-encompassing usage has its legitimate application, for all the types of groups called "party" interact more or less closely and at times may be as one. Yet both analytically and operationally the term "party" most of the time must refer to several types of group; and it is useful to keep relatively clear the meaning in which the term is used.[33]

III. Popular Concepts of "Party"

Key certainly identified the principal *scholarly* meanings of "party," but neither he nor any other scholar I am aware of has asked whether non-scholars have conceptions of party that differ from scholars'. It seems worth asking. An influential strain of contemporary philosophy argues that one of the best ways for scholars to clarify and legitimize their concepts is to see how the words they use are used in everyday language by ordinary people.[34] If there is something in this, and I think there is, perhaps it can help us understand "party" as well as more abstruse matters like "obligation" and "consent."

The Survey Research Center has shown us, in its findings summarized in Table 1, that most Americans have at least some degree of "party identification" (= express to interviewers some degree of preference for one party over the other).

By adding together the percentages of Independents and Apoliticals in each column of Table 1 and subtracting them from the total, we see that from 85 to 91 percent of the SRC's respondents expressed some preference for a party in the twelve national studies conducted from 1952 to 1964. For our present purposes the intriguing question is not *which* parties the respondents preferred, but *what* they preferred—that is, what perceived objects they were responding to in giving their answers. In other words, when a respondent tells an interviewer, "I am a strong Democrat," to what feature(s) of his cognitive map of politics does this affect attach? If we can answer this question we can go a long way toward identifying popular concepts of party in the United States.

Probably the ideal way to answer the question is to ask respondents directly some such question as: "You say you are a strong Democrat; what *is* the Democratic party in your view?"

33. *Politics, Parties, and Pressure Groups.* 5th ed. (1964), pp. 163–165. See also Frank J. Sorauf, *Party Politics in America* (Boston: Little, Brown, 1968), pp. 9–12.

34. See V. C. Chappell (ed.), *Ordinary Language* (Englewood Cliffs, N.J.: Prentice-Hall, 1964); and J. L. Austin, *Philosophical Papers* (Oxford: Clarendon Press, 1961).

Table 1. The distribution of party identification in the United States, 1952–1964

	Oct. 1952	Sept. 1953	Oct. 1954	April 1956	Oct. 1956	Nov. 1957	Oct. 1958	Oct. 1960	Oct. 1961	May 1962	Aug. 1962	May 1964
Strong Dem.	22%	22%	22%	19%	21%	21%	23%	21%	26%	25%	23%	24%
Weak Dem.	25	23	25	24	23	26	24	25	21	24	24	22
Ind. Dem.	10	8	9	6	7	7	7	8	9	7	7	7
Independent	5	4	7	3	9	8	8	8	10	9	11	10
Ind. Rep.	7	6	6	6	8	6	4	7	5	4	5	5
Weak Rep.	14	15	14	18	14	16	16	13	13	15	16	17
Strong Rep.	13	15	13	14	15	10	13	14	11	11	11	11
Apolitical (don't know)	4	7	4	10	3	6	5	4	5	5	3	4
	100%	100%	100%	100%	100%	100%	100%	100%	100%	100%	100%	100%
Number of cases	1,614	1,023	1,139	1,731	1,772	1,488	1,269	3,021	1,474	1,299	1,317	1,465

Source: Philip E. Converse, "The Concept of a Normal Vote," in Angus Campbell, Philip E. Converse, Warren E. Miller, and Donald E. Stokes, *Elections and the Political Order* (New York: Wiley, 1966), Table 2-1, p. 13.

But so far no student of voting behavior or parties has asked that kind of question. So I have tried a different strategy. The Survey Research Center has regularly asked its respondents four open-ended questions about the parties: "Is there anything in particular that you like about the Democratic party? (If yes) What is that?"; "Is there anything in particular that you don't like about the Democratic party? (If yes) What is that?"; and the same two questions about the Republican party. In their 1964 study the SRC asked these questions of a national sample of 1,571 respondents. For each they coded up to five responses in each of four fields (pro-Democratic, pro-Republican, anti-Democratic, and anti-Republican), and the results were made available through the Inter-University Consortium for Political Research.

Of the 1,571 respondents, 121 were classified on the party-identification scale as Independents; 11 expressed a minor-party preference or refused to say; 14 were classified as apolitical; and the party identifications of 10 were not ascertained. So a total of 1,415 respondents—90.1 percent of the sample—expressed some degree of preference for a major party. However, only 1,302 respondents—82.9 percent of the sample—offered at least one response to the four open-ended questions about party. So 113 respondents—7.2 percent of the sample—expressed some preference for a party without offering a clue to *what* it was they preferred.

Accordingly, our attention must be focused upon the 1,302 respondents who had something to say, however minimal, about what they liked and disliked about the Democratic and Republican parties. Using a three-column code, the SRC put the responses into ten main categories, divided into eighty-one subcategories and seven residual ("other") subcategories—each with its pro-Democratic, anti-Democratic, pro-Republican, and anti-Republican versions. My purposes required rearranging the eighty-eight subcategories into eight somewhat different main categories. They are as follows.

(1) *Groups of Leaders.* This includes all responses in terms of approval or disapproval of particular national, state, or local leaders, and all such general comments as "They have good leaders" or "I don't like their candidate(s)."

(2) *Managers of Government.* This includes all responses in terms of parties as groups of officials managing

government (mostly national). For example: "Democrats give us good, efficient government" (18 responses); Democrats waste too much money" (87); [35] "Republicans keep government spending down" (63); "Republicans are grafters" (19).

(3) *Associated with Good or Bad Times.* This includes responses in terms of the nature of the times when one or the other party is in power. Examples: "Times are good under the Democrats" (79); "There is always inflation under the Democrats" (1); "Times are good under the Republicans" (10); "The Republicans bring bad times" (45).

(4) *Advocates of General Philosophies.* This includes all sponses in terms of parties as groups of persons, in government and/or out, who stand for certain general political philosophies—but without reference to specific policies, legislative programs, or the like. Examples: "I like the Democrats because they're the liberal party" (31); "The Democrats are too socialistic" (69); "I like the Republicans' conservative philosophy" (115); "The Republicans are too conservative" (45).

(5) *Proponents of Specific Policies.* This includes all responses in terms of parties as groups of persons, in government and/or out, who push the adoption of more or less specific governmental policies. Examples: "The Democrats are for social security" (87); "The Democrats are pushing civil rights too hard" (64); "The Republicans are a better bet to keep the peace" (35); "The Republicans want to get us into a war"(22).

(6) *Champions and Enemies of Groups.* This includes all responses in terms of parties as groups of persons, in government and/or out, who champion certain groups in the population and/or oppose others. Examples: "The Democrats are for the common man" (322); [36] "The Democrats are tools of labor unions" (20); "Republicans are for all the people, not just special pressure groups" (21); "The Republicans are tools of big business" (160).

(7) *Organizations Conducting Conventions and Cam-*

35. Here and subsequently the numbers in parentheses indicate the number of responses coded in the particular category, though not necessarily given in the identical wording presented in the text.

36. This was the most frequently given single response of all.

paigns. This includes all responses in terms of the party organizations, national conventions, and presidential campaigns. Examples: "The Democratic party has a good organization, they stick together" (11); "The Democrats run dirty campaigns" (44); "I like the Republican platform [reason not specified]" (22); "The Republicans run dirty campaigns" (85).

(8) *Certain Kinds of People.* This includes all responses in terms of the personal qualities of persons in the parties, inside government and/or out, including expressions of feelings of identity with or hostility toward them. Examples: "We (my family) are Democrats" (197); "You can trust Democrats to keep their word" (13); "Democrats don't keep their promises" (19); "We (my family) are Republicans" (84); "The best people are Republicans" (15); "You can't trust Republicans" (32).

There were also a few responses in which I can discern no indication of what the parties are thought to be: "Don't change horses in midstream" (11); "The Democrats have been in too long" (11); "It's time for a change" (18); "I've just never been a Republican" (13).

The distribution of all 5,219 responses is shown in Table 2.[37]

Table 2 reveals a number of intriguing interparty differences in the distribution of favorable and unfavorable responses. If we combine the first and fourth columns (as favorable to the Democrats) and the second and third (as favorable to the Republicans), we see that 28 percent of the Democrat-favorable responses were in category 6 (champions and enemies of groups) compared with only 6 percent of the Republican-favorable. Another striking contrast is the fact that 25 percent of the Republican-favorable responses were in category 4 (advocates of general philosophies) compared with 9 percent of the Democrat-favorable. And a third is the fact that 16 percent of the Republican-favorable responses were in category 2 (managers of government) compared with 4 percent of the Democrat-favorable.

37. Note that the items in Table 2 are *responses,* not respondents, and each of the 1,571 respondents could have made five responses in each of the four columns, or a total of twenty responses (though none did). Hence the percentage in, for example, the first column, first row, is the proportion of all pro-Democratic responses which referred to the party's leaders.

Table 2. Distribution of references to parties, 1964

Type of reference	Pro-Dem.	Anti-Dem.	Pro-Rep.	Anti-Rep.	Total responses
1. Groups of leaders	7%	6%	12%	14%	10%
2. Managers of government	4	19	12	5	9
3. Associated with good or bad times	8	a	1	5	4
4. Advocates of general philosophies	8	22	29	10	16
5. Proponents of specific policies	22	29	16	12	20
6. Champions and enemies of groups	29	5	7	27	19
7. Organizations conducting conventions and campaigns	3	10	5	15	8
8. Certain kinds of people	18	8	16	10	13
9. No clear party referent	1	1	2	2	1
	100%	100%	100%	100%	100%
Total number of responses	1,822	1,132	983	1,282	5,219

a Less than .05 percent.

Source: Survey Research Center, University of Michigan, Study 473, Deck MC, data furnished by the Inter-University Consortium for Political Research.

This suggests that persons who like the Democrats and/or dislike the Republicans tend to think of parties as group-related entities, while persons with the opposite preferences tend to conceive parties as exponents of general philosophies and managers of government. However, limitations of time and programming resources prevented analysis of individuals' response patterns, so these relationships must, for the moment at least, remain only intriguing hypotheses.

For our present purposes, the fifth, or summary column in Table 2 provides the most significant clues. If we try to combine the various row categories to fit Key's scheme, we see that category 8 fits neatly in his "party-in-the-electorate," category 7 in his "party organization," and categories 2 and 3 in his "party-in-government." But category 1 fits both the latter two Key headings, and categories 4, 5, and 6 seem to fit all three—all of which is not very helpful.

There is another, more promising line of inquiry. If we choose as master categories (1) *parties-as-instruments* (i.e., parties conceived as devices for accomplishing or preventing specific governmental actions involving material gains or losses for particular persons and groups) and (2) *parties-as-symbols* (i.e., parties conceived as objects evoking generalized affective responses with little or no expectations of material gain or loss), the various popular concepts of party are more readily classified.[38] Under the first heading it seems reasonable to group categories 2, 3, 5, and 7 in Table 2; categories 4, 6, and 8 seem to fit the second heading; and category 1 probably includes responses of both kinds. Accordingly, 41 percent of the responses suggest mainly instrumental conceptions of the parties, and 48 percent imply mainly symbolic conceptions.

Given the limitations of the analytical methods used here, there is certainly no magic in these figures; nor am I even suggesting that more Americans conceive parties as symbols than conceive them as instruments. There seems little doubt, however, that for a great many Americans "the Republican party" and/or "the Democratic party" are primarily symbols evoking loyalty and identification and/or antagonism and alienation—not organizations of politicians established to achieve or hinder specific governmental actions. And I assume with some confidence (though no data) that the same is true of a great many Britons', Frenchmen's, Ghanaians', Nigerians', and Indians' concepts of *their* parties.

IV. Conclusion

If we classified sciences as we do nations, political science in general and the study of parties in particular would have to be labeled "developing" rather than "developed" (or, one hopes, "deteriorating"). Such a science cannot afford to let its inquiries be confined by rigid formal definitions intended more to fix boundaries than to encourage exploration. Pendleton Herring put the point well:

> To define is to issue a fiat. Definition means abstracting certain aspects from a complex factual context with the purpose of presenting these selected aspects as of essential importance. Hence in facing human behavior as involved and contradictory as that which is observable in political parties, it is hazardous to select one or two aspects as definitive of the whole. The pernicious nature of definition lies not in its inescapa-

38. The most stimulating recent discussion of the general nature and role of symbols in politics is Murray Edelman, *The Symbolic Uses of Politics* (Urbana, Ill.: University of Illinois Press, 1964).

bly partial character but in the tendency to view such formulations as in themselves social objectives. Hence when we observe that our political parties do not behave in accordance with our definitions, we sometimes conclude that the reality rather than the definition is at fault.[39]

If Herring is correct—and if, as I suggested at the beginning of this paper, the best test of a concept's validity is its fruitfulness in leading to new and better knowledge—then most students of party need to take a larger view of what a political party is. We need to strike out in at least two new directions. The first is to learn a good deal more about certain party-related phenomena than we now know. For example, we need to understand how parties are conceptualized by the people who identify with and support them (the inquiry reported here is only a very small sortie into a very large unexplored territory). We also need to study the nature and role of parties as symbols and loyalty systems as well as instruments for political action. And we need to investigate how these parameters vary in different nations, cultures, and times.

The second is to conceptualize parties as systems comprehending all activity and attitudes most directly connected with the labels which in each polity are generally regarded as denoting genuine political parties. And, most important of all, we need to investigate how each system's elements relate to each other. For example, we should certainly continue to study how the party's leaders and activists interact and influence each other's behavior. But we should also study how the party's ordinary members or primary voters relate to the leaders and activists—and to the supporters and identifiers—in the selection of candidates, design and execution of campaign strategy, formulation and implementation of programs, raising and spending money, and all of the party's other activities.

V. O. Key cleared the conceptual air for us by pointing out that "party" in fact has been used in four different senses and that none has or can have any official imprimatur as the only legitimate usage. Our job is to take the next step by further enlarging our working concept of the elements constituting the social systems called "parties," by seeking to understand these elements and how they relate to each other, and by being aware of what we are doing and why.

39. *The Politics of Democracy* (New York: Norton; 1940, 1965), pp. 100–101.

Leon D. Epstein

The Comparison of Western Political Parties

In a book honoring the founder of systematic comparative study of American state parties, it is appropriate to discuss the relation of that study to the burgeoning cross-national work in the field of political parties and closely related subjects. And it is appropriate as well as convenient to limit the field to Western democratic nations. Are the questions about American parties, as raised by V. O. Key notably in *American State Politics* and in *Southern Politics*, relevant for research across national lines in the Western world? Are the questions about other Western parties, principally British and European, relevant for American research? Stated broadly, these questions raise the problem of integrating two or more nearly separate areas of political science into a single context from which to generalize about parties in Western democratic nations. How meaningful, relative to conventional national studies, is cross-national research in this larger universe?

The Different Meanings of Comparative Study

Before directly approaching our principal questions, it is in order to comment on the intellectual development of modern comparative study. As organized political science, the beginnings date from James Bryce [1] and A. Lawrence Lowell.[2] Before the establishment of our academic guild, there was Alexis de Tocqueville.[3] Common to these scholars and consistent with their status as authors of classical comparative studies was the study of national governments other than their own but in the context of their own political systems. Surely there was something comparative, and consciously so, about their method, even when their attention was directed to a single nation at a time. Interestingly, this is most apparent in Tocqueville, who, despite his desire to generalize about democracy from the American experience, emphasized the way in which institutions and practices in the United States differed from the European. In this respect his work resembled the best efforts that followed. Comparison of the politics of another nation meant a stress on the distinctive, often on the interesting contrast, rather than on what was similar or familiar. The good book in this field was like a good foreign travel guide in that it led the reader to the curious and the novel rather than to what he already knew from his domestic experience.

It is a step away from the modern classics to much of the work that characterized "comparative government" in organized American political science during the first several decades of the twentieth century. The field and its label seemed pre-empted by what was really only the study of particular foreign governments—chiefly British and European—as distinguished from American government. The latter field was subdivided topically—constitutional law, state and local government, parties, public administration, and legislation. But each foreign government was dealt with as a whole, although primarily in legal and constitutional terms. Often several foreign governments were discussed in a single course or a single book, but almost always each was taken up successively as a subject.[4] There was at all levels, and crucially in research, a distinct separation between

1. In addition to his famous *The American Commonwealth* (Chicago: Sergel & Co., 1891), James Bryce later wrote a pioneering country-by-country comparison, *Modern Democracies* (New York: Macmillan, 1921).
2. *Government of England* (New York: Macmillan, 1908).
3. *Democracy in America*, ed. Phillips Bradley (New York: Knopf, 1948).
4. Exceptions were Carl J. Friedrich's *Constitutional Government and Democracy* (Boston: Ginn, 1946) and Herman Finer's *Theory and Practice of Modern Government* (New York: Holt, 1949), both of which were published in first editions in the 1930's.

the study of foreign government and the study of American government. Although there were always a few scholars actively interested in living up to the title of their field, whatever comparison took place tended to be limited to countries other than the United States. The tendency was confirmed in the 1930's and 1940's when many European scholars, including several of great distinction, joined American political science departments. They did add the prevalent European concern with the ideological basis of politics to the American preoccupation with institutional structures. But rather than bridging the gap that existed between the American and European political studies, the new specialists, combining their European expertise with a limited American experience, made the gap more obvious and more forbidding.

Although this geographical compartmentalization had its disadvantages, nothing could be more misleading than to ascribe it to the backwardness of individual political scientists in the first half of this century. In any balanced intellectual history of our discipline, the specialized work on national governments must be viewed as a step in the growth of knowledge. The comparative generalizations of the nineteenth century may have been in abeyance, but the new specialization reflected richness of detail and occasional depth of analysis. Knowing the language, the history, and the culture of a nation, as background for understanding political institutions, could be, and often was, advantageously stressed. The best political scientists studying European politics were really competent area specialists, concentrating on particular nations. None of these specialists had to be any more or less parochial than the larger number of political scientists who confined their attention to American politics. The absence of any significant comparative work was simply more noticeable in the case of specialists on European nations because they functioned under the label of comparative government and so might have raised higher expectations.

American politics itself was marked by the absence of comparative studies in one way that deserves special notice. Not only were the national politics and parties of the United States ordinarily treated in intellectual isolation from those of other nations, but studies of American state politics (and parties in particular) also tended to be isolated from each other. Until the 1950's these studies were usually of two kinds: strictly single-state studies, and encyclopedic textbooks illustrating institutional variations among the states. Systematic comparison of state parties and politics was largely unknown. The gap here is harder to explain than the absence of systematic comparison across national lines. American cross-state comparisons were unimpeded by language barriers, by major structural differences, or by great gulfs in historical experience. There were more constants in ideology, culture, and the general social order.

The evident reluctance to seize this opportunity might well lead to an inquiry about whether there have been inherent difficulties in the way of systematic comparative studies. The inquiry is suggested by the long absence of comparative trend analysis, either between national units or between state units. On the surface, this kind of analysis would appear feasible and convenient. Historical data on various political phenomena are available for states and their sub-units as well as for nations. Because the technical difficulties are not overwhelming, it is likely that the obstacles have been intellectual. This is another way of saying that political scientists have not been sure that they can say anything very meaningful at any one time about more than a single political unit, be it a state or a nation. The level of generalization required for comparative analysis may have appeared too broad or too speculative unless confined to the most microscopic problems. In turn, this suggests a lack of acceptable categories for analysis. What is relevant in the politics of one unit may not be so elsewhere. Even the classification of political phenomena may have little meaning if applied outside of the environment from which it has been derived. In that event, one may not see clearly what to study comparatively. The difficulty could be greatest for areas in which knowledge is already the most bountiful and the most specialized.

This possibility should help us to understand why the most innovate comparative analysis was first attempted, in the 1950's, for the developing areas rather than for the United States and Western Europe.[5] Not only could institutional elements be largely ignored, since they were so slight and impermanent, but such phenomena as parties could be subsumed under broad functional and behavioral headings intended to facilitate cross-national comparison. There were, in other words,

5. Gabriel Almond and James Coleman, *The Politics of the Developing Areas* (Princeton, N.J.: Princeton University Press, 1960).

fewer taxonomic inhibitions. Establishing meaningful categories for analyzing Western politics may be a more challenging task.

Nationally Oriented Research on Parties

For political parties, there is an earlier history of comparative research in the Western world. Ostrogorski[6] and Michels,[7] in their different ways, wrote comparatively about parties in outstanding books published before 1920; and Duverger[8] produced a third comparative classic just after World War II. These works, however, were exceptional in their scope. Most research on political parties in the United States and Europe was on a national basis. Apart from the difficulty of finding significant categories for comparative analysis, there is another explanation for concentration on national studies: Political scientists have naturally been concerned with policy questions, and these are for the most part national in character. For example, what kind of parties should there be in order to serve best the needs or purposes of a given national system? How should these parties be organized? Should they be stronger or weaker, more or less cohesive, more or less centralized in direction? Admittedly some of the same questions, if put broadly enough, have been asked about parties in more than one nation, but the form of the questions has depended heavily on the political scientist's sense of the problem in the nation with which he is primarily concerned. Even in a deliberately comparative work like Duverger's, the questions are highly national in character—that is, French questions, notably on the relation of legislative election systems to political parties.

The importance of national conditioning may be clearly discerned in the different foci of American and European studies. The emphasis among twentieth-century students of American parties has been on the inadequacy of those parties as political agencies. Their weakness in organization, their neglect of policy commitments, and their divisions at governmental levels have all been exposed and criticized. Occasionally, it is true, these apparent faults have been accepted as peculiarly American virtues.

6. M. Ostrogorski, *Democracy and the Organization of Political Parties* (New York: Macmillan, 1902).

7. Robert Michels, *Political Parties* (Glencoe, Ill.: Free Press, 1949), first published 1915.

8. Maurice Duverger, *Political Parties* (New York: John Wiley, 1954).

Much more often political scientists, while asking why parties in the United States are not stronger, have suggested ways in which they might become more effective. The theme is familiar in the influential responsible-party school of thought.

V. O. Key, himself, while not principally identified with the advocacy of responsible parties, illustrates certain typical American scholarly concerns, especially in his unconcealed desire for stronger parties. These concerns do not have to be explained by suggesting an unawareness of the questions raised about European parties. Understandably, Key's criterion was simply what seemed relevant in the United States. His subject matter, after all, was virtually all American. In Key's long and distinguished bibliography, only one article is devoted to politics outside of this country, and that is a piece on Canadian federalism relating to governmental grant policies rather than to parties. Parenthetical references to European—particularly British—parties occur from time to time, but only to sharpen by contrast a description or analysis of American phenomena. Although this does not have to mean that all of his findings are irrelevant for parties elsewhere, there can be no doubt that both by intent and result only American parties are being explored. The level of generalization is not cross-national. This may be stated as a plain fact rather than as a virtue or a deficiency. The point is that there are advantages as well as disadvantages in a strictly national context for studying parties.

One advantage is the inclusion of research subjects whose significance is simply not of cross-national concern. An obvious example is the relation of presidential and gubernatorial voting patterns in various states. Analyzed in detail by Key as part of his study of the connection between national and state parties, it could have no counterpart in other nations. Even in other federal systems where there exists something like comparable national and state party organizations, there is neither the same kind of executive-office election nor the simultaneous national and state elections characterizing American politics. A broader example is the American interest in the effect of the structural separation of powers on political parties. This interest has been largely reflected in analyses of how parties are frustrated as effective governing agencies, but it has also led to particular studies of the separate legislative and executive-oriented parties that have developed at both national and state levels. The whole subject of the elected executive's leadership, or attempted leadership, of legislators elected under the same party label involves a very different kind of inquiry from that of a prime minister's leadership of his parliamentary colleagues. Only in the broadest sense can there be common research questions on this subject, and it is by no means certain that these broad questions are more meaningful than those that are limited to a distinctive constitutional structure.

Still another topic emphasized by Key is the direct primary's influence on political parties. Again, this is an instance of an American institution that raises questions irrelevant almost everywhere else, but significant for understanding the organizational structure and limitations of parties in the United States. Of course, it is possible to view the American primary as one of several methods of candidate selection and so study it comparatively despite the unavailability in other nations of the intraparty electoral data provided by the primary. The effort appears worthwhile, but so does Key's research on the strictly American ground of the primary's impact over time on interparty competition. The value of primaries in general, as well as the respective merits of "open" and "closed" primaries, has remained an issue in American politics. No such issues have existed in other countries since direct primaries were almost never seriously contemplated, but for Key and other students of American politics there was a sufficient, even a compelling, American reason to study the question.

Turning to studies of Western European political parties, whether by American or European scholars, we can perceive a similar particularity determined by existing national circumstances. This is evident with respect to what is not studied as well as to what is. For example, there is little concern with one-party dominance, as opposed to interparty competition, in given areas. Instead, attention has been directed to the difference between multiparty and two-party competition, and to electoral procedures designed to encourage one or the other. Whether to have multimember proportional representation or single-member simple-plurality election, or another electoral variant, has been a live policy question in most European nations, and for the natural reason that there have usually been several rather than just two major parties. The student of parties becomes a student of election systems, and he tends to favor the election system most conducive to the number of parties he prefers. Multipartyism has had its intellectual defenders, and so therefore has proportional representation. Other political scientists have preferred a dualistic party model and so have favored a single-member, simple-plurality formula thought to be conducive to two-party competition. This difference in advocacy, however, is less relevant than the fact that the electoral question has been so prominent and apparently important. This fact has conditioned a great deal of Europan political research.

The state of party organization is another aspect of European politics that has made for a different approach from that followed in most recent American research. Instead of facing a situation in which parties had only weak and limited organizational structures, as was ordinarily the American situation by the 1940's, many students of European politics were studying nations some of whose parties had large and highly developed membership organizations. Consequently there was both a subject and a policy question not likely to occur to political scientists interested in American parties. European party memberships existed and so could be studied in their composition and their functions. Moreover, there was a question about what their role could or should be in a democratic political system. Significantly, the question was explored by Michels almost as soon as the first large membership party, the Social Democrats, became a major element in European, particularly German, politics. Understandably, the question has continued to command attention. Earlier, it is true, there had been an interest in the American-type party organization, characterized by patronage, that existed before any large European parties. The work of James Bryce and of Ostrogorski testifies to the interest of European as well as of American scholars in the American phenomenon. But there never arose any large American membership parties, of the European socialist type, and so, with the decline of patronage organizations (always hard to study systematically anyway), the whole subject of the character and role of party organizations became largely European. Students of American parties might advocate the establishment of membership organizations, but they did not have much by way of American phenomena to study. Nor did they have the European concern with the possibility that organized partisans might dominate the party's elected public officeholders.

For this reason there could be no American counterpart to Robert McKenzie's *British Political Parties*.[9] This important work had a distinctively European, or perhaps an almost distinctively British, subject and point of view. Written originally in the early 1950's, when Britain's Labour and Conservative parties were at their organizational peaks, McKenzie wanted to describe and analyze the relationship between these organized memberships and their respective parliamentary leaders. In Britain the organizations existed and they did raise a policy question; or at least the Labour organization raised such a question since it appeared to claim a policy-making role. McKenzie's work reflects this in two ways. First, he sought to show that the claim was not, in fact, asserted effectively and that Labour's parliamentary leadership maintained control over party policy-making at the governmental level. To this essentially empirical question McKenzie devotes much of his effort. It included a demonstration that Conservative and Labour party policy-making were much more alike than one would have been led to believe from respective party constitutions. McKenzie's second argument was that a subordinate role for an organized membership was the only role compatible with the British constitutional principle of parliamentary supremacy—that is, the supremacy of the elected members of the House of Commons. This point also involved empirical matters, especially the question of what British constitutional practice actually was, but it surely included a strong element of judgment as to what the practice ought to be. McKenzie simply did not believe that organized partisans should determine parliamentary party policy.

There are exceptions to the segregation of American-conditioned questions from European-conditioned questions. But even the exceptions show a basically national orientation of research. For example, American political scientists have occasionally asked how cohesive legislative parties or organized party memberships are achieved in European nations.[10] What they are looking for are the factors responsible for such political phenomena. In other words, what is the circumstance of a given European nation but not of the United States that makes for par-

9. (London: Heinemann, 1955 and 1963 eds.).

10. Lately, it is true, American political scientists have also studied the development of several American party membership organizations. James Q. Wilson, *The Amateur Democrats* (Chicago, Ill.: University of Chicago Press, 1962).

ticular party characteristics? The question is still an American one. Surely it is unlikely to be raised by a European student primarily concerned with Europe. On the other hand, Europeans have been known to ask, as did Duverger, why the United States does not have more highly organized parties of the European type. The question has also been asked in another way: Why does the United States not have a large socialist party? Inquiries of this type, like American questions concerning European parties, do not really involve cross-national research so much as an effort, often fruitful, to refocus one nation's research concerns in a different national environment.

Cross-National Possibilities

Most of what has so far been said constitutes a justification for essentially national research concerning political parties. There has been an explanation of why the bulk of scholarship has been national in its focus, and also a suggestion that this explanation provides an understandable and defensible basis for the predominant orientation. But there is still an argument for the possibilities of cross-national study. There may now be new and good reasons for believing in the growth of such possibilities, especially among Western nations. One reason relates to our enlarged research resources. Not only are techniques more highly developed, but there are an increasing number of political scientists whose efforts are heavily financed, making ambitious programs of cross-national research more feasible. Another reason for new opportunities is that Western nations appear to have more nearly common political phenomena now that they also appear to share more nearly similar socioeconomic circumstances. Specifically the United States and Western Europe may be more nearly a single political universe than they were a few decades ago. With the new affluence of much of the European working class, there is a less evident socioeconomic basis for the class-conscious ideological parties that characterized European politics in the first half of this century. One need not believe in anything so simple as the Americanization of Europe, or so sweeping as the end of ideology, to accept the increasing resemblance of the two once so distinct political cultures. This means that it is both more reasonable and more likely that common questions will be asked by political scientists.

No doubt some of the formerly European questions may become relevant in American studies, but if it is right to think of European politics as changing in response to a level of affluence approaching that of the United States, then one should expect the familiar American questions more frequently to be raised about European parties. The number of political scientists in the United States is overwhelming in relation to those in the rest of the world, and the body of their research findings on American politics provides an impressive storehouse of hypotheses for research elsewhere. The problem that remains is to discover which of these hypotheses are really suitable for cross-national study. To what extent does the national emphasis already stressed still limit the possibilities? One way to explore the matter is to ask which of several American inquiries, some identified with V. O. Key's study of American state parties, might now be relevant to Western democratic parties generally.

An inquiry of broad significance concerns the well-recognized American phenomenon of one-party dominance of regional or local politics. Its causes, or at least the factors with which it is associated, have been explored especially at the state level, so as to stress a relationship between the socioeconomic character of a constituency and the maintenance of party competition in that constituency (state or local). But American political scientists are not able to state this in terms so absolute as to say that there always have to be both a large urban working class and a substantial middle class of business, professional, or agricultural entrepreneurs in order to provide the bases for two separate parties in a given area. Whether any such division is essential must depend on whether it exists generally for the national arena in which parties are competing. In other words, two nationally competing parties could each have strong bases in those states or localities whose socioeconomic divisions approximate those of the nation. Exceptions can be expected for a variety of historical reasons, but the general tendency might still be discernible. If so, it is fair to ask whether the same association is found in other Western nations.

Insofar as attention is directed to national and state parties, the cross-national comparison must be limited to the few other federal systems in the Western world. Principally this means Canada and Australia, but Switzerland and possibly Germany could be included. Canada provides the most illuminating experience because, despite its similarities to the United States in other respects, that nation's two major parties compete less pervasively against each other at the provincial level than do the two American parties in the several states. Only some of this difference can be readily accounted for by the fact that the two Canadian parties do not monopolize the national arena in the manner of Republicans and Democrats in the United States. Third and fourth parties, it is true, compete nationally in Canada, but they do so to a large extent as extensions of their power in particular provinces. That power is related to the provincial weakness of one or the other (sometimes both) of the major national parties. Why should these major parties differ from their American national counterparts in the capacity to maintain themselves at regional levels? Or, when one party fails provincially, why is it replaced by a third or fourth party instead of by a one-party dominance of the other major national party as has been the American pattern since the demise, two decades ago, of midwestern progressivism as a separate party movement? [11] Put less nationally, what is being sought are the conditions making for one pattern of party competition as opposed to another in structurally similar federal systems.

There is no need, however, to confine the question to federal systems. The more general relationship between larger and smaller party arenas is involved, even though most American research has been directed to national-state party patterns accompanying a federal system. In unitary systems the relationship is between national and local parties, either at the single-member constituency level, as in Britain, or at the departmental multi-member (or multi-constituency) level, as in France. The point is to find the local basis for party organization and electoral mobilization below the national level. It must be admitted that national-local party relations in the British and French situations are not of the same order of significance as the national-regional relations in a federal structure. Local units rarely provide the same potential as do states or provinces for partially independent loci of political power for governing officials or their partisans. Therefore, considerable caution is required in attempts to compare even competitive patterns in the two different sets of circumstances. It is best to say that the possibilities for meaning-

11. These questions are raised in the author's "A Comparative Study of Canadian Parties," *American Political Science Review*, 58 (March 1964), 46–59.

ful comparison exist at a higher and looser level of generalization when federal and unitary systems are mixed. An obvious
way to make the situations more nearly alike in one respect is to
compare the national-local pattern of Britain, for example, with
the state-local pattern in the United States. One would then, however, have selected situations unlike in another respect. The presence or absence of the national level might well be crucial in
analysis.

Despite the difficulties in satisfactorily defining cross-national
categories, so as to allow a test of propositions derived from the
American setting, there does appear to be a general phenomenon
commanding attention. It is the existence within a large arena of
various smaller arenas whose party competition may vary from
that of the larger arena. The variation may be in the direction of
one-party dominance, or third-party strength, although the larger
arena is characterized by two-party competition. Or the variation
may, as seems likely for a multiparty nation like France, be in
the direction of having fewer serious competitors in given localities than there are nationally. In other words, what there is to
study is the degree to which the pattern of the larger arena pervades, or fails to pervade, in constituent units. It is easy to suggest possible causes (independent variables): size and nature of
the constituent units, historical regional differences, social and
economic homogeneity of the whole community, existence or degree of federalism, and a variety of other structural and cultural
factors.

The search for the circumstances associated with variations
from the larger arena's competitive party pattern does have a
policy-oriented purpose on a cross-national basis, as it does on a
cross-state basis in strictly American research. The latter, regarding two-party competition as a desirable norm, has sought the
causes for one-party dominance in given states in order to pre-
scribe changes in the desired direction. The fullest exposition is
in Key's *Southern Politics,* where the degree of historical Democratic party dominance is related directly to the Negro percentage of the total population and so to the white population's perceived need for single partisan representation at all levels of
government. While an extreme case, both in its racial circumstance and in its long-standing one-party manifestation, the
southern American states are by no means unique. Rather they
represent a species of a general phenomenon: a single highly

salient interest providing an overriding basis for the unity of a single party. The fact that no northern American state exhibits the same extreme one-party commitment can be explained by the absence of a single interest entirely comparable to that of the Deep South. Even without such intense motivation, however, certain northern states preserved fairly strong one-party dominance, based on the identification of heavily rural interest with the historically successful Republican party. Neither in these instances nor in the Deep South is there only a parochial American phenomenon. Its visibility and importance are accented by the federal structure, but the same is true for Canada. And there is no reason to think that even a nonfederal system would lack similar one-party pockets wherever there are distinctive regional interests. The quasi-federal situation of Northern Ireland within the United Kingdom is a case in point. The Conservative-affiliated Unionist party has served as the instrument of the pro-British Protestant majority, as against a pro-Eire Catholic minority. The Labour party has been precluded from fulfilling its usual role, in Britain, of representing industrial workers since to do so would split the Protestant majority in an attempt to unite workers and their supporters across religious and nationalist lines.

The Northern Ireland case comes to mind because, like American or Canadian one-party situations, it is identifiable with a definite governmental unit as well as with a single geographical entity. Elsewhere the phenomenon must also occur even if less readily identified. It is at least probable within any largely two-party national system employing the single-member, simple-plurality election of representatives. Britain, despite its relatively high national homogeneity, provides various examples. Most evident on a regional basis are mining constituencies which, in clusters, regularly produce large Labour party majorities. But there are also many individual cities, or constituencies within cities, where similar one-party predominance prevails. In fact, about two-thirds of Britain's parliamentary constituencies are ordinarily safe for one party or the other. The reason is clear enough. Each constituency is so small that it is also likely to be so homogeneous socially and economically as to provide a sufficient class or interest basis for only one strong party. The bases that exist nationally for two-party competition are most unlikely to be duplicated in microcosm in any large number of constituencies. This is as true for urban as for rural areas, except for an entire city that is itself about the size of a parliamentary constituency. Really large urban areas are likely to be divided into several constituencies corresponding to a de facto segregation along social and economic lines. In Britain as in the United States the older core districts are heavily working-class while the suburbs are heavily middle-class. As long as each of two leading parties derives its strength primarily from one or the other of these classes, constituencies are bound to be characterized by a high degree of one-party domination. The same might hold, although for a different set of constituencies, if party competition were primarily in terms other than class interests.

By suggesting the universal possibility of one-party politics at subnational levels and so the cross-national study of the phenomenon, the direct primary, so often associated with American one-party politics, is put in a new perspective, even though it cannot—for the simple reason stated earlier—be studied outside of the United States. What can now be asked is why the direct primary was not the response to local or regional one-party politics in other nations as it was supposed to have been in southern states and, just after 1900, in certain northern Republican states. One-party dominance in certain areas of other nations was plainly not a sufficient cause for the adoption of the direct primary. Nor did the absence of the primary in these nations lead to the growth of local and regional two-party competition in all of those places where there had been little or none. This could raise a new doubt about the extent to which the primary, once established in the United States, helped to perpetuate one-party politics. On *a priori* grounds, American political scientists might well have expected the primary to play such a role. Not only does the primary provide a democratic legitimacy by installing electoral competition at the intraparty level, when there might be little or no competition between parties, but it also constitutes an alternative outlet for any potential leadership group seeking to displace current officeholders. New aspirants for office need not attempt to gain election through a locally unpopular or moribund party. Nor need they attempt to form a third party. The primary opens the way for individuals or groups to mount electoral campaigns designed to capture the label of the dominant party. Victory for insurgents in such campaigns may be no easier to accomplish than victory in party conventions, but there can be no doubt that the direct primary has often been an important alternative to the still more difficult task of trying to secure office through the use of a minority party ticket (however easy it might be to secure nomination on such a ticket).

It is difficult to measure the extent to which the direct primary has deprived a minority party of its potential leaders and candidates. Two kinds of measuring attempts are possible. One is to study the degree of two-party competition in a state before and after the adoption of the direct primary. The other method is to compare the degrees of two-party competition in those states with the direct primary and in those retaining convention control of the nominating process. V. O. Key, as we know, tried both methods. The results, while necessarily inconclusive in light of all the other conceivable variables, have been generally consistent with the *a priori* view that the direct primary tends to inhibit interparty competition. The findings, however, do not go so far as to say that the direct primary precludes the development of interparty competition when there had been little or none before.

Even this limited causal link between the direct primary and inhibited interparty competition would be questioned insofar as one found as great and as persistent a one-party tendency in regions and constituencies of other Western nations as there has been in the United States. The absence of the direct primary in those nations would then make it harder to attribute causal influence to the primary in the United States. But it would not make such attribution impossible or entirely unreasonable. It might still be argued that *in American circumstances* the direct primary played a part in limiting interparty competition. That is all that anyone ever claimed. In other words, the hypothesis was exclusively national in the first place, and so in a sense not subject to destruction by cross-national findings.

Extending cross-nationally the study of degrees of party competition, or the absence of it, has other possibilities besides that of testing any causal effects of the direct primary. American political science has developed, on this and related subjects, broader generalizations more directly testable in Western nations. Most broad in its scope is the previously noted association of local and regional interparty competition with the duplication locally or regionally of the socioeconomic divisions supporting the respective national parties. The extent to which this association holds would be well worth cross-national inquiry. So would the related question of whether or not the frequently observed

American phenomenon of the metropolitan-nonmetropolitan party cleavage is reproduced elsewhere and, if so, under what conditions. Perhaps another way to put the point is to ask to what extent a given party includes both metropolitan and non-metropolitan bases of strength instead of having only one or the other base of power.

There is also a set of interesting questions that relate to the consequences rather than the causes of variations from the supposed interparty competitive situations. Assuming, from European as well as from American experience, that there are numerous variations of this kind, how do the adjustments to one-party dominance compare with the American adjustments? A particular aspect of this question involves the search for equivalents or near-equivalents of the American effort to use the direct primary as a means of electoral competition when there is no meaningful choice for local voters in the general election. Significantly, however, there appear to be no close equivalents in European nations. Little effort is made outside of the United States to provide large numbers of voters with a role in choosing party candidates, in either one-party or interparty competitive areas. Certainly there is no governmentally sponsored institutional effort at all analogous to American primaries. The reason, contrary to the American principle, is that a party's selection of candidates (what we call party nomination) is regarded as the business of a private association and thus subject to the same limited legal regulation pertaining to the choice of officials by corporations, trade unions, or clubs. This does not necessarily exclude the participation of relatively large numbers in the selection of candidates. A party, like any other private association, might have a large dues-paying membership authorized by the association's own rules to decide who should bear the party label in campaigns for public office. Party members themselves, or their chosen representatives, may gather at various constituency levels to select candidates. Or the members might even be given a chance to vote by means of a mail ballot or in person at party-maintained polling places. The latter, amounting to a privately operated primary, is rare among parties in Western nations; it has been used over a period of time and on a fairly large scale only in the Australian Labor party [12] and just sporadically else-

12. James Jupp, *Australian Party Politics* (Melbourne: Melbourne University Press, 1964), pp. 62–64.

where. But membership participation at candidate-selection meetings is common. One ought to be able to learn more about the numbers and nature of these participants. Viewing their function in relation to direct-primary participants would appear meaningful in terms of categories for cross-national comparison.

Although this study need not be limited to one-party situations, it would have a special importance in that connection. In any democratic system, it is assumed to be desirable that there should be a substantial opportunity for popular choice between individuals, or sets of individuals, seeking public office. This is a crucial minimum insisted on even by modern democratic theorists who have abandoned notions of popular decisions on policies and issues. Often the significant choice is thought to be between parties, or party slates of candidates, but this can hardly hold for the numerous constituencies in which one party is regularly dominant. Then, on the local level at least, there is a situation similar to (though admittedly not identical with) the legally constituted one-party nations, totalitarian or otherwise. One might therefore consider the cautious extension of a cross-national study to include, say, the candidate selection practices of the Communist Party of the U.S.S.R. along with the practices of locally dominant parties in Western nations. The comparison, it must be emphasized, is much more difficult to raise above the most general and superficial level than is cross-national comparison within the Western democratic universe—and that is difficult enough in ways already suggested. Among other difficulties, a Russo-Western study of candidate selection would encounter the basic difference in value attached to political competition by the two kinds of societies. Cherished in principle by Western democracies, open competition between groups of any kind (not just parties) is regarded as unfortunately divisive in Communist nations. Any provision for popular participation in candidate selection would probably have a very different purpose and be judged by very different criteria in the U.S.S.R. from those in a Western nation.

Returning to the limited concern with the Western democratic universe, one can perceive another research question growing in part out of the intra-American study of political parties. This is the degree to which respective party leaders are recruited differentially along class lines. "Leaders" here usually means elected public officeholders because of convenience in identifying and securing biographical information about them. But party organizational personnel need not be excluded. They are obviously important in nations with large membership parties. Although organizational personnel have not been neglected in American studies, most scholars, like V. O. Key, have been primarily concerned with the function of parties in recruiting candidates for public office. This typically American concern grows out of the desire for parties to be effective in obtaining and presenting candidates, particularly for a minority party in a two-party situation to be more effective in these respects. Effectiveness of this kind might be studied in several nations, but more fruitful cross-national research seems probable through an investigation of the degrees of socioeconomic distinctiveness of party leaders. One can perceive this in terms of a scale ranging from a homogeneous leadership group of, say, the professional middle class, characterizing each major political party, to a situation in which the major parties in a given nation differ sharply from each other in the socioeconomic origins of their leaders. The extreme instance of the latter is represented by a predominantly working-class leadership of one-party facing a predominantly middle-class (and perhaps upper-class) leadership of the other major party. Similar to the first or homogeneous recruitment by major parties is a situation in which each major party's leadership is drawn, and in approximately the same degree, from a mixed class background. This implies, as does a single-class source of all major party leaders, that party conflict is not along class lines.

Comparing party leaderships across national lines need not be confined to socioeconomic origins although these do appear especially revealing with respect to the difference between American and European recruitment patterns in the first half of the twentieth century and with respect to the more recent diminution of that difference. Other cross-national possibilities exist in categories already partially explored separately in the United States and in certain European nations. Ethnic and religious backgrounds are obvious subjects. Religion is almost too obvious in the case of continental European parties organized along denominational lines. Educational data, while simply measuring socioeconomic status when expressed in terms of years of schooling, can be used in ways to distinguish leaders by the kind of quality of their training—humanistic or technical, for example. Other opportunities for comparison can be found in age or generational characteristics and in psychological or personality attributes.

Recent Innovations

It is plain that the cross-national research possibilities just described are only modest and limited suggestions for the extension of certain largely American interests. Often the difficulties have been stressed as heavily as the opportunities. The basis for this cautiousness about cross-national research on political parties may be understood more clearly by looking at certain recent undertakings in the comparative field. The first thing to note is that with attention confined to "genuinely cross-national" work there are very few studies, and they are concentrated heavily on subjects readily lending themselves to quantification. Such studies may well be the beginning of a major trend in the comparative field, but so far they represent only a small portion of the total research in the politics of Western nations and they cover only a small portion of the total subject matter. It is really their innovative character, especially methodologically, that rightly commands attention.

Much of this attention on the part of students of political parties, along with almost everyone else in political science, has been given to a general cross-national analysis concerned with parties only among other political phenomena. The analysis involves the effort to associate particular national political systems, or features of political systems, with various national socioeconomic indices, and to express the association in statistical terms. One of the first and best-known instances of such cross-national correlation analysis was S. M. Lipset's attempt to associate the successful stabilization of political democracy with the economic and educational levels of advanced societies.[13] The method was similar to that applied within the United States to correlate degrees of party competition with the socioeconomic characteristics of the several states. For Lipset, nations rather than American states were the units of analysis. There must be a fairly large number of nations if there are to be quantitatively impressive results. Lipset used mainly the conventional Western

13. S. M. Lipset, *Political Man* (Garden City, N.Y.: Doubleday, 1960), chap. 2.

nations plus Latin America. Others used similar, if occasionally more refined, methods [14] for the more numerous new or developing nations, either as a separate group or as part of the totality of nations. The existence of over one hundred national units, each furnishing certain elementary statistical data on income, education, industrialization, and urbanization, encourages the correlation of such socioeconomic variables with simple, measurable political phenomena (for example, the number of parties) as well as with the more complex matter of the degree of democratic government. Considerable research resources have been invested in work of this nature, and the statistical ingenuity has been impressive.[15] The findings, however, are mainly suggestive (as is probably intended) of further inquiries in particular nations, often as deviant cases. A classic deviant nation is Germany. In Lipset's analysis, as elsewhere, Germany's twentieth-century experience with political democracy has not been as successful as the nation's socioeconomic status would lead us to expect. Therefore, one has to look to essentially national studies of Germany to learn what there is about the nation that might have made its experience exceptional.

Much closer to the special field of political parties is the cross-national study of voting behavior. It has attracted talent much as has strictly national voting behavior, and for similar reasons. For a generation equipped to use quantitative tools, voting behavior is a notably convenient subject because of its numerical manifestations. Not only is this true for actual election results, readily available in all Western nations (though not yet conveniently assembled on an international basis), but also for demographic data pertaining to districts in which votes are cast. This does not mean, however, that ecological analyses of voting is everywhere facilitated as it is in the United States. The ideal is to have small voting districts about which there are demographic statistics to relate to election results. But in Britain, for example, votes are counted only at the constituency level, not in individual polling stations, and so the analyst is limited in a way that he is not when dealing with American precincts, wards, or townships.

---

14. Phillips Cutright, "National Political Development," *Politics and Social Life,* eds. Nelson Polsby, Robert Dentler, and Paul Smith (Boston: Houghton Mifflin, 1963), pp. 569–582.

15. Arthur Banks and Robert Textor, *A Cross-Polity Survey* (Cambridge, Mass.: M. I. T. Press, 1963).

However, the difference is no longer a major obstacle to voting behavior research in general, now that ecological analysis has been largely superseded by the use of the more refined sample survey. Although this is particularly true of the United States itself, the survey has also come to be widely used in Western Europe on an independent national scale as well as in a limited amount of cross-national research.

Survey research interviews are hardly confined to voting behavior, but they have been widely used in this field and especially with respect to party voting behavior. Interviewing, it must be said, is not uniformly successful in every nation. This is only partly the result of the expected differences in the resources, the skills, and the diligence of the various national research organizations on which cross-national scholarship must depend. It is also a matter of differences between political cultures. In some, respondents are both more accessible and more forthcoming than in other countries. There is good reason to believe, for example, that numerous Italian citizens who actually vote for Communists do not reveal their party preference to pollsters. Thus there are exceptionally large percentages of don't-know or no-preference answers, and suspiciously lower Communist percentages than actual voting statistics indicate. To a lesser extent the same discrepancy appears in France. What may be reflected is a general tendency of a portion of the population to be alienated from participation in the survey as part of its alienation from the political order itself. Whatever the cause, there can be no question about the importance of the limitation imposed when substantial numbers will not reveal their party preferences.

Rightly, however, this limitation has not precluded a good deal of inquiry. Again, Lipset's work represents an early effort to use voting behavior data in a comparative context.[16] He did not confine himself to survey data but employed ecological analyses of election returns when, as for earlier periods, there were no surveys. Usually Lipset's method was selective rather than systematically universal. That is, he cited voting behavior statistics from various nations and for various periods in order to illustrate certain hypothetical generalizations. What is notable is that he cited many studies for several nations, even though he may not have cited all those in existence. The studies, however,

16. *Political Man*, chaps. 6–9.

had originally been conducted by various scholars and by various polling organizations as separate national inquiries. Although such studies often closely resembled each other in their subject matter (as, for example, in the relation between occupational status and party voting) and may have been influenced by each other, they were unlikely to raise identical questions and so were unlikely to produce strictly comparable findings. Particular propositions tested in one national polity were not precisely the ones tested elsewhere, and even if they were nearly the same, they would not have been tested in the same way. Thus it is hard to say that Lipset's use of separate national studies, no matter how carefully systematic they were individually, could be any more than illustrative of the hypothetical generalizations he advanced. Nevertheless, even as illustrations the many separate studies gave Lipset's analysis a novel breadth.

Subsequently, students of voting behavior across national lines have limited their analysis to a few nations within the Western universe and have concentrated on a few variables. These methods have been consistent with efforts to substitute selective systematic comparisons for the broader illustrative comparions used by Lipset. One of the best-known of these efforts is Robert Alford's use of pre-existing survey data from the United States, Britain, Australia, and Canada to determine the degree of class-based party voting in each of the four nations.[17] The surveys from which the data came were not, it is true, designed for Alford's comparative purpose. They were simply surveys that had been conducted in each nation over a period of years. But each survey had asked much the same questions both about party voting and about occupational class status. A comparable index of class voting could therefore be compiled for each nation, basically by measuring the proportion of manual workers, as opposed to nonmanualists, voting for the party (or parties) of the Left. The result was a rank order of nations, from high to low index of class voting: Britain, Australia, United States, and Canada. Much of the analysis showed how this rank order reflected, in reverse, the relative importance of nonclass determinants of voting, notably religion, ethnic background, and regionalism.

Still one step farther from Lipset's illustrative method, in both

17. *Parties and Society* (Chicago: Rand McNally, 1963).

its range and its systematic character, is the Converse-Dupeux comparison of French and American electoral identification with political parties.[18] Here there was a nearly common survey instrument, designed for the particular comparative study, and an examination focused on voters at a particular time in each country (rather than over a period of years and several surveys, as in Alford's work). The Converse-Dupeux method has the advantage of precision. Whatever disadvantages it may seem to have in this instance (as, for example, the limited time-span) are hardly inherent. With sufficient resources, the survey could be conducted in each nation over several years. Then the chief Converse-Dupeux finding—that more Americans than Frenchmen identify with political parties—could be tested to learn whether the low French figure was a consequence of the period of flux in party fortunes at the beginning of the Fifth Republic or whether it was a more durable phenomenon. Similarly the particularized survey could be employed in more nations than just two.

The really ambitious attempt along this latter line is the cross-national survey by Almond and Verba.[19] Their concern, however, was not primarily party voting, or even voting as such, but attitudes toward political participation in the broadest sense. These attitudes included views of party participation, but parties were plainly tangential interests for Almond and Verba. The reason for citing the work here is that its method is obviously adaptable to specialized purposes. That method, speaking generally, is the use of a common survey in several nations (United States, Britain, Germany, Italy, and Mexico) for a common research purpose—the testing of given hypotheses in several different national environments. Both the scale and the sophistication are impressive. So is the careful exposition of the methodological difficulties in the way of cross-national inquiries, particularly with respect to devising genuinely comparable questions and equally representative samples of respondents in radically different environments. The latter was chiefly a problem in Italy and Mexico rather than in the nations belonging to the more conventionally Western universe.

18. Philip Converse and Georges Dupeux, "Politicization of the Electorate of France and the United States," *Public Opinion Quarterly*, 26 (Spring 1962), 1–23.

19. Gabriel Almond and Sidney Verba, *The Civic Culture* (Princeton, N.J.: Princeton University Press, 1963).

Much less ambitious than the Almond-Verba study but clearly focused on parties is one of the very few other cross-national studies drawing on survey data. This is a Norwegian-American comparison by Campbell and Valen.[20] It is not a voting behavior study, but a more unusual work, in that it seeks to measure and to explain the difference in the frequency of working-class party activism in the two nations. The higher frequency in Norway is identified with the existence of a working-class party, within which workers can comfortably participate in a way that they could not in either American middle-class party. Other more far-reaching historical explanations are not excluded, and these might well emerge if data from other nations were included.

Admittedly this summary of recent innovative research does not entirely exhaust the list of what might be called genuinely cross-national studies. Casting the net a little wider, one can add, from a slightly earlier period, Gabriel Almond's *Appeals of Communism*,[21] comparing the attitudes of American, British, French, and Italian ex-Communists. Or, taking into account a major current undertaking, there are the ambitious and useful efforts to compile electoral data on comparable bases for democratic nations.[22] Possibly a number of other studies involving systematic cross-national research are just appearing. It is doubtful whether they are yet sufficient in number or in scope to preempt the field of comparative politics in general or of comparative parties in particular. This is another way of saying that essentially national studies are still employed to answer most research questions, notably the policy-oriented questions. While not methodologically innovative in the sense of systematic cross-national design, many of these national studies may now be less parochial than seemed to be the case in the past. Comparison, even within a given national study, may be conscious in the manner of Tocqueville, and so differ from most of early

20. Angus Campbell and Henry Valen, "Party Identification in Norway and the United States," *Public Opinion Quarterly*, 25 (Winter 1961), 505–525.

21. (Princeton, N.J.: Princeton University Press, 1954).

22. Stein Rokkan has been the major initiator of efforts in this and other areas of cross-national data gathering. A first production is Richard L. Merritt and Stein Rokkan, eds. *Comparing Nations: The Use of Quantitative Data in Cross-National Research* (New Haven, Conn.: Yale University Press, 1966). See also Seymour M. Lipset and Stein Rokkan, eds. *Party Systems and Voter Alignments* (New York: The Free Press, 1967).

twentieth-century American political science. Unlike Tocqueville, however, most recent efforts have focused on particular subjects among which parties have been prominent. Nor have the consciously comparative studies of single nations always been the product of students from nations other than the one being studied. Even scholars studying their own nations have come to ask questions of a broad and general nature, or questions borrowed from another context.

The number of such studies in the parties field alone is so large that it is hard to mention any without seeming to discriminate unduly. McKenzie's standard work on British parties has already been noted. Philip Williams' detailed French study is another important example.[23] So is the Valen-Katz work on Norwegian party organization.[24] Still more specialized examples are the political party studies by Guttsman for Britain and by Seligman for Israel.[25] Another kind of specialized treatment is Austin Ranney's intensive study of candidate selection by British parties, so designed as to test the American-held proposition that Britain's cohesive parliamentary parties are strongly associated with centralized party control of the process of choosing parliamentary candidates.[26] The proposition, incidentally, is disproved. One more similarly deliberate comparative study of a British subject deserves mention. It is Roland Pennock's analysis of British agricultural policy designed to demonstrate that Britain's strong party governments have been more effectively pressured for farm subsidies than have American governments.[27]

Even so abbreviated a list of party studies illustrates the range of questions that are asked in single-nation studies. The end of their usefulness is hardly in sight. They may well be stimulated by suggestions emerging from broad cross-national analyses. There really seems no likely substitute for exploration, in depth, of the national context in which parties or other political phe-

23. *Crisis and Compromise* (London: Longmans, 1964).

24. Henry Valen and Daniel Katz, *Political Parties in Norway* (Oslo: Universitetsforlaget, 1964).

25. W. L. Guttsman, *The British Political Elite* (London: Macgibbon and Kee, 1963), and Lester Seligman, *Leadership in a New Nation* (New York: Atherton Press, 1964).

26. *Pathways to Parliament* (Madison: University of Wisconsin Press, 1965).

27. "Agricultural Subsidies in England and the United States," *American Political Science Review*, 56 (September 1962), 621–633.

nomena are found. To some extent the subject-matter is intractably national. This hard fact does not, and should not, prohibit meaningful cross-national analysis or the borrowing of research questions from one national environment to ask in another. But the national character of politics does suggest, much more strongly than the state character of politics in the United States, that the comparative method must complement and not supersede studies of particular systems. Caution is in order especially for those of us who seek to generalize about political parties within the Western universe, not to mention still wider fields. It is hard to match the level of knowledge and insight that characterizes the best of the national studies, and to be as directly relevant to the policy questions arising in national contexts.

Duane Lockard

State Party Systems and Policy Outputs *

Among the rich hypotheses and generalizations in V. O. Key's *Southern Politics* is his observation that a one-party system tends to serve the interests of the haves of society better than those of the have-nots:

A loose factional system lacks the power to carry out sustained programs of action, which almost always are thought by the better element to be contrary to its immediate interests. This negative weakness thus redounds to the benefit of the upper brackets. All of which is not to say that the upper brackets stand idly by and leave to chance the protection of their interests. A loose factionalism gives great negative power to those with a few dollars to invest in legislative candidates. A party system provides at least a semblance of joint responsibility between governor and legislature. The independence of candidacies in an atomized politics makes it possible to elect a fire-eating governor who promises great accomplishments and simultaneously to elect a legislature a majority of whose members are committed to inaction.[1]

* I am particularly grateful to my colleagues, Michael Danielson, Edward Tufte, Stanley Kelley, Charles Berry, Richard Quandt, and Charles Hermann, for their helpful criticisms of an earlier draft of this essay. I was also helped greatly by my former research assistant, John Strange, and by Stephen Salmore, a Princeton graduate student.

1. V. O. Key, Jr., *Southern Politics in State and Nation* (New York: Knopf, 1949), p. 308.

He goes on to say, in one of his most frequently quoted paragraphs: "The great virtue of the two-party system is, not that there are two groups with conflicting policy tendencies from which the voters can choose, but there are two groups of politicians. The fluidity of the factional system handicaps the formation of two such groups within the southern Democratic party, and the inevitable result is there is no continuing group of 'outs' which of necessity must pick up whatever issue is at hand to belabor the 'ins'." [2]

Although Key made no systematic attempt to analyze the variations in public policy among southern states with strong and continuous factions, as opposed to those with looser factional systems, he did point out that Virginia and North Carolina— both with "tightly organized factional systems as southern politics goes"—had more responsible government than the other states in the South. He attributed this in part to the capacity of a "cohesive faction . . . to discipline wild-eyed men." [3] In the absence of such control he expected the poor to suffer and the rich to gain on the crucial issues of taxation and expenditure, levels of education and public services, public regulation and controls.

Unfortunately Key never systematically followed up this intriguing facet of state politics. Other political scientists working on the problem have, with few exceptions, been skeptical about the validity of the generalization that party competition induces higher payoffs for the have-nots. By ranking the states according to the extent of competitiveness of parties and comparing that ranking with expenditures for programs especially important to the less well-to-do, they did find some correlation between party competition and payoffs; but when they compared the wealth of states with payoffs they found similar or higher correlations. [4]

2. *Ibid.*, pp. 309–310.
3. *Ibid.*, p. 306.
4. See particularly Richard E. Dawson and James A. Robinson, "Inter-Party Competition, Economic Variables, and Welfare Policies in the American States," *Journal of Politics*, 25 (May 1963), 265, and "The Politics of Welfare" in *Politics in the American States*, Herbert Jacob and Kenneth N. Vines, eds. (Boston: Little, Brown, 1965), 371; Thomas R. Dye, "The Independent Effect of Party Competition on Policy Outcomes in the American States," paper presented at the 1965 Annual Meeting of the American Political Science Association (mimeo.) ; his much more elaborate treatment of this subject, published since the present article was written, *Politics, Economics, and the Public* (Chicago, Ill.: Rand McNally, 1966) ; and Richard I. Hofferbert, "The Relationship between Public

That wealth affects the capacity of states to respond to the needs of the indigent is certainly an easy proposition to accept, but one would expect that certain characteristics of the political system would also have an impact on the responsiveness of the state. For example, there is considerable evidence that political leaders in competitive states will try to persuade legislators of their party to accept liberal policy proposals "because of the next election." The "theory" (if one may call it that) is simply that fear of the next election may induce action in behalf of the poor since the politicians' visibility and possible accountability (or fear thereof, which is probably more significant) are greater in competitive than in noncompetitive states. But some scholars seem to deny this. They contend that socioeconomic factors, not political variables, are the true determinants of the payoff for the poor. Thomas Dye, for example, uses correlational analysis in an attempt to prove this point; he reports that party competition had little independent effect on public policies in 26 of 28 different "policy outcomes" he examined. His research, he says,

suggests that the linkage between socio-economic inputs and policy outcomes is an unbroken one, and that characteristics of political systems do not independently influence policy outcomes. Political systems are, by definition, the structure and processes which function to make public policy, but these systems do not mediate between societal requirements and public policy so much as they reflect societal requirements in public policy. Political system characteristics are much less important than socio-economic inputs in determining policy outcomes.[5]

Perhaps the profession has assumed too much and proved too little about the significance of political systems for public policies, but before abandoning Key's hypothesis and reshaping this facet of the political science venture into an investigation of the socioeconomic variables and their correlation with policy payoffs, it seems worthwhile to take another look at the kinds of relationships that can be found between political systems and policy. Thus it is the object of this essay to reconsider the evi-

Policy and Some Structural and Environmental Variables in the American States," *American Political Science Review*, 60 (March 1966), 73.

5. Dye, "Independent Effect of Party Competition," p. 16. The exceptions—where party competition appeared to have some significance—were "state participation in the financing of public activities, particularly education. The state proportion of educational expenditures and the state proportion of total state and local government expenditures was lower in the more competitive states, indicating that the local proportion of these expenditures was higher" (at p. 14).

dence and arguments about the Key hypothesis. After a brief review of some of the arguments offered by others, we shall examine not only policies that can be statistically ranked but also other statutes, the presence or absence of which may be important to the have-nots (as, for example, laws concerned with minimum wages, right-to-work laws, antidiscrimination policies, and small-loan regulations). In addition, an attempt will be made to examine more closely the particular states that deviate from expectations implied in the hypothesis—i.e., states that have low competition but high payoffs and states with high competition and low payoffs. Instead of relying solely on statistical correlations, attention will also be given to the information known about the political systems of individual states.

To introduce subjective aspects of state politics is admittedly to sacrifice some precision. But the statistical evidence makes it conclusively certain that only a part of the deviation from expected performance could be explained by competition. Therefore, resort to less quantifiable data about state politics may offer some explanations where statistically manipulable data do not.

Measuring Competition

One serious problem of research on this subject is the difficulty of measuring with precision the degree of interparty competition. A number of methods have been used, and they produce different results because they rely on different time periods and offices, and they include or exclude other factors such as the frequency of turnover of party control. For the most effective assessment of state politics in the present context, none of these ranking systems seems appropriate [6] because none of them takes into account the extent of party voting in the legislature or the character of factions within those states in which one party predominates. Bringing these factors into the classification system is difficult, however, for the obvious reasons that, in the first place, they are not statistically quantifiable, and secondly, the data on the degree of party voting are not very reliable for some states.

6. Some of the purely statistical rankings may not merit as much precision as is attributed to them since in a given period a state may change drastically in political orientation (e.g., Maine 1950–1965), and the resulting averages may therefore be quite misleading.

Table I. Patterns of state party competition [a]
(arranged alphabetically in groups)

GROUP I COMPETITIVE PARTIES, MUCH PARTY VOTING IN LEGISLATURE

Connecticut
Massachusetts
Michigan
New Jersey
New York

GROUP II COMPETITIVE PARTIES, CONSIDERABLE PARTY VOTING IN LEGISLATURE, BUT NOT AS MUCH AS IN GROUP I

Delaware
Indiana
Ohio
Pennsylvania
Rhode Island

GROUP III COMPETITIVE PARTIES, MODERATE PARTY VOTING IN LEGISLATURE

Colorado
Hawaii
Illinois
Montana
Wisconsin

GROUP IV COMPETITIVE PARTIES, LITTLE PARTY VOTING IN LEGISLATURE

Alaska
California
Maryland
Minnesota
Washington

GROUP V SOME COMPETITION, LITTLE PARTY VOTING IN LEGISLATURE

Arizona
Nevada
New Mexico
Oregon
Wyoming

GROUP VI LITTLE COMPETITION, LITTLE PARTY VOTING IN LEGISLATURE

Idaho
Kentucky
Missouri
Utah
West Virginia

GROUP VII ONE PARTY DOMINATION, PARTY VOTING RARE

Iowa
Kansas
Maine [b]
Oklahoma
New Hampshire [b]

GROUP VIII ONE-PARTY DOMINATION, MORE THAN IN GROUP VII, AND PARTY
VOTING EQUALLY RARE

Nebraska
North Dakota
South Dakota
Tennessee [b]
Vermont [b]

GROUP IX NO PRACTICAL COMPETITION IN INTRA-STATE POLITICS,
BIFACTIONAL DIVISION FREQUENT

Georgia [b]
Louisiana [b]
North Carolina [b]
South Carolina [b]
Virginia [b]

GROUP X NO PRACTICAL COMPETITION, MULTI-FACTIONAL DIVISION
FREQUENT

Alabama [c]
Arkansas [c]
Florida [c]
Mississippi [c]
Texas [c]

---

[a] Based upon the closeness of electoral competition for the Presidency, the Governorship, and party representation in the state legislature 1944–1960; the degree of Party voting on legislative roll calls; the extent of bi- or multi-factional alignment. There is no precise statistical measure of these combined factors due to the vagueness of roll call data and the shifting patterns of factionalism. Therefore no effort is made to rank the states from 1–50, since the rankings would be too arbitrary to be statistically reliable.

[b] States where bi-factional division in the dominant party is common, although in most cases this is less true today than in the past.

[c] States where multi-factional division in the dominant party has been common.

Nevertheless we do know a good deal about this from the work of Malcolm Jewell and others, so it was decided to arrange groupings of states according to the closeness of party competition on the basis of five factors: voting for president and governor, party representation in legislatures, the degree of party voting cohesion in legislative roll calls, and the extent of bi- or multifactional alignment in the less competitive states. Table I presents the 50 states grouped into ten categories, with the listing within each group alphabetical rather than statistical, since in my opinion the data do not lend themselves to closer measurement. (See also Appendix A-3 for a more schematic representation of this classification.)

Admittedly the impressionistic character of the data on which some of the groupings were made leave the categories open to dispute. Further, the categories would be hard to replicate. But, since the factional and roll call cohesion factors are at the heart of Key's argument, no other alternative seems adequate.[7] In any event the measures of competition used here do not vary more from the other commonly used rankings than these rankings vary with each other.[8]

Party Competition, Wealth, and Public Policy

The assessment of the impact of competition on policy is complicated by the fact that there is a high degree of correspondence

Table II. Party competition and income by states

Competition	Median family income as of 1959		
	Highest 20 states	Middle 10 states	Lowest 20 states
Highest 20 states	17	3	0
Middle 10 states	3	5	2
Lowest 20 states	0	2	18
	$\tau_c = .79$ [a]		

Source: *U.S. Statistical Abstract 1963*, p. 340.

[a] This and all the following tables are significant at least at the .05 level of meaning. For the method of calculation see Hubert M. Blalock, *Social Statistics* (New York: McGraw-Hill, 1960), pp. 321–324.

7. Most rankings omit four states that are included here—Alaska, Hawaii, Minnesota, and Nebraska—the first two for lack duration of elections as a basis for judging, and the second two because of their nonpartisan elections for state legislature. Alaska and Hawaii have now had a sufficient number of elections for judgments to be made (and elections subsequent to that of 1960 were used to verify the impressions reported in the table). In Minnesota the legislature is organized on a partisan basis. Nebraska's nonpartisan system comes closer to representing actual nonpartisanship in practice, but increasingly in recent years partisanship has become a factor. In any event the one-party politics of southern legislatures is essentially as nonpartisan as Nebraska's. Therefore the inclusion of Nebraska seems justified.

8. Compare, for example, Austin Ranney's ranking in Jacob and Vines, *Politics in the American States*, p. 65, with that of Hofferbert, "The Relationship between Public Policy and Some Structural and Environmental Variables . . . ," (see fn. 4 above), p. 65.

between high levels of party competition and state wealth. (See Appendix A-1 for state income variations.) This is indicated by the data in Table II. The same kind of similarity occurs when one measures state performance in various programs that may loosely be called ones that benefit the have-nots. For example, if one establishes an index of the progressivity of state tax systems, there is a slightly higher correlation between tax progressivity and income than between competition and the tax system but the difference is small.[9] Tables III and IV show that relationship. (See Appendix A-2 for the variations in tax progressivity.)

Table III. Competition and state tax progressivity

Competition	Tax progressivity		
	Highest 20 states	Middle 10 states	Lowest 20 states
Highest 20 states	13	2	5
Middle 10 states	3	3	4
Lowest 20 states	4	5	11
	$\tau_c = .33$		

Source: See fn. 9.

Table IV. Family income and state tax progressivity

Income	Tax progressivity		
	Highest 20 states	Middle 10 states	Lowest 20 states
Highest 20 states	12	1	7
Middle 10 states	4	5	1
Lowest 20 states	4	4	12
	$\tau_c = .26$		

Source. See fn. 9 for tax factor; *Statistical Abstract* 1963, p. 340 for income.

9. The index was established by noting the percentages of gross state revenue collected from income taxes as opposed to sales, gross receipts, and property taxes. A finer distinction was drawn among the sales tax states by noting the range of exemptions (for food, medicine, and clothing) permitted. Returns from severance taxes were deleted. The data were gathered from a report of the National Education Association entitled "State Taxes in 1963," dated February 1964. Since 1963 several states have changed their tax laws, but no attempt has been made to take these into account. For detail see Appendix Table A-2.

Similar correlations between competition and income appear for many other state expenditure programs that aid the less-well-to-do—workman's compensation, unemployment compensation, aid to the blind, aid to dependent children, and general assistance to the indigent. This is illustrated in Tables V and VI which show that the relationship between competition and per capita welfare expenditures of state funds (excluding federal and local monies) for six different welfare programs is slightly higher than the relationship between income and welfare.[10]

As the foregoing illustrates, there is a fairly high correspon-

Table V. State per capita welfare expenditures and party competition

Competition	Per capita welfare expenditures		
	Highest 19 states	Middle 10 states	Lowest 19 states
Highest 19 states	14	3	2
Middle 10 states	2	3	5
Lowest 19 states	3	4	12

$$\tau_c = .47$$

Source: See fn. 10.

Table VI. State per capita welfare expenditures and income

Income	Per capita welfare expenditures		
	Highest 19 states	Middle 10 states	Lowest 19 states
Highest 19 states	11	5	3
Middle 10 states	5	3	2
Lowest 19 states	3	2	14

$$\tau_c = .45$$

Source: See fn. 10.

10. The welfare rankings for the states are taken from the work of Richard E. Dawson and James A. Robinson, "The Politics of Welfare" in Jacob and Vines, *Politics in the American States*, p. 394–395. The six programs involved were aid to dependent children, old age assistance, aid to the blind, aid to the permanently disabled, general assistance, and unemployment insurance. They exclude Hawaii and Alaska as therefore do Tables V and VI. Their rankings are based upon average payments per recipient for the six programs.

dence between high income and high competition in the states, and this creates some difficulty in determining which of the two factors has the greater impact on policy payoffs. That is, where high income levels and high competition tend to occur together, the drawing of statistical inferences about the relative importance of the two factors has to be done with considerable care. Thomas Dye, in the paper previously referred to, draws his conclusions on the basis of simple and partial correlations between his 28 different policy variables and income and competition. He found that when he controlled for "economic development" of a state there was little apparent effect of party competition, but that, when he controlled for competition, economic development still had a significant effect on policy.[11] By a somewhat different method Richard Dawson and James Robinson arrived at a similar conclusion. They used rank order correlations of competition, income, and other factors with welfare policies, and concluded that "political variables make a difference for policies about well-being, but socio-economic variables make a greater difference."[12] It is interesting, however, that when Dawson and Robinson controlled for income and the proportion of foreign-born population that in two of the six categories (achieved by dividing the states into top, middle, and low third in income and in foreign-born population), party competition showed a higher correlation with payoffs than either income or foreign-born population.[13]

In order to check further the respective influence of the income and competition factors I devised another test. Assuming that income certainly could be expected to have an influence on payoffs, I divided the per capita expenditures on six welfare programs[14] by the per capita income of the states, and then compared the results with levels of party competition. This is shown in Table VII.[15] The influence of party competition is ap-

11. Dye, "Independent Effect of Party Competition," p. 15.

12. Dawson and Robinson, "The Politics of Welfare" (fn. 4 above), p. 409.

13. The same authors carried out slightly different procedures in their earlier article, "Inter-Party Competition, Economic Variables, and Welfare Policies in the American States" (fn. 4 above), and they arrived at roughly the same conclusion. They were somewhat stronger then in denying the relevance of party than in their article on "The Politics of Welfare" in the Jacob and Vines volume.

14. The welfare data are the same as those noted in fn. 10 above.

15. In this table Hawaii and Alaska were eliminated since the data are for 1961, shortly after they became states. Since this left me with 48 states, I drew

parent. The τ_c value produced by this distribution is .34 and is highly significant in statistical terms.

It is also noteworthy that John Fenton came to a more or less similar conclusion in his analysis of the problem. He found that education expenditures were more significantly related to income than to competition; but for several measures of welfare, and for aid to dependent children specifically, there was a considerably higher association with competition than income. He found that

Table VII. Per capita general welfare expenditures by state income levels compared with party competition

Per capita payoffs divided by per capita income (1961)	Level of State Party Competition		
	Highest third	Middle third	Lowest third
Highest third	10	5	1
Middle third	2	6	8
Lowest third	4	5	7
	$\tau_c = .34$		

Source. See fn. 10 and *Statistical Abstract*, 1963, p. 329; for 1961 per capita income.

75.4 per cent of the variation in the case of aid to dependent children could be explained by competition and only 6.1 per cent by income. This was done by multiple correlation, which minimizes the problem of interrelationship of the income and competition variables.[16]

In short, there appears to be grounds for believing that the hypothesis has some validity, although admittedly the case is not conclusively "proven" by these statistical devices. The fact remains that some states do not perform as expected: Minnesota pays off more than it might be expected to do, given its moderate

my categories of competition together to make three groups. This required the assignment of three states more or less arbitrarily because they were at the end or the beginning of the alphabetically arranged groups of states. California and Maryland became the last states in the top third, and West Virginia became the first state in the bottom group.

16. John H. Fenton, *People and Parties in Politics* (Glenview, Ill.: Scott, Foresman and Co., 1966), p. 44.

income and moderate competition; Michigan comes off badly, despite its highly competitive parties and its relatively high income. This makes it necessary to look in more detail at state-by-state performance to see whether we can find explanation of the significant variations from expected performance.

In order to test these variations I divided the states into three categories: (1) those with income groupings higher than their competition groupings; (2) those with identical (or within one-group deviation, higher or lower) competition and income groupings; and (3) those with income groupings lower than their competition standing. In the first category there are eight states. In four of them the higher income levels, one may assume, helped induce the state governments to enact laws paying off at a higher level for three of five programs used for comparison. (The test used for significant deviation is a variance of two or more groups higher or lower in payoffs than competition groups for three or more of the five programs used: tax progressivity, aid to dependent children, aid to the blind, general assistance, and unemployment compensation.) Those states (with their competitive groups noted) were California (IV), New Hampshire (VII), Utah (VI), and Virginia (IX). Two other states, Alaska (IV) and Nevada (V), had *lower* payoff groupings than their competitive standing. In the two remaining states, Maryland (VI) and Texas (X) there was no significant difference between the competitive position and payoffs—that is, for neither state was there a two-group deviation for three or more categories.

In the second category (where competition and income groupings do not vary more than one group) there were 33 states, and in 22 of them there was no significant variation between the competition grouping and the payoffs. In eight of the 33 states there was a *higher* payoff level for three or more programs: Idaho (VI), Iowa and Kansas (VII), Nebraska and North Dakota (VIII), Oregon (V), Minnesota and Washington (IV). In three states there were *lower* payoff groupings than competition standing: Michigan (I), New Mexico (V), and Ohio (II).

In the final category of nine states (in which the income groupings were below the competition standings), six states had *lower* payoffs than their competition levels: Indiana, Pennsylvania, and Rhode Island (II), Massachusetts (I), Montana (III), and West Virginia (VI). In the remaining three states there was no significant difference between the payoffs and the competition levels: Florida (X), Kentucky (VI), and Tennessee (VIII).

How can one explain these deviations? Considering the first category—where the states of California, New Hampshire, Utah, and Virginia had higher payoff rankings than their competition—there is little similarity among their political systems. In California, during most of the post-World War II years, there was relatively little party cohesion in the legislature, but at least the state was not often plagued with divided party control between the governor and one or both houses of the legislature. In the period 1954–1966 there was only one two-year term with divided control (17 per cent of the twelve-year period). New Hampshire likewise had only four years of the twelve with divided government, and Virginia, of course, never experienced it. In Utah, however, half the period had divided control prevailing. It is noteworthy too that in Nevada, where despite a high income level there were relatively lower payoffs, there was divided government (mostly due to Republican control of the Senate) for 83 per cent of the period 1954–1966. Alaska, as of 1966, had never had divided government, and yet it too had a lower level of payoffs despite its higher income levels. The failure of Maryland and Texas to have higher payoffs in view of their higher income can perhaps be explained in part by the multifactional politics that both tend to have, especially so in the case of Texas. Only one-third of the sessions of the Maryland legislature had divided control, so that offers no explanation. It is important, however, that in three of the four cases with higher than expected payoffs the states did not have divided control often and that in one of two with lower payoffs divided control was common. (More will be said of divided control later.)

For the states where the income and competition levels were nearly or exactly identical some very interesting variations occur. There were three states in which the payoffs were strikingly below the norm—Michigan (four out of five categories), New Mexico and Ohio (three out of five each). Michigan and Ohio are among the most competitive of the states, and New Mexico is in the middle range, so competition per se is no explanation. It is striking, however, that in the case of Michigan only one term of the legislature during 1954–1966 had unified party control; consistent battling between governors and legislatures of opposite parties has contributed greatly to the lower payoffs, particularly on the key issue of revenue. Although Michigan is among the top five states in competition, it has a tax system ranked with the most regressive five at the bottom of the scale, and even for unemployment compensation Michigan was in the third group. Aspects of Ohio politics also contribute importantly to its lower payoff rankings, for, as John Fenton points out, Ohio has a party system that is oriented toward patronage and is dedicated to keeping issues out of politics. Noting that Ohio has been inclined toward Republicanism during its history, he says, however, that it was not this that made the state conservative. "Minnesota and Wisconsin were dominantly Republican states before the Great Depression, but the governments were not notably conservative. The conservatism of Ohio's elected officials and government emerged out of the issueless character of the state's politics wherein the parties failed to provide the voters with meaningful policy alternatives in elections." [17] It is symptomatic of Ohio's style of politics (and significant for the low payoffs) that a highly conservative Democrat, Frank Lausche, was governor for ten years between 1944 and 1956. At least one writer on New Mexico's politics claims that it too has largely issueless politics; this may help to account for its low payoffs.[18]

Equally interesting are the states with similar competition and income levels and significantly higher payoff groups. All are states in the northwestern quadrant of the country, running from Minnesota on the east to Washington on the west, and none farther south than Kansas. They are listed in Table VIII below. Here, of course, neither competition nor income explains the variations.

Nor does divided party control provide an answer. Minnesota has had division in every session since 1954, and North Dakota, Oregon, and Washington have fairly high rates of divided control while the others have fairly low rates. For Minnesota, Oregon, and Washington one can point to their relatively liberal orientations. Of Minnesota John Fenton says,

In summary, Minnesota's political leadership, political opinions, political competition, and governmental programs all make a logical pattern.

17. John H. Fenton, *Midwest Politics* (New York: Holt, Rinehart and Winston, 1966), p. 148.
18. See Frederick C. Irion, "New Mexico: The Political State," in *Western Politics*, Frank H. Jonas, ed. (Salt Lake City: University of Utah Press, 1961), pp. 223–246, esp. p. 235.

The state has a history of issue-oriented politics, originating in the pro-
tests of farmers and small businessmen against exploitation by big business. The voters found that political protest paid, for when they de-
manded action their candidates generally provided programs designed to
erase the reasons for their grievances.[19]

Oregon and Washington also have quite liberal histories,[20] and
North Dakota, with its Nonpartisan League and its militancy
during the Depression (and officials like the late Senator William Langer), may reasonably be said to have had a liberal
background.

Idaho, Iowa, Kansas, and Nebraska are harder to explain,

Table VIII. States with higher payoffs when competition and
income levels identical

States	Competition group	Income group	% Divided party gov.	Tax prog.	ADC	Aid to blind	Genl. asst.	Unemp. Comp.
Idaho	6	6	33	2	2	6	n.a.	3
Iowa	7	7	33	4	5	2	7	6
Kansas	7	6	33	6	4	3	3	4
Minn.	4	5	100	1	2	1	2	6
Nebr.	8	8	n.a.	9	6	2	6	9
N.D.	8	8	50	5	3	7	5	7
Oregon	5	5	67	1	3	2	5	5
Wash.	4	3	67	10	2	1	2	4

Source: For Welfare Categories, see *Statistical Abstract*, 1962, p. 299. For Unemployment Compensation see *Book of the States*, 1962–1963, pp. 526–529.

partly because relatively little has been written about the intrica-
cies of their politics. Daniel J. Elazar has placed three of these
four states in what he calls the category of "Moralistic Political
Culture," by which he means a set of common political norms
which stress the value of public activity for a "notion of the public good and properly devoted to the advancement of the public
interest." [21] He distinguishes this from the "Individualistic" and

19. Fenton, *Midwest Politics*, p. 109.
20. On Oregon, see John M. Swarthout, "Oregon: Political Experiment Sta-
tion," in Jonas, *Western Politics*, pp. 247–271; on Washington, see Hugh A.
Bone, "Washington State: Free Style Politics," in Jonas, *ibid.*, pp. 303–333.
21. Daniel J. Elazar, *American Federalism: A View from the States* (New
York: Crowell, 1966), p. 90.

the "Traditionalist" cultures which tend to dominate respectively in areas where heavy European immigration took place and in the South. Nebraska he lists as a mixture between the Individualistic and Moralistic cultures. The difficulty with this supplementary explanation, however, is that South Dakota, Colorado, and Montana also have Moralistic cultures but do not excel in payoffs. Perhaps more detailed information on the political patterns of the four high payoff states would help explain their deviation.

It might be added that Wisconsin, another of the issue-oriented states of the Midwest identified by Fenton, comes close to falling into the above category. Its competition ranking is 3, and its income position the same, but its five rankings for the payoffs (in the same order as in Table VII) are 2, 2, 2, 1, 2. Wisconsin's liberal tradition and its pioneering role in social reform obviously have contributed to raising its level of payoffs above its competition and income levels.

The final category for evaluation are those states with income groupings below their competition levels. There are nine states in this group, and for three of them (Florida, Kentucky, and Tennessee) there was no significant variation in payoffs either up or down. None of the states had higher payoffs than their competition ranking, but six largely competitive states fell *below* their competition ranking in their payoffs. Data on them are in Table IX.

The interesting thing about this group of states is that the one border and two southern states with relatively noncompetitive parties had payoff levels that generally matched their competi-

Table IX. States with lower payoffs and with income groups below those for competition

				Policy Payoff Groups				
States	Competition group	Income group	% Divided party gov.	Tax prog.	ADC	Aid to blind	Genl. asst.	Unemp. Comp.
Indiana	2	4	50	9	7	5	8	7
Mass.	1	3	50	2	3	1	3	5
Montana	3	6	100	3	5	6	5	9
Pa.	2	4	67	4	6	6	5	5
R.I.	2	5	67	6	3	4	5	4
W. Va.	6	8	50	7	7	10	8	10

tion levels, while the five with relatively high competition and West Virginia with moderate competition had significantly *lower* payoffs. Take Indiana, for example. It is in the second group in competition and the fourth in income but the average payoff rank for the five programs was 7.2; in all five it was significantly lower than both its income and competition levels. Pennsylvania was likewise low in all five categories, although not as drastically as Indiana. Montana was low in four of five categories, but this may to some degree be accounted for by the fact that its income level is three ranks below its competition level. It is logical to expect the simple factor of inability to pay to come into play here. Much the same thing is true of Rhode Island, whose income ranking is three levels below that for competition.

In the states where the income level does not vary so extremely from the competition level, however, one must seek other sources of explanation. In the case of Indiana, Fenton describes in some detail the extent of corruption and interfactional dispute within the parties, but he observes that the parties there are somewhat better organized and more competitive than Ohio's.[22] In some respects he found Indiana's payoffs in accord with its higher competition levels (as compared with Ohio), but he reports general underfinancing of Indiana's welfare programs. For half of the twelve-year period 1954–1966 Indiana had divided party control, however, as did Massachusetts and West Virginia. In Pennsylvania and Rhode Island there was divided rule two-thirds of the time, and in Montana every session of the period had divided control.

It is quite significant, then, that in a high proportion of the cases where states deviate significantly from the expected there is much divided party control where the states fail to meet expectations, or, conversely, little or no division where the states perform as expected, or excel. This factor may therefore be of more importance than some observers have believed. Two scholars in recent papers have expressed some doubt about the significance of party division in the course of analyses of the probable impact of the removal of malapportionment in state legislatures. Herbert Jacob finds a low correlation between the extent of divided government and the degree of malapportionment, noting, however, that Michigan and New Jersey are exceptions to this

22. Fenton, *Midwest Politics*, chap. 6.

rule.[23] Richard I. Hofferbert comes to about the same conclusion. Interestingly, neither of them controls for competition in gauging the relationship between apportionment and divided government. To test this point, I used Hofferbert's classification system for competition and calculated the percentage of time during the period 1954–1966 that there was divided government in the non-southern states. It turns out (see Table X) that there is

Table X. Party competition and degree of divided partisan control, 1954–1966

	Average per cent of divided control
Top third of states in competition	64.0
Middle third of states in competition	51.5
Bottom third of states in competition	39.1

far more likely to be divided control where competition is high.[24] It is easy to see why malapportionment might cause this to happen more often in the competitive than in the noncompetitive states, since only where there is likely to be a close election is there likely to be divided control in any but the most extreme cases of malapportionment or landslide elections. Thus it may well be that close examination of the legislative politics of some of the competitive states which have low payoffs would indicate that one of the most serious barriers to the achievement of results through competition is that the apportionment system tended to short circuit the process.

Furthermore, one has a number of specific situations to illustrate the way in which malapportionment has blocked liberal policy outcomes through vesting control of one or both legislative houses in a different party from that of the governor. New Jersey, for example, had until 1965 an apportionment system that constitutionally gave the upper chamber to the Republican party, and through that control small county Republicans regu-

23. Herbert Jacob, "The Consequences of Malapportionment: A Note of Caution," *Social Forces*, 43 (December 1964), 256; and Richard I. Hofferbert, "The Relationship between Public Policy and Some Structural and Environmental Variables . . ." (see fn. 4 above).

24. Hofferbert excludes not only the South but Nebraska, Minnesota, Alaska, and Hawaii, ending up with 35 states in his table. See *ibid.*, p. 78.

larly blocked a number of significant pieces of legislation for a decade or more. Yet when a landslide and temporary reapportionment coincided in 1965, New Jersey Democrats took control of the governor's office and both houses and enacted a flood of legislation that delivered the state from some "wrong" payoff categories (in terms of its wealth and competitive parties). The same thing happened the year before in New York State, and earlier (without reapportionment) in Connecticut (the 1959 session). In Michigan, divided party control has had much to do with Michigan's being among the states with the most regressive tax policies in the nation, as first Governor Williams and then Governor Romney were unable to make any progress toward breaking the tax impasse. Many other examples could be cited to illustrate the consequences of division of party power and of its absence.

Some Nonquantitative Payoffs and Political Systems

Something further about political systems of the states may be inferred from investigating the incidence of other laws than those with quantifiable payoffs. The have-not elements of the society also benefit from the passage of such legislation as minimum wage laws, antidiscrimination statutes, small-loan laws, and the absence of right-to-work laws. As it turns out, in three of the four categories there is a significant correlation between competition and these statutes, the exception being small-loan laws—for reasons detailed below.

As of 1966 there were 14 states with minimum-wage laws providing for minimum rates of at least $1.00 per hour and applying to nearly all workers.[25] Ten of the fourteen were in the first four groups in terms of competition.[26] The remaining four states (with their competition groups) were Idaho (VI), Maine and New Hampshire (VII), and Vermont (VIII). It is interest-

25. U.S. Bureau of Labor Standards, "Brief Summary of State Minimum Wage Laws," Fact Sheet 4A, January 1965. Since this tabulation was made, New Jersey has enacted a law providing wide coverage—a law, incidentally, long blocked by the Republicans, who before 1966 controlled the Senate. The New Jersey law is included here.

26. The ten states were Alaska, Connecticut, Hawaii, Massachusetts, Michigan, New Jersey, New York, Pennsylvania, Rhode Island, and Washington. This, incidentally, includes all five of the top group of states in competitiveness, but—consistent with earlier findings—Indiana and Ohio are missing (along with Delaware) in the second most competitive group.

ing to note that of these states the latter three are tending in recent years toward greater competition than was usual in their pasts, and it is significant too that all three are New England states, which have relatively more liberal orientations than some other less competitive states. Moreover, it is interesting that two of these New England states enacted minimum-wage laws after they were becoming somewhat more competitive than they had previously been. (Maine's law dates from 1959 and Vermont's from 1957.) The existence of competition, however, does not assure the passage of minimum-wage laws since half the twenty most competitive states have not enacted them. But it is significant that the states with the laws are overwhelmingly the competitive ones.

Antidiscrimination laws likewise tend to be passed where competition exists, and to be passed, if at all, in less competitive states at much later dates. In the fifteen years between 1945 and 1960, sixteen states enacted Fair Employment Practices laws and none of them was in the bottom half of the states in terms of competition. Eleven of the highest 15 states in competition had enacted such laws by 1960 (the exceptions—not then having an FEP rule—were Illinois, Hawaii, Indiana, and Montana). More recently, between 1961 and 1966, another twelve states enacted FEP laws, and seven of them were among the more competitive half of the states. The less competitive states enacting FEP were Kansas, Missouri, Utah, New Hampshire, and Nebraska. The striking fact is, however, that 19 of the top 20 states in competition have passed FEP laws.

In an even more sensitive area of antidiscrimination policy—housing—a total of 16 states have enacted laws (all since 1959). Those 16 states include only one in the lower half of the competition levels (New Hampshire).[27] Again 11 of the 15 most competitive states were among those passing laws against private housing discrimination (including nine of the top ten— Delaware being the exception).[28]

Right-to-work laws were enacted largely due to the much-debated Section 14(b) of the Taft-Hartley Act of 1947 which

27. It might be added, however, that the New Hampshire law did not have an auspicious beginning, since the legislature refused to grant funds for operation of the enforcement agency.

28. For details see Duane Lockard, "The Politics of Antidiscrimination Legislation," *Harvard Journal on Legislation*, 3 (December 1965), esp. pp. 10–11.

forbids the closed shop but permits the union shop except where states prohibit it. Although they have been proposed in every state, right-to-work laws have been enacted in very few of the competitive states (and have been repealed later in most of them), while the reverse is true in the least competitive states.[29] Among the more competitive states only Arizona, Nevada, and Wyoming now have right-to-work statutes (all are in the fifth category of competition). Delaware and Indiana enacted the laws, but later repealed them (Delaware in 1949 and Indiana in 1965). Conversely, among the less competitive states, all those of the old South—with the exception of Louisiana—have the laws along with Iowa, Kansas, Nebraska, North Dakota, South Dakota, and Utah. While it is true that the states with right-to-work laws tend to be those with relatively low levels of industrialization, and accordingly relatively weaker labor union movements, it does not follow that this is the sole explanation for the presence of these laws in the less competitive states. There are several states with much party competition and with low levels of industrial employment (as measured by the percentage of employees in occupations other than agriculture) that have never enacted the laws (e.g., Minnesota, Montana, Wisconsin). And, on the opposite side, several noncompetitive states have a moderate degree of industrialization but have the laws nevertheless (e.g., Florida, Georgia, and Texas). Admittedly this is not a matter of complete correspondence since several states with competition rankings in the bottom half of the scale do *not* have the laws (nine of them to be exact), but that sixteen of the less competitive states do have them and almost none of the competitive ones do is highly suggestive.

One further area of legislation of importance to the poor was tested—small-loan regulations. This is a matter of considerable importance to the indigent for they are often victimized by loan sharks or by legitimate businesses that charge exorbitant rates —often as high as or higher than 36 per cent per year. But there does not appear to be any correlation between competition and the closeness of state regulation.[30] Very possibly this is be-

29. U.S. Bureau of Labor Standards, "Brief Summary of State Union Regulatory Provisions," Fact Sheet 7-C, November 1965.

30. For a wealth of detailed evidence on state practices, see Barbara A. Curran, *Trends in Consumer Credit Legislation* (Chicago: University of Chicago Press, 1965).

cause of the effort to drive out illegal loan practices by permitting high interest rates and charges for legitimate lenders. Indeed the draft of the Uniform Small Loan Law proposes a rate
not exceeding three per cent per month (!) on loans not in excess
of $100.[31] Thus there is a wide variation in types of regulations
among the states; some of the more competitive and urbanized
states have highly detailed regulations that actually allow quite
high rates, whereas some less competitive states have flat prohibi-
tions on usurious rates of interest but do not provide detailed
regulation. The latter may be harder on the indigent borrower
than the former, although on the surface the opposite appears to
be true. In any event, if there is a difference between the competitive and noncompetitive states in small-loan policies it is not apparent without detailed analysis of the operation of laws rather
than their formal provisions alone.

Conclusions

What all this leads to is the point that V. O. Key made often
in his career: never forget that the political process is human,
that it depends upon notions in men's minds, and that statistical
inference must always be made with utmost caution. He particularly argued this in an article on social determinism in electoral
behavior, and again in his last two books.[32] Some of the social
determinism research, he wrote, "threatens to take the politics
out of the study of electoral behavior." [33] The same can be said
of some of the research on his hypothesis about party competition: by concentrating on the quantifiable variables the political
reality has been overlooked. How can one discount the evidence
that abounds in case studies and in analyses of political decisions of the fear that is struck in party leaders by the uncertainties of the next election. Are we to ignore the innumerable instances when party leaders plead with their legislative followers
to go along with this or that liberalizing policy for the sake of

31. See *ibid.*, pp. 144–157, sec. 13(a).
32. V. O. Key, Jr., and Frank Munger, "Social Determinism and Electoral
Decision: The Case of Indiana," in *American Voting Behavior*, Eugene Burdick
and Arthur J. Brodbeck, eds. (Glencoe, Ill.: The Free Press, 1959), p. 281;
V. O. Key, Jr. *Public Opinion and American Democracy* (New York: Knopf,
1961); and *The Responsible Electorate* (Cambridge, Mass.: Harvard University
Press, 1966).
33. Key and Munger, "Social Determinism and Electoral Decision." p. 281.

the party's interest in the next election? Not infrequently politicians press for policies they dislike personally because they do identify with the party and hope to avoid retribution at the polls. Since the governorship is a major political prize—as well as the most conspicuous state office—party politicians strive to enact policies they believe necessary to attract votes. Accordingly representatives of the have-nots have opportunities to frighten leaders into action that in the absence of competition might be much less common.

If one wished, one could cite an overwhelming catalogue of such cases. From my own intermittent political activity in Connecticut I can recall literally dozens of times when I heard governors and party leaders (of both parties) plead with legislators to enact a particular liberal measure because the image of the party depended upon it. And in many cases these were actions that the pleader was not particularly anxious to support personally (for example, civil rights matters) but which they felt it necessary to seek. I also recall hearing a governor of New Jersey plead urgently with state senators of his party to support revision of the rules of the senate because this was an item of reform on which he and they had campaigned. He stressed that default on the promise would set up the opposition in the next election, but he certainly also had in mind that the rules changes would facilitate the delivery of the sweeping program that he was about to propose. Wherever the party organization is strong enough to be a factor in persuading legislators to vote with the leadership, one should expect the plea for the party image to be of at least some significance. To be sure, there are reverse cases where a political party in control of a single house of a legislature will wantonly hold up legislation that might make the opposition party's governor look well in the next campaign (e.g., Michigan); but even that is an evidence of the political system's having an impact on policy making and it has virtually nothing to do with the socio-economic variables that some investigators place their prime reliance upon in interpreting policy outcomes.

It may well be, however, that Key placed too much emphasis on the party system per se for producing results in behalf of the have-nots. The political party is, after all, a part of a larger political system, and, as we have observed, there are many factors that can inhibit the functioning of party organizations to the policy ends Key anticipated. An important one is the apportionment system, which may enhance the possibilities of deadlock government through divided political party control. In time, as the full effect of the Supreme Court's decisions on state malapportionment is felt, this factor may be somewhat reduced in significance, but clearly in the past—and the past record is our only basis for judging the effects of competition—divided government was an important restraining factor in many competitive states.

Another important consideration is the political tradition of the particular state. By political tradition I mean the set of attitudes and beliefs that pervades a state's political life. Beyond the obvious factors of liberality or conservatism of belief in state political communities, there is a pervading atmosphere that obviously conditions the way in which a political system operates. Corruption is condoned or condemned; public service opportunities loom large in political life, or there may be a frankly opportunistic self-gain philosophy; who the enemies of the public interest are varies with political history, and so on. As Erik Erikson has wisely observed

A historical decision . . . is really a very condensed moment in historical actuality, for here the resources of the maker of the decision and of those who must accept and sustain it fuse in one instant. To understand this, historians *and* psychoanalysts must learn to grasp fully the fact that while each individual life has its longitudinal logic, all lives lived independently within a given historical period share a kind of historical logic—and a-logic. Much of this is contained in the way and in the images by means of which men identify with each other, identify themselves with their institutions and their leaders and their leaders with themselves, and how, as they thus identify, they repudiate . . . their adversaries and enemies.[34]

What is true for historians is equally true for political scientists: the potential for comprehension of political reality through tracing historical and psychological factors in a community has hardly been tapped. This may sound archaic in an age when the cybernetic revolution provides such rich opportunities for research in quantifiable data, but it may also stand as a warning that a certain artificiality can be imported into a research problem if important but nonquantifiable variables are defined out of the problem.

34. Erik H. Erikson, *Insight and Responsibility* (New York: Norton, 1964), pp. 206–207.

Likewise, facets of the party system other than pure competition can have a decisive effect on policy-making. The degree of centralization of a party may affect the extent of party discipline and the cohesiveness of voting in a legislature, which in turn can have an impact on the way decisions are made and therefore upon their content. The extent and character of factions have a similar impact: some kinds of decisions have been impossible in New Jersey because of the peculiar factional patterns that prevail there. The same decisions have been more readily made in Connecticut and New York, where the factional patterns are different.

Some aspects of the governmental system—also a part of the political system, broadly defined—affect the policy-making process. For example, constitutional restraints on state expenditures, borrowing, and taxation may have an inhibiting effect on policy initiation. The dominance of a legislature by a governor, or conversely its relative independence, may be important. The degree of relative authority of the bureaucratic ranks may have importance too, since the bureaucracy and its clientele may acquire enormous strength and independent power to forward their goals and thereby affect public policies fundamentally.

If we rely primarily on socioeconomic factors to explain policy differences, how then shall we account for the high income state that has low payoffs—and vice versa? Clearly only by examining the political system of any state as an intervening variable of the greatest importance can we provide answers. The character of a state's political leadership, its political traditions, its pressure group patterns, as well as the party system and other forces must all be taken into account. This is not to deny that socioeconomic factors themselves affect the political system. Obviously the introduction of numerous European immigrants into the politics of the northeastern states was a significant determinant of the political patterns of those states, just as the arrival of southern Negroes has been more recently. Patently some socioeconomic factors that are not quantifiable—e.g., attitudes toward government—also affect not only the political system but also the policies it produces. In a sense, therefore, the debate about whether the political system or the underlying social and economic situation is the more important influence is futile. In the real world the two forces are invariably intermixed. What the researcher must do is to look even more deeply into the political system of individual states and particularly to examine in depth how decisions were made that proffer some assistance to the migrant farm laborer, the crippled, or the insane. This essay has cast some doubt upon the generalization that socioeconomic variables in isolation are the key ones. Finding the data on and interpreting the ways in which socioeconomic forces and political system characteristics combine to influence policy outcomes is a task that remains to be done.

Appendix

Table A-1. Median family income, 1959

Group I	$	Group VI	$
Alaska	7326	Montana	5403
Connecticut	6887	New Mexico	5371
Nevada	6736	Kansas	5295
New Jersey	6786	Idaho	5259
California	6726	Missouri	5127
Group II		**Group VII**	
Illinois	6566	Iowa	5069
Maryland	6309	Virginia	4964
New York	6371	Vermont	4890
Michigan	6256	Texas	4884
Hawaii	6366	Maine	4873
Group III		**Group VIII**	
Massachusetts	6272	Nebraska	4862
Washington	6225	Florida	4722
Delaware	6197	Oklahoma	4620
Ohio	6171	West Virginia	4577
Wisconsin	5926	North Dakota	4530
Group IV		**Group IX**	
Utah	5899	Louisiana	4272
Oregon	5892	South Dakota	4251
Wyoming	5877	Georgia	4208
Indiana	5798	Kentucky	4051
Colorado	5780	North Carolina	3956
Group V		**Group X**	
Pennsylvania	5719	Tennessee	3949
New Hampshire	5636	Alabama	3937
Rhode Island	5589	South Carolina	3821
Minnesota	5573	Arkansas	3184
Arizona	5568	Mississippi	2884

Source: *Statistical Abstract,* 1963, p. 340.

Table A-2. The states ranked by progressivity of tax systems as of 1963 tax collections

Rank state	Per cent of revenue from		
	Sales, gross receipts, and property	Income tax	Sales tax and exemptions
1. Oregon	22.6	54.0	No sales tax
2. New York	27.8	57.5	No sales tax
3. Delaware	25.0	46.6	No sales tax
4. Minnesota	32.7	41.2	No sales tax
5. Alaska [a]	33.2	38.9	No sales tax
6. Massachusetts	33.4	38.3	No sales tax
7. Idaho	34.6	35.5	No sales tax
8. Wisconsin	33.4	47.0	S.T. (FMC) [b]
9. Virginia	41.8	39.2	No sales tax
10. Vermont	44.9	31.2	No sales tax
11. Montana	54.5	25.2	No sales tax
12. New Jersey	55.8	8.1	No sales tax
13. Maryland	54.6	31.1	S.T. (FM)
14. California	57.8	24.7	S.T. (FM)
15. North Carolina	55.8	28.3	S.T. (M)
16. Colorado	50.5	29.1	S.T.
17. Utah	58.7	20.6	S.T.
18. Iowa	60.0	17.3	S.T.
19. Connecticut	68.5	14.0	S.T. (FMC)
20. Pennsylvania	66.2	11.3	S.T. (FMC)
21. Kentucky	64.4	20.5	S.T.
22. North Dakota	59.7	11.6	S.T. (M)
23. Missouri	63.4	18.5	S.T.
24. Kansas	63.4	16.4	S.T.
25. New Mexico [a]	66.0	9.5	S.T.
26. Hawaii	68.9	28.3	S.T.
27. New Hampshire	62.7	3.7	No sales tax
28. Oklahoma [a]	66.0	12.3	S.T.
29. Rhode Island	72.5	10.0	S.T. (FM)
30. South Carolina	71.0	19.5	S.T.
31. Georgia	73.3	19.3	S.T.
32. Alabama	73.1	12.3	S.T.
33. Arkansas	71.5	13.0	S.T.
34. Louisiana [a]	70.7	7.1	S.T.
35. Tennessee	71.8	8.4	S.T.
36. Mississippi	73.9	9.5	S.T.
37. West Virginia	77.8	7.6	S.T.

Table A-2 (*continued*)

Rank state	Per cent of revenue from		
	Sales, gross receipts, and property	Income tax	Sales tax and exemptions
38. Wyoming	72.5	0	S.T.
39. Texas [a]	72.5	0	S.T. (FM)
40. Ohio	74.9	0	S.T. (F)
41. Nebraska	86.1	0	No sales tax
42. Indiana	83.3	c	S.T. (Tax Credit)
43. Florida	75.3	0	S.T. (F)
44. Maine	75.8	0	S.T. (F)
45. Arizona	81.4	10.1	S.T.
46. Michigan	70.8	0	S.T.
47. South Dakota	74.1	.8	S.T.
48. Nevada	78.5	0	S.T.
49. Washington	82.0	0	S.T.
50. Illinois	84.4	0	S.T.

Source: "State Taxes in 1963," National Education Association pamphlet dated February 1964.

a Excluding from total revenue the returns from severance taxes, on the assumption that this is a tax the legislature would consider transferable to ultimate consumers beyond state borders. The percentages of total revenue from severance taxes by state are Alaska 8%, Louisiana 36.6%, New Mexico 14.5%, Oklahoma 11.1%, and Texas 18.1%.

b Refers to exemptions from a general sales tax as follows: (F) food, (M) Medicine, (C) clothing.

c Indiana income tax revenue began in July 1963 and was not recorded here. Later tabulations will raise the state higher in the ranking. There are no direct commodity exemptions on the sales tax, but a $6 credit on the income tax is allowed for sales tax paid on food and drugs.

Table A-3. Patterns of state party competition [a]

Cohesion of voting in legislature	Very competitive parties	Some competition	Little competition	One-party domination	Heavy one-party domination	No Competition	
						Bi-factional	Multi-factional
Extensive party voting	I Conn. Mass. Mich. N. J. N. Y.						
Much party voting	II Del. Ind. Ohio Pa. R. I.						
Moderate party voting	III Colo. Hawaii Ill. Mont. Wisc.						

continued

[a] States are arranged alphabetically in each group.

Table A-3 (continued)

Cohesion of voting in legislature	Very competitive parties	Some competition	Little competition	One-party domination	Heavy one-party domination	No Competition	
						Bi-factional	Multi-factional
Little party voting	IV Alaska Calif. Md. Minn. Wash.	V Ariz. Nev. N.M. Ore. Wyo.	VI Idaho Ky. Mo. Utah W. Va.				
Party voting RARE				VII Iowa Kan. Maine Okla. N. H.	VIII Nebr. N. D. S. D. Tenn. Vt.		
No party voting						IX Ga. La. N. C. S. C. Va.	X Ala. Ark. Fla. Miss. Texas

Merle Fainsod

The Dynamics of One-Party Systems

By a one-party system we mean a political regime in which a single party monopolizes power and opposition parties are outlawed. So defined, one-party systems must be distinguished from one-party dominant systems such as those of Mexico and India where minority parties continue to operate legally and compete for electoral support. While the result in either case may be to produce a single ruling party, one-party dominant systems at least provide a recognized channel through which opposition to the dominant party may express itself and take form. Nor should it be forgotten that powerful tendencies toward one-party dominance manifest themselves in even the most vigorous systems of competitive politics. As Professor V. O. Key, Jr., observed in *American State Politics,*

Not only are many states dominated by men bearing the label of a single party, in many of them all sorts of barriers have been erected against the achievement of power by the lesser party. Doubtless among politicians, as among businessmen, some sort of deep urge toward monopoly exists. No matter how ringing their affirmations of faith in the great American two-party system may be, party politicians endlessly devote themselves to the contrivance of ways and means by which the opposition

221

will not have much of a chance." [1] The aspirations which find their focus in one-party rule are rooted in deep-seated human drives.

The primary concern of this essay is with the dynamics of one-party systems rather than with one-party dominant systems. Its thesis can be simply stated. One-party systems are established to achieve a variety of objectives and reflect different social interests; the only quality which they have in common is that they attempt to monopolize political action and deny the right of other parties to exist. They seek to perpetuate their rule by anchoring their power on a corps of party activists, who undertake to dominate government, the police, the armed forces, the channels of mass communication, and every form of social organization. But their capacity to survive depends on more than their organizational skills in integrating their societies and their ruthlessness in suppressing opposition. They cannot ultimately escape the divisive issues of the societies in which they are operating or insulate themselves from the forces of change. Over the longer run, they are unlikely to remain viable unless they obtain acceptance of their legitimacy, learn to manage intra-party and social conflict without imperiling the dominant role of the party, and pursue goals in both domestic and foreign policy which respond to the expectations of their subjects and do not endanger the party's base of support.

To test these propositions, five types of one-party regimes will be examined: 1) the Soviet case as the archetype of Communist one-party systems; 2) Fascist one-party systems as exemplified by Mussolini's Italy and Hitler Germany; 3) the Falange in Spain as a proto-Fascist instrument of a conservative military dictatorship; 4) the modernizing tutelary one-party systems of which Turkey between 1923 and 1945 will serve as an example; and 5) the post-colonial one-party systems, illustrated by African experience.

Of these five types, the Soviet regime has thus far proved the most durable. [2] Born to make revolution and bound together by strong doctrinal ties, the Communist party has always placed a

1. V. O. Key, Jr., *American State Politics: An Introduction* (New York, 1956), pp. 273–274.

2. For descriptions of the system, see Merle Fainsod, *How Russia is Ruled* (Cambridge, Mass., 1963) and F. C. Barghoorn, *Politics in the USSR* (Boston, 1966).

high premium on centralized, disciplined organization and penetration of the society over which it presides. Its high potential for system maintenance is perhaps best illustrated by its determination to assimilate the activist and leadership elements of Soviet society into its ranks. The membership policy of the party has been consciously designed to enlist leading representatives in every sector of Soviet life—the officer corps in the armed forces and the police, the functionaries who occupy important posts in administration, the directors of production in industry, agriculture, and trade, the scientific and technical intelligentsia who man the command posts in the academies, the universities, and the technical institutes, and the cultural bureaucrats who dominate the mass media, literature, drama, music, and the arts. At the same time, the party seeks to preserve its links with the masses by recruiting so-called leading workers—foremen and skilled craftsmen in the factories, collective and state farm chairmen, agronomists, accountants, and brigadiers from the countryside, and corresponding ranks elsewhere. Since career opportunities and the perquisites that go with them depend on party approval, the ambitious find party membership a sine qua non for advancement. The insistence of the party on enrolling leadership elements in every segment of Soviet society is one of the greatest sources of its strength.

In order to safeguard its dominating position, the party at an early stage assumed control of the strategic levers of power in government and society. By insisting on party membership as a condition of access to positions of influence and by permeating the armed forces, the police, and every branch of administration and the economy with party cells and party controllers, the party leadership sought to assure that its authority would go unchallenged. Under Stalin the role of the party organization was reduced to an instrument of his personal dictatorship, but since his death the party has re-emerged as the paramount force in Soviet society.

From its earliest days the party has also taken its responsibility to guide, direct, and mobilize the energies of the masses with the utmost seriousness. It has utilized its control of the mass media, educational institutions, and a highly developed network of oral agitation and propaganda to shape the minds and attitudes of the population. It has concentrated maximum efforts on capturing the loyalty of the youth by enlisting their more active members in organizations such as the Pioneers and the Komsomols. It has developed a large variety of party-dominated mass organizations which serve as transmission belts to convey the party message into every segment of Soviet society. Despite the apathy and indifference which these party-inspired efforts sometimes encounter, and indeed help generate, they leave their deposits by saturating the society in party values.

Reinforcing these positive agencies of indoctrination are the organs of repression which are available to deal with those who deviate from prescribed codes of behavior. While mass terror has ceased to play the major role which it did under Stalin, the security police are still very much in being, and they serve to intimidate the heterodox by their very presence. Controlled by the party to a degree that they were not in Stalinist times, they remain available to cope with those who challenge the party's supreme authority in any sphere of Soviet life. At the same time, cruder forms of repression have given way to more sophisticated forms of manipulation in dealing with actual or potential dissent. The area of permissible within-system criticism has been broadened, and efforts have been made to quiet restiveness among the intelligentsia by judicious combinations of the carrot and the stick.

An important measure of the stability of the regime is its apparently improved ability to manage intra-party conflicts and succession crises without putting the authority of the party in peril. In the wake of Lenin's death the party was rocked by a series of bitter factional struggles which spread out into the party cells and threatened to spill over into the streets. The final consolidation of Stalin's power involved the slaughter of his opponents and a series of mass purges which consigned millions of his victims to the concentration camps. By contrast, the succession struggle after Stalin's death, while accompanied by the execution of Beria and his entourage, was a relatively peaceful affair. It was contained within the upper echelons of the party, and though Khrushchev's opponents were disgraced and demoted, they were left to finish out their days in peace. The removal of Khrushchev in turn was smoothly engineered at the Presidium and Central Committee level, without any involvement of the party rank and file, and, in form at least, in strict conformity with the party rules. Lest these contrasts convey too roseate a picture of the triumph of legality, it should also be noted that each succession struggle has exacted a heavy price in shaking confidence in the regime itself. Stalin's charges that most of Lenin's closest comrades-in-arms were traitors and scoundrels, Khrushchev's condemnation of Stalin as a bloodthirsty tyrant, and the attack on the deposed Khrushchev as an incompetent hatcher of hare-brained schemes were hardly calculated to breed trust in a party which produced such leaders. Perhaps the most serious residue of past succession struggles is the doubt it casts on the legitimacy of the regime itself.

What can be said of the success of the Communist party in achieving legitimacy? For some the pragmatic fact that the party has occupied the seats of power in the Soviet Union for more than a half-century will seem answer enough. Yet, if by legitimacy is meant wide-spread popular commitment to a particular system of rule, no one-party system, however long-lasting, can be certain that it enjoys such support in the absence of opportunities to opt for an alternative. Yet there are other, perhaps less satisfactory, tests of legitimacy which cannot be dismissed as without significance. The willingness of a people to defend a regime against its enemies, the extent to which it dispenses with terror and repression in dealing with dissent, and its ability to enlist the energies of its people in constructive enterprises may all serve as ancillary measures of its legitimacy. Judged by this mixture of criteria, the record of the Soviet regime may still appear to be ambiguous, and the central role of terror in Stalin's formula of governance hardly points to a substantial measure of popular support for his measures. Yet even the alienation and fear evoked by Stalin's purges and concentration camps must be balanced against the patriotic pride aroused by his industrial achievements, by the victory over the Nazis, and the vast expansion of Soviet power in the aftermath of World War II. Perhaps the single most important factor in validating the party's claim to legitimacy has been its palpable success in transforming the Soviet Union from a relatively backward society to a modern industrial super-power.

Still another measure of the viability of a one-party system is the degree to which it meets the daily needs of its people. Under Stalin improvements in living standards were deliberately sacrificed to build the sinews of economic and military power, while extensive reliance on repression served to hold popular discontent in check. His successors have allocated a greater share of national resources to provide more food, housing, and consumer goods. Faced with the problem of stimulating the growth of an increasingly complex economy, they apparently concluded that Stalinist terror had reached a point of diminishing returns and that tangible rewards had to be provided if creative energies were to be unleashed. By shifting to greater reliance on incentives and amenities rather than repression and fear, they hoped to narrow the gap between rulers and ruled and broaden their base of support. While the concessions thus far made available fall short of popular aspirations, they nevertheless represent a welcome improvement and may serve to dull the edge of mass discontent.

A final factor contributing to the survival power of the party has been its foreign policy successes and military triumphs. Since the Civil War period there has been only one moment of peak danger—the initial Nazi onslaught on the Soviet Union —when the life of the regime appeared to hang in balance. But the party held together in its hour of greatest crisis, and with victory in World War II, it greatly expanded its territory and emerged as one of the world's two great super-powers.

In sum, after a half-century of experience as the ruling element in society, the Communist party gives every outward sign of being securely entrenched in power. It has enlisted leading elements of Soviet society in its ranks, consolidated its controls over all key posts in government, penetrated important social formations, survived a series of succession crises, and achieved the kind of legitimacy which derives from an impressive record of industrial progress, military victories, territorial gains, and, more recently, an increasing degree of responsiveness to the welfare aspirations of its own people. In contrast to the Communist regimes of Eastern Europe, which bear the stigma of having been established as Soviet client states and which seek their legitimacy in emancipation from Soviet controls, the Soviet regime from its earliest days has been able to draw strong support from identification with a native fund of patriotic sentiment. In contrast to its Communist Chinese neighbor, which has still to demonstrate its potential for rapid industrialization and which is caught up in the convulsions of frustrated revolutionary expectations and its first succession crisis, the Soviet regime gives evidence of having become a relatively mature industrial power in which the framework of the social structure has begun to congeal while the impulse to social transformation and revolution has weakened.

Yet secure and taken for granted as the party's monopoly may appear to be, the same cannot be said of the prerogatives of the party functionaries who man the key posts in the party machine and who reserve to themselves the power to define policy for it. Limitations on their authority have been bred by the very revolution over which they have presided. In directing a complex industrial society and in determining its priorities of development, they must increasingly depend on those who possess the professional skills to manage it. In inescapable fashion, the professionalisms of military technology, industrial management, and every branch of science and engineering impinge on the capacity of the party leadership to coordinate them. Within the ranks of the party there is a continuously troublesome problem of relating the overall authority of full-time party functionaries to the jurisdiction of other party members who exercise professional authority in specialized fields.

As Soviet society has become more professionalized and differentiated, the outlines of an influence-group structure have begun to emerge. The armed forces, the police, the managers of industry and agriculture, the scientific community, and the cultural intelligentsia all have their specialized interests to defend, and since they cannot be promoted outside the party, the party has itself become an arena in which these competing interests must be adjusted and reconciled. One of the results has been to introduce a strong adaptive ingredient into the party leadership's mobilizing and coordinating role.

There are still other forces at work which contribute to limit, if not to undermine the authority of the party functionaries and the party which they direct. As the custodians of a doctrine which claims to embody infallible truth, they find their credentials contemptuously rejected by their powerful Chinese neighbor, and they no longer speak for a united Communist world. As spokesmen for the "wave of the future," they see their revolutionary dynamism arrested, and their expansionist ambitions limited by the imperatives of survival in a thermonuclear age. As the putative possessors of an exclusive formula for rapid industrialization, they have watched their growth rate slacken as planning and management problems have become increasingly difficult and complex. Even where they have relaxed restrictions on the cultural intelligentsia and gone part way to satisfy popular expectations of higher living standards, they discover that they have only whetted appetites which demand still more.

What do these developments portend for the future of the Soviet one-party system? [3] There are some who see these pressures as operating to transform what was once a monolithic party into a pluralistic party in which interest groups will be free to maneuver and legalized factions may emerge. There are others who go farther and visualize the eventual appearance of a two party or multiparty system as the party leadership finds it impossible to confine the plural energies of Soviet society within the bounds of a single party. There are still others who predict that a weakening of party leadership will set the stage for a military coup d'etat and the emergence of a military dictatorship in the next stage of Soviet development. There are yet others who visualize the transformation of what was once an ideologically inspired party into a technical and managerial élite, governing in authoritarian and scientifically rational fashion, and guided by production and welfare goals.

Without undertaking to predict the shape of things to come, it is, nevertheless, possible to identify certain forces which are likely to influence the development of the Soviet one-party system in the years ahead. First, it can be safely posited that a party which has built its power on the suppression of opposition outside the party and factionalism within, will not willingly abdicate its power short of a major catastrophe such as military defeat or an equivalent domestic disaster. Second, it can also be assumed that no party, whatever its pretensions to monolithism, can escape individual and group rivalries, and that these rivalries will inevitably reflect the changing configurations of interests inside the party as they are shaped by the tasks it assumes. Third, in ministering to the needs and directing the destinies of a highly industrialized country, the Soviet Communist party must

3. For examples of the variety of views on the future of the Soviet system, see Isaac Deutscher, *Russia, What Next?* (London, 1953) and *Russia in Transition and Other Essays* (New York, 1960); Barrington Moore, Jr., *Terror and Progress, The USSR* (Cambridge, Mass., 1954); A. B. Ulam, *The Unfinished Revolution* (New York, 1960); Harry Braverman, *The Future of Russia* (New York, 1963); Leonard Schapiro, ed., *The USSR and the Future* (New York, 1963); Z. Brzezinski's article "The Soviet Political System—Transformation or Degeneration?" in *Problems of Communism* (January–February, 1966), and comments on the article by a number of authors in subsequent issues of the same journal.

perforce accord greater weight and authority to those elements in the party who possess the knowledge and technical skill which make an industrial society work. Fourth, as the economy and the society become more complex and differentiated, the influence of professionalism will probably increase, and tendencies toward a dispersal of authority and influence are likely to become more clearly manifest. Fifth, given the commitment of the Soviet regime to technical progress and scientific advance, the need for a social environment conducive to innovation and creativity is likely to intensify and exert its demonstration effect outside scientific walls. Finally, the disillusionment bred by the Sino-Soviet dispute and the spread of polycentric tendencies in the Communist movement, with its self-evident lesson that there are not one, but many Communist truths, should contribute to undermine the dogmatic certainty on which party monolithism rests. If these propositions have any validity, they would point to the emergence over time of a looser, more pragmatic, and pluralistically based party in which the differentiated interests of an industrial society find freer expression and the party sees its role as the management of their interrelationships. They may, but they do not necessarily, pose a threat to the Soviet one-party system as such.

II

When one turns to the Facist one-party systems, or rather their Italian and Nazi prototypes, the record is behind us, and the forces which brought them to their doom can now be readily identified. Dedicated to conquest and military adventure, both overreached themselves and met destruction on the battlefield.

The dynamics of their disintegration provide interesting contrasts with the relative stability of Soviet rule. Both Italian Fascism and Hitler's Nazi party gave the impression in their time of being firmly established power structures. Like the Soviet Communist party they appeared securely entrenched without any visible challengers on the horizon. A closer examination of the two regimes unfolds a much more complex pattern. The Italian case in particular reveals the weaknesses and vulnerabilities of the Fascist one-party system.[4]

4. A brief but authoritative summary of the Fascist era in Italy is available in H. Stuart Hughes, *The United States and Italy* (Cambridge, Mass., 1953), pp. 62–142.

For all of Mussolini's totalitarian theorizing, Italy under his rule remained a quite incompletely totalitarianized society. Mussolini used his Fascist party to seize the machinery of government, but unlike his Soviet predecessors, he did not tamper with the existing social and economic structure. While not at first averse to using leftist-sounding slogans to rally working-class support, his primary appeal was to the propertied classes. Indeed, his historic role was to lead a counter-revolution to protect the existing order. By promising a virile and rejuvenated Italy that would overcome parliamentary immobilism, rescue the nation from depression, and usher in a new era of prosperity and national greatness, he hoped to overcome the attraction of socialism and communism. His millenial vision was designed to provide an alternative to social revolution.

Italy at the end of World War I, with its mass unemployment, inflation, class conflict, and sense of injured pride at having been denied the fruits of Allied victory, provided fertile soil for Mussolini's demagogy. He marched to power by enlisting the support of unemployed war veterans ready for desperate action, members of the salaried middle class threatened with loss of status, and rich industrialists, church dignitaries, landowners, and other pillars of the established order who feared a workers' revolution. After organizing his own private army and carrying terror into the streets, he shifted the battle to Parliament. There, with the blessings of the Royal House, the willing and unwilling connivance of his coalition partners, and the use of violence and electoral trickery, he managed by 1926, some four years after the march on Rome, to transform the Chamber of Deputies into a single-party monopoly and to consolidate his power as head both of the party and the Government.

Outwardly, Mussolini's Italy appeared to be the very epitome of the totalitarian one-party state. Its ideology of corporatism purported to be an all-embracing proclamation of the unity of the state and the harmony of class interests. The party, in theory at least, represented the paramount force in the state and society, though it operated under the unquestioned direction of its leader—the Duce. On paper Fascist party controls seemed impressively pervasive. A large part of the youth was enlisted in party-dominated organizations. The mass media functioned as instruments of the party, and party controls penetrated higher educational institutions and professional organizations. The workers were enrolled in Fascist syndicates, and the party had its own militia and instruments of terror to deal with the dissident.

In practice these controls fell far short of completeness. The limits on Fascist control were evident at every level of Italian society. Though the Royal House collaborated with Mussolini, it remained a counter-symbol of legitimacy, and in the final reckoning became the immediate instrument of Mussolini's undoing. The military were seduced by Mussolini's dreams of aggrandizement and grandeur, but they maintained a professional solidarity which proved resistant to party penetration. The Lateran Treaty and Concordat of 1929 won Mussolini great popularity among the Catholic clergy, but when Mussolini undertook to dissolve Catholic youth and university organizations in 1931, the outcry of protest from the Church was powerful enough to force him to concede a degree of autonomy for Catholic youth activities. Industrialists and large landowners had reason to be indebted to Fascism because of its effectiveness in curbing labor unrest, but they too retained a considerable degree of independence, despite occasional harassment by venal Fascist bureaucrats. Beneath the façade of synthetic unity and artificial enthusiasm, popular support for the regime steadily eroded. As economic conditions worsened, the attitude of the mass of workers and agricultural laborers could best be described as one of weary scepticism and smoldering resentment. The urban white collar groups too suffered disillusionment. Some, to be sure, achieved comfortable berths as Fascist bureaucrats, but, since these positions tended to be filled by the older generation, the younger members of the professional and intellectual classes discovered fewer outlets for their talents and became increasingly alienated and radicalized. As the Fascist era moved into its final phase, an aging regime of self-serving bureaucrats, buttressed by the repressive technical apparatus of a police state and resting on the conditional support of the propertied classes, found itself more and more isolated from the mass of the people.

Yet it is a measure of the power generated by even an incompletely totalitarianized state that it required a total and crushing military defeat to topple it. Once it became clear that defeat was inevitable, the days of Fascism were numbered. The collapse of the regime was in effect engineered by those who had been among its strongest supporters. The King and the aristocracy

gathered around him, the officer corps following Marshal Bado-
glio, the industrialists, and the so-called moderates in the Fascist
party led by Grandi and Ciano joined in jettisoning Mussolini in
the hope of salvaging what they could out of a military debacle.
Rallying around the Monarchy as the only remaining symbol of
legitimacy, they made Mussolini the King's prisoner, and though
he was subsequently rescued by the Nazis and persuaded to set
up a new Fascist republic of the north under Nazi auspices, he
ended his days a hunted fugitive, executed by his own country-
men in a final savage judgment on the failures of the Fascist
era.

The Nazi regime too collapsed as the result of military defeat,
but to the bitter end it remained a much more formidably regi-
mented instrument of totalitarian power than Mussolini's Fascist
movement.[5] Hitler, unlike Mussolini, had no competing symbol
of legitimacy with which to contend; after President von Hinden-
berg's death on August 2, 1934, the title of President was
merged with that of Chancellor, and Hitler joined in his person
the combined offices of Party Leader, Chancellor, Supreme
Commander-in-Chief of the Armed Forces, and Head of State.
He personally dominated the party machine and the institutions
of government and society to a degree far beyond Mussolini's
reach, and, at least until the tide of battle turned in Russia, his
impressive record of diplomatic and military triumphs com-
manded a measure of genuine popular support which Mussolini's far less successful military ventures never achieved.

Like the Italian Fascists, Hitler's Nazi party offered itself as a
symbol of national regeneration and revitalization. Both rejected
liberalism and Marxism and exalted national values. But where
Mussolini turned to anti-Semitism belatedly and possibly even
reluctantly, Hitler from the beginning made it a cardinal element in his program. Building on a myth of racial Aryan purity,
he elaborated the notion of the Germans as a superior race distinguished by its heroic feats and martial valor. Unlike Mussolini, whose expansionist ambitions were at first relatively limited,
Hitler's vision was one of unlimited expansion, with the German
master race imposing its rule on "inferior" Slavs and other
second-rate people.

Like Mussolini, Hitler marched to power by exploiting the

5. For an excellent treatment of the Nazi regime, see Alan Bullock, *Hitler—
A Study in Tyranny* (New York, 1953).

frustrations of national humiliation and economic depression. His promise to erase the shame of Versailles tapped a massive reservoir of outraged national feeling. He countered the appeal of Communists and Social-Democrats by offering his own brand of National-Socialism and mobilized anti-Semitic sentiment across class lines by charging the Jews with national betrayal and economic exploitation. In essence his panacea for economic depression was a program of full employment achieved through re-militarization. His remedy for social ills was to make the German Volk an armed camp dedicated to plunder and conquest. From the beginning, his popular following was greatest among the peasantry and middle strata of German society, but at the height of his power his diplomatic successes and military triumphs won him widespread support in all classes of the German nation.

The party on which he relied to enforce his will was in a special sense his personal creation. Once he had rid himself of the more radical elements in the 1934 purge of Roehm and other storm troop leaders, Hitler's leadership in the party went unchallenged. Surrounded by sycophantic satraps who vied for his favor, he played them off one against another and avoided even the suggestion of an heir apparent. While not himself much interested in the details of administration, he nevertheless reserved to himself a final right of review in matters large and small whenever he was so minded. His manner of dividing authority among his subordinates involved the establishment of rival administrative empires, frequently overlapping and working at cross-purposes, but insuring that the reins of power remained securely in his hands.

The Nazi drive for the consolidation of power over government and society followed a pattern made familiar by its Italian Fascist predecessor. Beginning with a coalition with the nationalist Right which installed Hitler as Chancellor of the Reich, the Nazis used terror to intimidate their political opponents and to secure Parliamentary approval for a suspension of the rights guaranteed by the Weimar constitution. Operating under a mask of pseudo-legality, they moved swiftly to transfer dictatorial power from the Reichstag to the Cabinet, outlawed all other parties, assumed supreme power in the states, Nazified the civil service and the courts, and seized control of the instruments of mass communication. The Army High Command posed a more difficult problem, since it had force at its command. There Hitler's first task was to disarm suspicion of a Nazi takeover. The purge of Roehm removed the fear that his Storm Troopers would inundate the army and fanned illusions among the officer corps that Hitler offered no threat to their independence. Concerned as some of them continued to be by the growing power and autonomy of Himmler's S.S. units, they nevertheless found comfort and reassurance in the rearmament program which Hitler sponsored. Once his authority was securely established, Hitler exploited the rival ambitions of the generals to promote those whom he could trust and to weed out the potentially disloyal. The oath of allegiance which the generals swore, not to the Fatherland, but to Hitler personally, symbolized their subservience.

The Nazi totalitarian machine, despite its brief life, showed itself a far more formidable engine of power than Italian Fascism. In Italy, the officer corps, the industrialists, the large-landowners, and the Church maintained some degree of independence, even when their interests were intertwined with those of Fascism. By contrast, Nazi controls proved far more effective. The powerful tradition of professional solidarity in the German officer corps was never effectively mobilized to resist Hitler's demands, even when its leading generals were most dubious about his plans. Whatever doubts about the future individual industrialists and landowners may have entertained, they lent themselves readily to Hitler's designs and functioned as his willing adjutants. Such pockets of resistance as developed in the churches were brushed aside, and the universities were taken over with relative ease. The most powerful labor movement in Europe with its millions of Social-Democratic and Communist voters was subjugated with hardly a trace of defiance. The Nazi terror apparatus with its network of concentration camps and death factories operated with a frightening technological efficiency and ruthlessness which left little room for opposition.

This is not to say that the Nazi regime did not have its underground resistance groups and its conspiracies to dispose of Hitler, beginning as early as 1938. But the fact remains that as long as Hitler marched from success to success, he carried his people with him, and those who distrusted or opposed him found themselves paralyzed by his victories. It was only when the tide of battle turned after Stalingrad and inevitable defeat stared Germany in the face that conspiracies began in earnest to salvage what still could be saved from the wreckage of the Fatherland. As many as seven attempts on Hitler's life were planned during 1943. All were failures; only the bomb planted by Graf von Stauffenberg at Hitler's headquarters in East Prussia on July 20, 1944 came within a hairbreadth of killing him. The conspiracies found their leaders in the more aristocratic remnants of the old officers corps and their support among a few courageous church figures such as the Catholic Bishop of Münster and the Protestant pastor Niemoeller and among a handful of older civil servants such as Kr. Karl Goerdeler. Their failure even in the hour of impending catastrophe is a measure of the spell in which Hitler still held the army and the nation. Only when Berlin had been reduced to rubble and the Fuehrer himself had committed suicide did the Nazi regime collapse. The melancholy lesson which emerges is that both the Fascist and Nazi one-party systems proved powerful enough to cow their internal enemies; it was the external enemies that they manufactured that demolished them. To suggest that they might have survived much longer had they been more prudent and less venturesome is perhaps beside the point. The furies which drove them to their doom were implicit in their imperial dynamism.

III

By contrast, the longevity of the Franco regime in Spain could be explained at least in part by its caution and lack of dynamism. Conservative in outlook and authoritarian rather than totalitarian in its organization, the Franco establishment did not fit the usual conception of a one-party system, even though over much of its life, only one party, the Falange, was legally permitted to function. Perhaps it could best be described as an aborted one-party system in which the pretensions of the Falange to play a major role in political and social life received only limited recognition. In essence Franco Spain was a military dictatorship dominated by the Caudillo and dedicated to the preservation of the traditional establishment. Its power was based on an alliance of élite interest groups—the church hierarchy, the officer corps, the large landowners, the bureaucracy, and the more well-to-do business and professional groups. Since it was interested in neither internal change nor external expansion, it sought to limit the disruption of existing Spanish society by modernizing forces. Its techniques of control placed less emphasis on mobilizing mass enthusiasm and positive support for the regime, and more on the maintenance of political apathy and compliance with the regime's dictates. This it undertook to do by censorship, repression of any form of organized opposition, and a calculated policy of diverting the masses from political activity by engaging their energies in processions, spectacles, sports, and circuses.

The role of the Falange in Franco's power structure was at best ambiguous and always subordinated to his impressive manipulatory skills. Indeed, the Falange can best be understood as a party in search of a role which it was never able to define and in pursuit of a power monopoly which it was never able to establish. Originally launched under the leadership of José Antonio Primo de Rivero, who dreamed vaguely of leading a movement of national regeneration which would abolish social strife and political discord, the Falange supported the military rebellion against the Popular Front Government and provided militia units which played a minor role in the Civil War. Some months after José Antonio's execution by the Loyalists on November 20, 1936, the party was in effect taken over by Franco and declared the official party of the new Spanish State. From the beginning it functioned as his personal tool, rather than as an independent power in its own right. In the words of Stanley G. Payne, the historian of the Falange, "Franco conceived of the [Falange] as the party of the State, but he never thought of his regime as a real party-State . . . Whenever its political pretensions threatened to disturb the internal equilibrium worked out by the Caudillo, he quickly cut the party down to size." [6]

The uses to which Franco put the Falange varied with his changing needs. In the aftermath of the Civil War and during World War II, it provided the ideological rhetoric which rationalized the values of the "new Spain" and of the syndical system in which workers were enlisted. Its feminine section took over the administration of social services, while restive Falangists were placated with jobs in local government and used as a counterforce against the possibility of a monarchist restoration. With the defeat of the Axis powers, Franco sought to rid himself of his Fascist image by further reducing the role of the Falange. By the

6. Stanley G. Payne, *Falange—A History of Spanish Fascism* (Stanford, Calif., 1961), p. 200.

end of the fifties the Falange had largely become a paper organization; aside from its patronage function, it had virtually ceased to exist. The basis of Franco's power remained his capacity to articulate and aggregate the interests of the élite formations—the Church, the army, the upper bureaucracy, and the more affluent business and professional groups.

Yet for all of the maneuvering finesse of the aging dictator, there were signs on every hand that the power of the traditional establishment was crumbling. Unrest and illegal strikes on the part of workers and farm laborers were mounting. Students, professors, and members of the secular intelligentsia were more and more alienated from the regime. The more liberal elements in the Church appeared increasingly critical of the regime's rigidity. Looking to the future, it was difficult see how these pressures for change and modernization could be long denied, despite the reluctance of the Caudillo himself to part with supreme power.

IV

By contrast, modernizing tutelary one-party regimes at least hold out the possibility of pluralizing their authority as their political energies spill over single-party boundaries. The road to such development is cleared of an important barrier when the leaders of the regime proclaim their authority as temporary and profess to administer a tutelary custodianship preparatory to the establishment of a constitutional order. Here the experience of modern Turkey is particularly interesting since it provides one of the very few examples of the voluntary transformation of a one-party regime into a competitive party system.[7]

The one-party regime of the Republic People's Party which was presided over by Mustafa Kemal (later Atatürk) from 1923 until his death in 1938 and by Inonü from 1938 to 1945 emerged as a reaction to the defeat of the Ottoman Empire in the

7. Particularly useful studies include Bernard Lewis, *The Emergence of Modern Turkey* (London, 1961); Frederick W. Frey, *The Turkish Political Elite* (Cambridge, Mass., 1965); Kemal H. Karpat, *Turkey's Politics—The Transition to a Multi-Party System* (Princeton, 1959); and two outstanding essays by Dankwart A. Rustow, one on "The Development of Parties in Turkey," in J. La Palombara and M. Weiner, eds., *Political Parties and Political Development* (Princeton, 1966), pp. 107–133, and the other on "Turkey: The Modernity of a Tradition," in L. C. Pye and S. Verba, eds., *Political Culture and Political Development* (Princeton, 1965), pp. 171–198.

First World War and found its rallying point in Kemal's brilliant leadership in the war of independence which followed. His successful defense of the territorial integrity of Turkey against the threats of foreign occupation and annexation made Kemal, who served as Commander-in-Chief of the Army, the embodiment of the forces of patriotic unity. Relying on his overwhelming popularity, he proceeded to abolish the Sultanate and to transform Turkey into a republic with himself as president. He also assumed the leadership of the Republic People's party, which quickly established a political monopoly.

In the initial stages of consolidating his power, Kemal tended to move cautiously, avoiding divisive religious issues in the interest of rallying maximum national support. Once he was securely entrenched in power, he moved swiftly to enact a wide-ranging program of secular reform. Beginning with the abolition of the Caliphate and the religious courts, he unified and modernized the educational system, westernized the legal system, adopted the Latin alphabet, gave women the suffrage, and embarked on a state-sponsored system of industrialization to build national strength.

This dramatic and far-reaching program of modernization necessarily generated opposition in the more traditional sectors of Turkish society. When opposition appeared, Kemal and his followers did not hesitate to use force and coercion to speed the pace of change. But they also placed heavy reliance on Kemal's prestige as a national hero to overcome resistance. Kemal's primary support came from army officers, the modernizing sector of the bureaucracy, the urban Westernized élites, the secular professionals, and the students, while opposition to the reforms tended to be greatest among religious leaders and the tradition-minded peasantry who were still subject to their influence. The party operated as the spearhead of social transformation. Its strongest organizational detachments were concentrated in the large cities and urban centers, though it also sought to project its influence into the rural areas by relying on a growing army of secularly trained village school teachers.

Kemal's own conception of tutelary authoritarianism did not exclude the possibility of an opposition party, at least as long as it remained faithful to the principles of the state which he had founded. Indeed, it was at his own express suggestion that an opposition Liberal party was established in 1930. But the experiment foundered when the Liberal party threatened to become too popular. It was quickly dissolved on the ground that it was attracting the support of religious reactionaries.

The decision to open the way to a real opposition party and to permit it to challenge the Republic People's party in a free electoral contest was taken, not by Kemal, but by his successor, Inonü. The circumstances which contributed to this decision may throw light on the more general problem of transforming a one-party into a competitive party system. Long before Kemal's death in 1938 there were signs that the popularity of the Republic People's party was waning. The Great Depression of the thirties produced economic stagnation. The government's policy of state industrialization imposed heavy burdens on the peasantry. Some leaders helped to discredit the party by utilizing their positions to advance their own personal interests. Despite growing popular disillusionment, the party leadership clung tenaciously to its monopoly through the pre-war and war years and appeared quite uninterested in encouraging challengers to its supremacy.

While the defeat of the Axis powers in World War II contributed to create a political climate more receptive to democratic experiments, it was the appearance of an organized opposition within the ruling party, led by such figures as Bayar and Menderes, that set the process of parturition in motion. The first reaction of the party leadership was to expel the dissidents, but soon thereafter President Inonü, in opening the Grand National Assembly on November 1, 1945, expressed the hope, echoing Kemal's earlier views, that an opposition party might be established which would be suited to the country's needs. Encouraged by these words, the dissidents brought their opposition into the open, found support in local associations of the ruling party, and utilized friendly newspapers to criticize the government and prepare the way for the creation of an opposition party. Further stimulated by the weak response of the government to the attacks which were launched against it and encouraged by evidence of public sympathy with their cause, the oppositionists under the leadership of Celal Bayar launched their own Democratic party on January 7, 1946. Its establishment was now formally welcomed and approved by the Republican People's party, possibly on the assumption that the new Democratic party offered no real threat to Republican dominance. If this was the prevailing assessment, it soon proved quite misguided. In the elections of May 1950 the Democrats won a sweeping victory and remained in power until 1960, when they were thrown out of office by a military coup. After a brief period of military rule in 1960–1961, party competition was restored.

What conclusions can be drawn from the Turkish experience with one-party rule? For one thing, it suggests that there are no insuperable barriers to the peaceful transformation of a one-party regime into a system of competitive party politics, provided that a proper conjuncture of circumstances occurs. To begin with, the leaders of the ruling party must be prepared to weaken or dilute their monopoly of political power. They may do so, as was partially true in the Turkish case, because of a desire to placate foreign opinion and to win new friends in the West. They may believe that a one-party regime is no longer viable because of the insoluble problems it faces and the enemies it has made. They may operate on the assumption, mistaken or not, that they are creating the appearance of opposition, rather than opposition itself. And, perhaps most important of all, they must be persuaded that the values and goals which they have sought to impress on the life of the nation will not be fundamentally overturned if the opposition comes to power.

It is the last point that perhaps deserves special emphasis in the Turkish case. Divergent as the future paths of the Republican and Democratic parties turned out to be, both accepted Kemal's revolution as common ground. The leaders of both parties were part of the same Turkish élite. While the leaders of the Democratic party subsequently went to much greater lengths to woo the support of the peasant masses, neither party sought to activate the radical potential of the industrial working class. In short, the emergence and recognition of the Democratic party did not in its time precipitate a crisis of participation in which the pressure of new demands from a newly activated section of the electorate threatened a fundamental overturn of the Kemalist social order. In the transition from a one-party to a competitive party system, politics remained a family affair. Had more fundamental issues been at stake, it is at least doubtful that the transition would have been so smooth.

V

We turn finally to the post-colonial one-party regimes of national integration. In this category the new states of sub-Sahara

Africa present the most challenging array of difficult problems. Perhaps the paramount characteristic of the present African political scene is its fluidity; even the most informed specialists on Africa despair of developing a typology of political movements that will do justice to it. The scholarly literature on African one-party states has tended to draw a fairly sharp distinction between revolutionary-centralizing or solidary one-party regimes such as Guinea, Mali, and, to a lesser degree, Ghana under Nkrumah, and the more pragmatic-pluralist types which emerged in states such as the Ivory Coast and Senegal.[8] While this distinction can certainly be defended in terms of the rhetoric employed by the respective leaders of these regimes and even has a certain basis in reality, the differences between these types do not appear as sharp as they are sometimes stated. The actual control exercised by most African one-party regimes over their societies falls far short of their pretensions.

If African one-party systems are compared with their Communist or Fascist prototypes their weaknesses are readily apparent. Party organizations, while impressive on paper, do not in fact function as disciplined instruments of the central leadership and struggle to embrace a congeries of centrifugal tribal pressures which constantly threaten to tear them apart. The idea of loyalty to a party-state remains alien to large sectors of the traditional community still oriented to tribal and kinship attachments. Control of the governmental apparatus, the police, and the armed forces is at best tenuous and subject to sporadic challenge by dissatisfied groups. The capacity to mobilize mass support is limited by lack of communication facilities and transport. The underlying reality is one of diffused social authority which the party can only with great difficulty penetrate and contain.

Weak as the African one-party systems may appear to be when contrasted with the totalitarian parties, they nevertheless represent significant efforts to build new aggregations of power on the African scene. To measure their achievements and failures, one must understand the problems which they face. As the inheritors of the colonial legacy and the artificial boundaries

8. See, for example, James S. Coleman and Carl G. Rosberg, Jr., *Political Parties and National Integration in Tropical Africa* (Berkeley, 1964), esp. pp. 5–6, and the essay by Rupert Emerson, "Parties and National Integration in Africa" in La Palombara and Weiner, *Political Culture and Political Development,* pp. 267–301.

which it imposed, they confront the task of building nations out of refractory tribal material and substituting new allegiances for old. As the successful survivors of the struggle for ascendancy within the freedom movements, they seek to hold on to power, cope with disgruntled opponents, and meet the new challenges of development which post-colonial governing parties cannot avoid. The talents which they have demonstrated as freedom-fighters do not necessarily equip them for the new responsibilities they have assumed. Catapulted into the modern world with meager human and material resources, they not infrequently find themselves frustrated by their inability to fulfill the extravagant promises of increased well-being which helped to bring them to power. With independence come disillusionment and the tendency of one-party regimes to turn to force to suppress the opposition which they cannot co-opt or buy off.

The rhetoric of African one-party ideology stresses unity and an identification of interest binding leader, party, and state. As Nkrumah put it at the height of his glory, "The Convention People's party is Ghana," and he considered himself the epitome of both. Leaders of African one-party systems without exception defend their monopoly of power as a necessary instrument of national unification and integration. The alternative, they insist, is tribal fragmentation and divisive conflicts which new nations can ill afford. Since the primary task of the party is proclaimed to be nation-building and national development, those who oppose the rule of the party are denounced as traitors to the national cause.

When one turns from rhetoric to practice, the lofty goals of the party take on a different guise. Ideally, the party should, in Nyerere's words, be "open to all" and strive for a blend of policy which gives recognition to the interests of every sector of society. But this is far easier said than done. In fact, African one-party regimes vary widely in their sources of social support, and all of them develop their favored clients and their neglected, or excluded groups. Thus on the more conservative side, Houphouet-Boigny's *Parti Democratique de la Côte d'Ivoire* (PDCI) has drawn its primary support from the relatively well-to-do cocoa planters and tribal chiefs, while at the other end of the political spectrum Sékou Touré's *Parti Democratique de Guinée* (PDG) undertook to emasculate the power of the chiefs, while relying on workers and the lower middle strata as its main base of support. Whatever be the political and economic orientation of the party, it tends to become a patronage machine, which distributes favors to the faithful in order to consolidate their support. Since state and party frequently appear indistinguishable, the tendency of leaders of one-party systems has been to treat state resources, not as a trust to be administered in the interest of the nation, but rather as a patrimonial fund to reward followers and dependents in the party itself.

Any attempt to generalize about the dynamics of African one-party systems must begin with a caveat that we are dealing with phenomena that are still in process and that the experience thus far is both brief and various. Nevertheless, certain discernible trends have emerged which deserve to be noted. First, there are clear indications that most of the so-called one-party regimes have still to achieve the organizational discipline which would make them effective instruments for controlling their societies. With the possible, but by no means certain, exceptions of Guinea, Mali, and Tanzania most lack the mobilizing and penetrative power to do more than attempt to reshape the traditional social structure. The dramatic collapse of the apparently powerful Convention People's party after Nkrumah's downfall only serves to underline the organizational weakness of many of the African one-party systems.

Second, the euphoria of the early post-independence days has begun to give way to the realization that neither charismatic leaders nor the parties through which they rule can work any developmental miracles. Indeed, what has happened all too frequently is that the one-party state has become an instrument for perpetuating the domination and filling the coffers of the first generation of successful nationalist leaders. Conspicuous displays of newly acquired affluence have tarnished the reputation of the freedom fighters and excited the envy of groups denied access to the fleshpots of power. Since many of the entrenched leaders are still young and determined to hold onto power, there is no room at the top for an only slightly younger, and frequently better-trained generation, impatient to assume the responsibilities for which they think themselves equipped. Meanwhile, other claimant groups—government employees, soldiers and police, labor unions, cash crop farmers, and unemployed young men who have fled the bush to crowd into the cities—press their grievances, and confront African one-party leaders with a spiraling set of demands which they are frequently powerless to satisfy.

Thus, the party becomes an increasingly ineffective instrument for assimilating and mediating the claims which are made on it.

With mounting dissidence, a third factor comes into play. The rulers turn increasingly to the use of repression and dependence on the police and military to suppress discontent. As the party declines in significance, organizations capable of exercising force assume an increasingly strategic role. Since the Army commands the preponderance of force, the road is opened to military take-overs, and as recent experience makes clear, it is the military coup d'etat which usually brings civilian one-party regimes down. Indeed, the rash of military coups in recent years has suggested to some observers that this is by way of becoming the institutionalized form of government change on the African scene.[9] As the military assumes a central role in African politics, the future of one-party systems appears increasingly in doubt. In some cases, such as Ghana, the military have promised a restoration of civilian government after a caretaker phase to be devoted to rooting out corruption and restoring the economic health of the nation. But even if such promises are honored, the possibility of renewed military intervention is likely to persist as an omnipresent shadow. The prospect in many cases may well be a succession of free-booting praetorian regimes concerned above all to enjoy the perquisites which come with seizures of power. Yet the inability of such regimes to provide either a framework of order or welfare suggests that they too are unlikely to be long-lasting. Successor political arrangements will necessarily reflect local conditions. Where traditional sources of tribal authority persist and remain powerful, they will probably continue to fill the political vacuum. Where the forces of change release new social energies and politicize and activize previously inert groups and new social strata, the demand for effective representation of their interests is likely to intensify and will not easily be contained within tribal agglomerations, military regimes, or even one-party systems. Whether the new African states can develop the institutional machinery to integrate the claims of the more modern and traditional sectors of their societies still remains to be deter-

9. See Aristide R. Zolberg, *The Structure of Political Conflict in the New States of Tropical Africa,* Paper prepared for delivery at the 1966 Annual Meeting of the American Political Science Association; and the same author's *Creating Political Order—The Party-States of West Africa* (Chicago, 1966).

mined. Their capacity to respond to this challenge may be the true measure of their successes or failures at nation-building.

VI

What conclusions emerge from this examination of the dynamics of one-party systems? The experience reviewed in this essay suggests that the organizational features which one-party systems have in common tells us very little about their durability or the direction and nature of their development.[10] One-party systems not only vary widely in their organizational effectiveness; they also differ greatly in the goals they set themselves, the interests they serve, the environments in which they operate, and their ability to cope with the responsibilities they have assumed. Given this diversity, their life histories necessarily take different forms.

The five types of one-party systems examined here illustrate the variety of developmental patterns which can be subsumed under a one-party rubric. It is a rare case when a one-party system gives way without violence to a system of competitive party politics, but Turkish history demonstrates that it can happen when a monopoly party disintegrates into factions, and these factions in turn become the nuclei of opposing parties. The Spanish Falange, on the other hand, represents the case of an aborted one-party system; when it no longer served the purposes of Franco's military dictatorship, it was, in effect, put on the shelf. The Fascist and Nazi one-party systems came to an abrupt end as casualties of military defeat; their fate was sealed by the recklessness of their course. The post-colonial one-party regimes have still to prove that they are viable political formations; their fragility and dubious prospects are emphasized by the number that have already fallen victims to military coups.

Even that most powerful and long-lasting of all one-party systems, the Soviet Communist party, finds itself challenged by the task of maintaining its authority and defining its role in a milieu of increasing professionalism, intensified bureaucratic competition, rising intellectual ferment, and cumulative demands for

10. For a suggestive discussion of this theme by Raymond Aron and others, see "Can the Party Alone Run a One-Party State?" in *Government and Opposition*, 2 (January–April 1967), 1965–180.

improvements in living standards. While there is no present indication of any disposition on the part of the party leaders to abandon the party's political monopoly or even to tolerate the organization of opposition groups within the party, they cannot escape the problems of responding to the changing social aspirations of an increasingly industrialized and professionalized society or relating themselves to the variety of interests which it has been spawning. One-party systems, no matter how powerfully entrenched, provide no magic formula for dealing with the complexities of social and economic change or the new crises of political participation which they precipitate. It is when one-party systems ignore them that they nurture the seeds of their own undoing.

Index

Index